Financial Joy

Banish Debt, Grow Your Money and Unlock Financial Freedom in 10 Weeks

Ken & Mary Okoroafor

QUERCUS

First published in Great Britain in 2024 by

QUERCUS

Quercus Editions Ltd
Carmelite House
50 Victoria Embankment
London
EC4Y 0DZ

An Hachette UK company

A CIP catalogue record for this book is available from the British Library.

TPB ISBN 978-1-52943-425-5
eBook ISBN 978-1-52943-426-2

10 9 8 7 6 5

Illustrations by Robert Brandt
Cover design by Anna Morrison

Printed and bound in Great Britain by Clays Ltd, Elcograf S.p.A.

Papers used by Quercus are from well-managed forests and other responsible sources.

Praise for *Financial Joy*

'In this brilliant book, Ken and Mary have created a perfect blend of inspiration and practical steps to help ANYONE get their financial lives in order. Read it, apply it and experience the joy of financial control. Highly recommended!'
— **Pete Matthew**, Creator of Meaningful Money

'The most joyful money book out there. Money and joy can sometimes feel like the antithesis, especially if we believe that the two are mutually exclusive. In *Financial Joy*, Ken and Mary show us how to shift from this mindset, but not only that, they give us the practical tools to put the new concept of Financial Joy into practice.'
— **Selina Flavius**, author of *Black Girl Finance*

'This book is a real gift for those genuinely committed to sorting out their finances and attitude to money. Packed with practical information and research, the authors hold your hand through the challenges of navigating your way to a positive financial attitude. It's the Marie Kondo of getting your financial house in order.'
— **Brenda Emmanus OBE**

'Throughout many of our lives, the narrative around money and finances has been clouded by fear and misinformation, but it doesn't have to be that way. That's precisely why *Financial Joy* is a revelation – it's THE definitive guide for personal financial understanding, planning and freedom. This book doesn't just educate; it empowers and transforms your financial journey into one of clarity and confidence. Beyond just growing wealth, the idea of crafting a financial life filled with joy and free from regrets. A must-read for anyone ready to rewrite their financial story.'
— **YolanDa Brown OBE DL**, award-winning musician, broadcaster and Chair of the British Phonographic Industry

'This is a book to savour, and Ken and Mary have organized it so you can do just that. In it you'll find a journey of ten weeks, each designed to take you ever closer to financial freedom the way it should be done: Joyfully.'
— **JL Collins**, author of the international best-seller *The Simple Path to Wealth* and *Pathfinders*

'If you want to learn how to build a life of financial freedom, this book is a thorough step-by-step guide on how to achieve it, no matter what your life circumstances are.'
— **Kristy Shen**, author of *Quit Like a Millionaire*

'An entertaining gem of a book whose financial advice is timeless. Reading the book is like sitting down with two caring friends who believe in you and want you to succeed financially. There's no doubt in my mind that if you need just one book to guide you successfully on your money journey, this is it.'
  – **Chad Carson**, host of the *Real Estate Investing with Coach Carson* podcast

'If there's one book you read this year, it should be *Financial Joy*. Ken and Mary hold your hand through a comprehensive overhaul of your financial life and guide you to the hidden treasure trove of joy buried inside you.'
  – **Julien and Kiersten Saunders**, authors of *Cashing Out* and creators at richandregular.com.

'*Financial Joy* is a refreshing roadmap to designing your ideal life – one that skillfully integrates financial wisdom with well-being and purpose. This book is perfect for anyone seeking to transform their relationship with money and live their purpose with more freedom.'
  – **Bob Lotich**, CEPF®, financial coach & author of *Simple Money, Rich Life*

'A joyous read of two determined, financially joyous humans wishing to share the simple message of wealth, happiness and behaviour change. A delightful read and highly recommended to people of all ages who need a firm but loving reminder that financial freedom is doable.'
  – **David McQueen**, CEO of QSquared

'Ken and Mary are the financial wizards we all need in our lives! Relatable, inspirational, and full of practical advice . . . *Financial Joy* really is the book we all need to read in order to live a happier and more financially free life'
  – **Anna Williamson**, broadcaster, author, counsellor and life coach

'This is one of the most important books on money and finance you'll read.'
  – **Timothy Armoo**, entrepreneur, investor and global speaker

'A simple, detailed and fun road map to help you build wealth no matter your starting point. It will change how you feel about your money and help you change your life.'
  – **Jillian Johnsrud**, author, podcaster and coach

We dedicate this book to our great sons, Joshua and Elias.
We love you forever and thank you for being patient,
getting involved in the process and encouraging us when things
got tough as we wrote this book. We're proud of you and it's
our prayer that this book will be a lasting legacy and inspiration
for you, your future children and their children.

Contents

● ●

Part 3:

Looking ahead to financial freedom

● ●

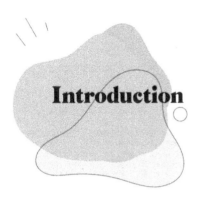

Introduction

WOULD YOU RATHER BE WEALTHY OR HAPPY?

It was a beautiful sunny morning in June and we were excited, because we were on our way to a creativity summer camp with our children, aged eight and ten. The idea was to design your dream invention and when we arrived we were each given an iPad, asked to identify a real-life problem we wanted to solve and then to draw a colourful prototype for what a solution might look like. It was fun and stimulating, but during a break the organizer came up to us and said something that was completely unrelated to the session and completely unexpected. He said, 'You have an energy around you both. It's an energy of contentment. You seem happy with where you are in life. What do you both do for a living?'

Although surprised by the comments of a complete stranger, we looked at each other and smiled, because we understood exactly what he was trying to say, even though he couldn't quite put his finger on it, because he didn't know our story. This wasn't the first time we'd been told this. People have even said that we not only look happy, but we are looking younger than we are. The summer camp organizer wanted to know our secret, but our secret isn't that we are still madly in love with each other after 12 years of marriage, although we are, it is simpler than that. We understand the power of money as a tool to design a financial life filled with joy.

Our finances play such a crucial role in everyday life and underpin other very important areas, such as health, relationships and our spiritual lives. When we ask our communities how they feel about money, the most common responses are: stressed, worried, frustrated, anxious, disillusioned or overwhelmed. This is driven by day-to-day challenges, such as the rising cost of living, taxes and the odd life event that can put your plans back a few steps. You may be living paycheque to paycheque, be deeply in debt or navigating 'point-of-no-return' events like redundancy, having children, getting a mortgage, divorcing or even emigrating to a new country and starting again. These 'point-of-no-return' events create uncertainty about the future and can either push you deeper into despair or act as a slap-in-the-face catalyst to change your life forever.

Although working hard to thrive financially or build wealth is a good thing, too many people are sacrificing the very things that matter most in life: well-being, health, family life, relationships, purpose and enjoying life in the present without guilt. What if you could have both wealth and happiness rather than sacrifice one for the other? And what if you could get a taste of both now and not later? This is what creating your life of financial joy is all about and it's accessible to everyone, no matter where you are right now in your finances. This book will help you turn your life around to create the financial life you want, while prioritizing your well-being, purpose and fun.

HOW DO WE KNOW?

We both come from very humble beginnings, but we achieved financial independence at the age of 34 and became mortgage free in seven years. There is nothing special about us and we've never inherited money or won the lottery. However, one thing we did have going for us was that our lives couldn't really get any worse. This helped us over time to develop a burning desire and a vision that drove a ten-year plan to change our financial lives. In that time, we chose to pursue our goals differently from how we'd seen others do it.

Rather than the extremes of 'you only live once' (YOLO) or extreme frugality, we chose to put joy at the centre of our finances, and make well-being and fun a central part of the purpose of our income. In the decade when we slowly built our wealth, we also created beautiful memories by travelling to 28 countries, while also starting a family and raising children, levelling up our careers and taking risks to invest and start side hustles. This resulted in a balanced, richer and more fulfilled life with no regrets.

In order to design your life of financial joy, you must first take stock of where you've come from. This is where we've come from.

OUR STORY

Hi, I'm Ken. Here is my story:

On 22 July 1998, aged 14, I boarded my first-ever flight and emigrated to London, UK, from Lagos, Nigeria. I was so excited to be moving to the UK from what was a highly politically unstable and unsafe Nigeria. In my head the streets of the UK were paved with gold and I even imagined we'd live in a five-bedroom house next to Buckingham Palace. Of course, I didn't know it at the time, but this was a point-of-no-return event that would drive my determination to achieve financial independence 20 years later.

The reality of the UK hit me hard. Not only was the reception cold, I quickly realized that I was leaving behind everything I'd ever known and starting life in a new country with a new culture and people. My dream of a five-bedroom house did come true, except my family of six (Mum, Dad and four children) were in one bedroom in a house we shared with strangers.

That night, I slept on the floor with my siblings while my parents slept on the bed, and I woke up to day one of the ten years I spent simply surviving. The streets of the UK were not paved with gold, but instead filled with corner shops. Loneliness set in because I didn't have any friends and I feared opening my mouth to speak with my strong Nigerian accent, because I didn't want to stand out or get picked on.

Things got worse around six months later when our visitor visas expired and we became what I'd later understand to be 'overstayers' even though my dad was British. This meant that on top of having no money, we were without 'papers' and couldn't get a job, use the NHS or claim any benefits. We were trapped. We couldn't return to Nigeria and couldn't live like others in the UK.

Pause for a moment to imagine a life where you have no money, and yet you and your family have no legal way of making a living to put bread and milk on the table. I remember feeling like we were worse off than the poorest citizens of the country. Then you throw in the shame that comes with knowing deep down that you have nothing going for you or anyone that can help you.

I started secondary school in Year 11, in the worst school in the borough. Again, I felt completely out of place. Other students had established friendships, but I found solace in my books. I had no identifiable document to my name and I began to see education as a possible way to create my own identity one day.

If you think my situation was bad, spare a thought for my mum, who moved to the UK in her mid-forties to start again with four children and no money. She had a thriving career in Nigeria, having graduated with a political science degree from the prestigious Nigerian University of Ibadan and a master's degree in public administration. She had then worked her way up to become an Assistant Comptroller of Immigration, but she gave all of that up for a 'better life' for her children in the UK.

Given the restrictions we faced as immigrants, she took on three cash-in-hand jobs doing dishwashing, packaging and cleaning. I vividly remember washing the dirty pound coins she'd get as tips from builders at the canteen she worked at in Canary Wharf. Every penny mattered so we could have food on the table. In a recent conversation with Mum about those jobs, she said, 'I did it with joy because it would not last forever.'

My dad had been in the UK for about five years before we arrived. He was a qualified vet in Nigeria, but he found his qualifications were worthless in the UK, so in addition to taking other jobs he worked on a supermarket checkout to provide for his family, while also studying to level up his qualifications.

Although my parents are now well accomplished in business and financially independent at retirement, life was very hard initially. On top of the lack of money back then, I was being bullied at school by the cool kids who not only wore the latest 'garmz', but also got all the girls. My pocket money was £1 ($1.28) a week and I really struggled to make that stretch at school. My luck started to change when one day I found a bundle of free school meal vouchers that a staff member had dropped in the playground. It felt like my prayers had been answered. For the first time, I got to have burgers at school and those vouchers kept me going for months.

Although the UK felt like a hostile place racially and culturally, I started to notice that it held great promise. Things seemed organized. For example, buses actually showed up and were often on time. The trains ran properly and, provided I could afford to pay for things, I could get by, even as a young

Black man. This began to shift my relationship with money as I started to see the UK as a land of opportunity if I worked harder than others.

We'd now upgraded from living in one room to renting a council flat from someone else. This one shift alone, from one bedroom for our entire family to a three-bed flat, represented significant progress. I realized that there was a strong correlation between having some money and living a good lifestyle, so I set out to find my first cash-in-hand job.

Driven by the motivation to fit in at school and buy my first pair of trainers that weren't fakes, I got a cleaning job at a paper factory in Walthamstow, East London, hoping no one from school would ever see me there. My first pay packet was £80 ($102) for a week of work and it was the most money I'd ever made in my life. I still remember being handed the brown envelope. As an attention-starved teenager, I immediately quit my job, went to the shopping centre and spent £40 ($51) to buy the brightest Reebok Classics I could find in Neon Blue. Although I didn't attract any girls, earning my first £80 taught me that I could make some money if I set my heart on something.

Passing my GCSE exams built my confidence and taught me that I had what it took to make it in the UK. With those results, I got into college and worked very hard studying maths, chemistry and biology A levels, while also trying to fit in socially. I got an A grade for my A level maths, but didn't know what I wanted to do with my life, so my teacher suggested accountancy was a good profession to pursue.

Again, almost as though God was opening doors for me, through the clearing system I got a place to study accountancy and economics at City, University of London. However, this was still a challenge, because we couldn't afford the £1,100 ($1,400) a year tuition fee and I couldn't get a student loan due to residency issues. My parents literally had no spare money after paying for the essentials, so the university kindly agreed I could pay £400 ($500) a term, although even this resulted in many arguments between my parents as they had to find that extra money each term to support me.

Going to university turned out to be a game-changing opportunity because, after three years of hard graft, I graduated in 2005 with a first class honours degree, a first in my family's history. I went on to train as a chartered accountant with a top ten firm and for the first time ever, I started to earn proper income with a payslip. Going from my first pay packet of £80 a week to a trainee contract paying £22,000 ($28,200) a year was a huge leap.

I suffered lifestyle inflation and suddenly wanted the world to see that I was successful. I wasted money on a flashy Mercedes Coupé on finance and bought a Rolex watch and Cartier bracelet. Although I looked successful on the outside, my bank account had no money in it and I lived from paycheque to paycheque. I'd had enough.

Fast forward to 2009, another point of no return in my life, and I met my beautiful wife, Mary, in the most unlikely of places, at a property seminar, after reading Robert Kiyosaki's book, *Rich Dad Poor Dad*. In the same year, after three years of hard work, I also qualified as a chartered accountant and started my career in the asset management business. Meeting Mary coincided with the end of my decade of survival and the beginning of my decade of thriving.

Mary and I started dating, but the one key event that would change our lives forever was that we decided to create a ten-year plan (more on this later) even before we got married. Between 2009 and 2017 I went from being a newly qualified accountant to a chief financial officer (CFO) for a venture capital business. As I fought for my place in the world and rose in my career, so did my income, which doubled every three years.

However, something else happened during this decade of thriving.

As my income rose, my lifestyle became simpler and simpler, and cost less, creating a buffer of money to invest in what would become a great bull market. I hustled like crazy in this decade, starting a number of side hustles and joint venture businesses, while keeping up with my demanding job and becoming a parent to our two boys. In addition, I dreamed of completing an Executive MBA at the University of Cambridge and achieved this in 2016.

For Mary and I, financial freedom was a must, but we didn't want the fact that we'd become parents to stop us from achieving this goal and also having fun along the way. I'd seen enough evidence that this could become a reality as I'd read lots of books and American blogs, and joined Financial Independence Retire Early (FIRE) communities in the UK, and by 2017, we achieved financial independence. Later that year, we decided that we wanted to start sharing what we'd learned as a family via a blog at www.thehumblepenny.com, as we couldn't see Black couples, families or minority communities in this space.

This step of faith to start the Humble Penny became a calling and when Covid hit, it all got too much for me. The demanding CFO job, a growing side hustle (which now included a YouTube channel and Financial Joy Academy), homeschooling during the lockdown and mental health pressures led to me quitting my accountancy career in 2020 to focus on educating others via the Humble Penny.

This shift to do what we love as a new career was only possible because we'd achieved financial independence and also paid off our mortgage. As far as I was concerned, the only way was up with our work with the Humble Penny and the best part was that I got to do what I love with my beautiful wife, Mary, whom I love so dearly.

But this journey has not been easy or smooth. I've experienced redundancies, jobs I hated, failed ventures, poor investments, recessions, systemic racism, failed relationships, health scares, residency problems, deportation threats and so much more. However, even with all this and the many things I haven't even shared yet, I managed to design my life of financial joy. My mission now is to share the ideas, tools and frameworks that will help you design yours, no matter what that looks like and irrespective of where you are now in your finances.

Hi, I'm Mary. Here is my story:

I grew up and lived for 27 years in a tough inner city council estate in Hackney, East London, an economically disadvantaged area and a far cry from the gentrified Hackney of today. Born to immigrant parents who arrived in London in the late 1970s, I was the youngest and had three older brothers.

As a child, I remember watching shows like *Blue Peter* and realized that the schools depicted on the TV were a stark contrast to my own. I longed for the educational opportunities portrayed on screen. However, my reality was quite different. My primary school was plagued by frequent expulsions, absent teachers and disruptive learning environments. Secondary school and college provided a slightly better experience; I got the A level grades I needed to do a BSc multimedia technology and design at Brunel University.

Money was rarely talked about at home. The only time I heard it discussed was when relatives in Nigeria would call, requesting financial support – an occurrence that happened regularly. While trying to build wealth, my parents would regularly send money back home to support their family, which they still do to this day, even as pensioners.

My earliest memory of money was observing my parents' sensible spending habits. They prioritized essentials, forgoing family holidays and dining out. However, birthdays were always celebrated with memorable parties, filled with friends, family and an abundance of home-cooked food. Living within their means, my parents avoided credit card debt and embraced a frugal lifestyle. Witnessing their dedication and my brothers' entrepreneurial pursuits from a young age, I eagerly followed suit.

At 14, I began a paper round and, with my brother, even crafted music CDs, which I sold in my secondary school playground. Throughout my school days I had part-time retail jobs and, although I didn't necessarily need the money, I relished seeing my savings account grow each month.

On my 17th birthday, I organized a party at my older brother's luxury river-view penthouse in London's Docklands. Back then, having a penthouse was a big deal – the prevailing aspiration was to secure a spot on the council housing waiting list – and my eldest brother stood out as an anomaly in our community. While his peers struggled to obtain qualifications, their futures clouded by lack of opportunity and resources, crime, mental health issues, poverty, imprisonment or even premature death, he had a degree, a successful job and a side hustle building, configuring and selling computers. Financially, he was doing exceptionally well.

Unfortunately, the economic landscape shifted in 2000, leaving my brother without a contracting job for the first time in years. He had to move back home and sleep on the living room floor, saving up for a deposit to purchase his own property. This experience served as a profound lesson for me. I vowed to delay moving out until it was really necessary and, instead of renting, to become a homeowner and landlord. I would eventually stay at home until I got married.

While my parents contemplated a return to Nigeria, our neighbours were purchasing their council homes at affordable rates. By the time my parents decided they would stay in the UK, our own property had surged in value and their mortgage became five times that of our neighbours.

This experience ignited my thirst for knowledge and financial literacy. I delved into money books, attended business seminars and scribbled copious notes.

Growing up amid my siblings' entrepreneurial endeavours, I had always harboured the desire to start my own purpose-led business. Two of my brothers ran a media company and I worked there during my placement year, helping to design clients' websites.

After uni, my first graduate job was short-lived due to a redundancy during the 2008 global financial crisis. Undeterred, I secured another corporate role within three months and eventually landed a position at one of the top five accountancy firms as an e-business analyst. In 2009, amid another wave of redundancies, I managed to avoid the cut, but witnessed the distress and uncertainty my colleagues endured during the gruelling redundancy process. Two more rounds of redundancies would occur in the four years that I was there. Each time I was unaffected, but some of my colleagues were not so lucky.

This further solidified my belief that employment alone could not guarantee financial security. I vowed never to rely solely on a job for my income. This conviction resonated deeply with the teachings of *Rich Dad Poor Dad*. The book's concepts, particularly the cashflow quadrant, and the value of being a business owner and investor, articulated the thoughts I had struggled to express. I wanted financial independence.

Having accumulated significant savings from years of hard work, I felt compelled to make my money work harder than simply leaving it in a cash ISA, but I didn't know where to even start. Without hesitation, I attended a *Rich Dad Poor Dad* property seminar advertised in the newspaper in October 2009 and it was there that I met my amazing husband, Ken.

In 2011, we tied the knot and embarked on an exhilarating journey of faith together, committed to creating lasting memories and taking a different approach with our finances. While three months pregnant, in 2012, I had an opportunity to manage a new branch of our family-run nursery business, while still working at the accountancy firm. Colleagues questioned my sanity, but with the corporate world's uncertainties, the need to code-switch and not seeing a future there, I was ready for a change. Although I cherished my team and enjoyed a decent salary, I craved more.

Embracing the chance to manage the nursery and assume various roles, I pursued a childcare qualification. In the midst of these responsibilities, I gave birth to our two boys, who would accompany me to work each day at the nursery. It proved to be a fulfilling and challenging taste of entrepreneurship, while saving us thousands in childcare costs.

For seven years I devoted myself to the nursery until Ken and I started a passion project in 2017 that eventually transformed into a side hustle – the Humble Penny. Juggling parenting, the nursery, marriage and the Humble Penny became overwhelming, prompting my decision to transition to full-time work on the Humble Penny in 2019.

My journey has been shaped by my faith, my upbringing, the challenges I have faced, the lessons I have learned from economic setbacks and my unwavering drive for financial independence. With the Humble Penny, I seek to empower individuals to take control of their finances and design their own lives of financial joy.

OUR WORK

The Humble Penny started life on 3 December 2017 as a 99p blog. It came from a strong desire to do something meaningful that would help others financially; people who didn't start life with trust funds. We chose the tagline 'Create financial joy', because when we thought about our relationship with money, all we ultimately wanted was to use money to design a life of freedom and options, with no stress, but filled with the small experiences and things that bring us joy.

Given that we ran this as a side hustle alongside our day jobs, the Humble Penny was a two-hour-a-day experiment. Over time, it started to grow as more people came across our simple and relatable stories and ideas. That blog grew and started attracting tens of thousands of visitors a month, leading us to start a YouTube channel to help us reach more people through our work. To date, the Humble Penny has helped over five million people across the world to improve their relationship with money.

Given we were receiving daily emails from lots of people for coaching and couldn't help everyone at once, in 2020 we decided to take a big leap and launch Financial Joy Academy, a first-of-its-kind, step-by-step membership platform to help at least ten thousand 'dream-makers' achieve financial independence in a decade.

It's an online community of like-minded people and we created it as a low-cost and accessible way to provide all the tools, courses, expert masterclasses, in-person events, ongoing biweekly coaching from us and accountability you need to achieve your wealth-building, investing or business goals.

Our community of dream-makers have taken control of their finances, started money-making side hustles, received five-figure promotions, become debt free, got on the property ladder, entered joint ventures to buy investment properties, grown stock market investments as beginners (some by over 20% in a year), developed an abundance mindset, created lifelong friendships from accountability partners and more.

The ultimate goal of our work is to not only help you to create financial joy in your life, but we also want to create a ripple effect that will help our children's generation to create financial lives that they love.

WHO IS THIS BOOK FOR? CALLING
ALL DREAM-MAKERS!

A lot of people around us, across the country and all over the world are stressed and fed up with the status quo of spiralling living costs, declining real wages, higher taxes and so on, and they have deep uncertainties about the future.

They also have dreams, such as getting on the property ladder, becoming debt free and mortgage free, increasing or diversifying their incomes, doing fulfilling work, starting or enjoying family life, planning for a comfortable retirement and, ultimately, having financial security while enjoying life.

We've written this book for singles or couples (with or without children) who are typically aged between 20 and 55 and range in financial circumstances from those who have no money at all to those who have some financial security already.

However, we're writing it through our lens as a couple with young children who were once single and have been through many trials and tribulations of life, from poverty to financial freedom, at our current age of 40.

We've written this book to give you a practical ten-week, step-by-step plan, motivation and inspiration for how to turn your life around, re-write your story and join a growing community of dream-makers who are taking small but consistent steps to change their lives financially.

Whether you're currently just about making ends meet, living on your overdraft, in debt and stressed, a complete beginner when it comes to investing, fed up with your career, relying solely on one income and desperate for another, making a good income but uncertain how to stop running the rat race or feeling like time is running out to prepare for retirement, you too can become a dream-maker with the help of this book.

That's because becoming a dream-maker starts in the mind. What unites us all is our core desire to get into the driving seat, turn our lives around and design meaningful lives of financial joy – and you won't be undertaking this journey alone, because we're here with you every step of the way.

Please note: While the examples and context in this book will primarily focus on the UK, the principles and strategies discussed can be applied universally, providing value to readers around the world.

THE KEY PRINCIPLES OF FINANCIAL JOY

Financial joy is a mindset and model that can be used by anyone who earns or spends money to take control of their finances, grow their money and design a financial life they love, while prioritizing the experiences and things that bring them joy.

It is a practical ten-week programme that cuts out all the jargon, complexity and shaming to provide you with a step-by-step plan that's encouraging, empathetic and empowering, so that you can design a financial life that's not only richer, but more meaningful and without regrets.

Financial joy is for everybody and it's accessible to you now not later. Here are three simple rules to remember on the journey: Take control of your finances, grow your money and create joy. Let's now break these three simple rules down into the ten key messages of the book.

Principle 1. You need the three seeds of mindset, skillset and toolset

Most people have deep-rooted mindset problems that prevent them from improving their skillsets. They also don't have the toolsets – the game plans, for example — to guide them and help them to beat the fear of failure and achieve their goals. This book will give you the three seeds of mindset, skillset and toolset.

Principle 2. Becoming wealthy and happy are not mutually exclusive

We will introduce you to new research in this area and show you that you don't have to choose either wealth or happiness, but that you can have both and enjoy both without comparing yourself to others.

Principle 3. You can start where you are now, and turn your life around

You might look at your life right now and feel like it's too late for you. The truth is, where you are now is a good enough place to begin turning your life around and you have what it takes to create new opportunities in your life irrespective of age, gender, race, religion or location.

Principle 4. Your money story is emotional and complex and that's okay

Your money story and blueprint are deeply connected to not only your parents, but also your grandparents. The good news is that you can upgrade the money story and blueprint that you have today, but first we need to work on healing your money wounds and shifting your money mindset and habits.

Principle 5. Financial literacy is not enough – you need to change your behaviour

In addition to financial literacy, we will dig deeper to understand money psychology, the behavioural biases holding you back and what it takes practically to change your behaviour in order to achieve lasting outcomes with your finances.

Principle 6. The vision you have for your life is a design problem that can be solved

We will show you why having a vision, writing it down and making it plain creates an unstoppable drive towards achieving your money goals.

Principle 7. Faith is a currency in your finances

Money is energy and faith is the currency in our finances. This isn't about religious beliefs, but about how you take faith walks in situations that are both under or outside your control and trust the process.

Principle 8. Growing your income starts by breaking the employee mindset

We will show you how to break those limiting beliefs and guide you through various options to learn new skills that will help you to grow and diversify your income streams.

Principle 9. Enjoying your money now – without guilt – is a great idea

We believe that you should consistently spend some of your money intentionally on the things or experiences that bring you joy, while being confident that you're working towards your ultimate financial freedom. We will show you how to create your Joyful Spending Plan.

Principle 10. Financial joy is for everyone and available to you now

Although financial freedom is a great goal to have, it is not the only goal on the money journey. Yours could be that you want to become debt free or build an emergency fund or have some financial flexibility. Whatever your goal is, this book will help you to put joy at the centre of it, so that you can start living your unique life of financial joy now, rather than later.

WHAT YOU'LL GET OUT OF THIS BOOK

Our goal with this book is to keep things simple, positive and practical, so that you can follow our ten-week, step-by-step plan to design your own life of financial joy.

Saving to travel? Want to get on the property ladder? Or would you like to create an extra stream of income for more financial security in your life? This book will help you create a game plan for your goals, while also leaving room to enjoy your money and your life, guilt free.

In addition, we'll share relatable real-life interviews, the most recent research and expert insights to bring everything together into a well-rounded plan for you.

The book is split into three parts:

Laying the foundations for financial joy: First, we will work on how to remove fear, improve your money mindset and behaviours, write your vision and take control of your finances.

Building financial joy: Next, after mastering your day-to-day finances, we will focus on how to become braver and grow your money.

Looking ahead to financial independence: Finally, we will look at how to aim for financial freedom and retirement, while enjoying your money and doing what brings you joy.

Within each part, the programme is broken down into weekly goals, with useful information, lessons and action steps. We designed the book like this to ensure that the goals are all achievable and you can transform your attitude to money in just a few weeks.

After reading this book, not only will you have better control of your money than most adults, you'll also have full clarity and a plan to design your unique life of financial joy.

Buckle up for an exciting ride, because implementing everything we share over these ten weeks will change your financial destiny forever!

IMPORTANT DISCLAIMER

Nothing we share in this book constitutes financial advice.

Ken was professionally involved in the investment business for 14 years, worked his way up to become a CFO, is a qualified chartered accountant

(ACA – ICAEW) and holds an MBA from Cambridge University's Judge Business School. However, beyond our professional expertise, everything we share comes from our lived experience of working towards and achieving financial independence as a couple in a decade.

That includes everything we've learned from mentors, other experts and our parents. For example, Mary learned about business from her brothers and frugal living from her parents and their Yoruba Ijebu culture, while Ken learned about entrepreneurship from his enterprising mum and her Igbo culture.

We've seen the extremes of wealth and poverty first hand through our travels to over 28 countries. Ken was also born and raised in Nigeria, where there isn't the safety net of a social security system, and we come from working-class immigrant backgrounds, so we've been resource-poor ourselves.

Through working our way up our corporate jobs, we've met others who are extremely wealthy, too. For example, Ken's work as a CFO in the venture capital business, where he helped raise tens of millions of pounds, meant he often interacted with high-net-worth millionaires and billionaires.

In addition, through our content we have coached thousands of people and taught millions how to achieve financial freedom. We have also received tens of thousands of positive comments, emails and progress reports about the different areas we cover in this book, so we know that our methods work.

All these unique experiences give us a unique perspective and enable us to bring something fresh to you through this book. We're confident that everything we share will help you move forwards on your money journey and, beyond that, design your life of financial joy.

STAY IN TOUCH

Please feel free to follow and DM us on social media – we are @TheHumblePenny and @FinancialJoyAcademy on YouTube, Instagram, Facebook, X and TikTok. Follow us on LinkedIn by searching for 'Ken Okoroafor' and 'Mary Okoroafor'.

You can also join over 40,000 monthly readers of our weekly newsletter at our website at www.thehumblepenny.com, where you can also email us directly at Book@thehumblepenny.com

Finally, remember that this is your unique journey and it's not a comparison game or a sprint. Your life of financial joy can only be created by you, so say yes to it and start creating it today, one week at a time.

To our success, dream-maker!

Love, Ken and Mary

PS. Thank you from the bottom of our hearts for reading our book. It's a dream that we're now authors. Please take a photo of yourself with the front cover of the book or a picture of the book in an interesting location and share it with us on Instagram – you can DM us @thehumblepenny or send it via email to Book@thehumblepenny.com – telling us what part of the world you're reading from. Use the subject line, 'Financial joy book pic'. We'd love to hear from you and share your photo on our socials.

PART 1

Laying the foundations for financial joy

GOAL: Remove fear, improve your money mindset and behaviours, write your vision and take control of your finances by getting into the driving seat of your life.

Week 1:
Design your life of financial joy

A life of financial joy is intentional and coherent with who you are, what you value and what brings joy to your life today.

I remember it like yesterday. I (Ken) woke up confused, looked around, and wondered where I was and why I was sitting on the floor in my pants. Everything seemed blurry and I couldn't remember how I got there.

Three hours before, at 12.31 a.m., I'd arrived home from work after a gruelling 15-hour shift, trying to meet my deadlines as a CFO at an investment business. The lonely two-hour journey from London back to Kent had taken a further toll on me, and I'd had to walk home from the station in the bitter cold, through dimly lit streets with only foxes for company.

I remember thinking, is this the life that I always dreamed of? After all those years of working my way up the career ladder, here I was. Not only had I not spent time with my wife and children that evening, but I hadn't seen them properly for days and, although I didn't know it then, things were about to get worse.

I got home and crashed out next to Mary. Three hours later I got up to use the bathroom and, as I would learn later, I immediately collapsed and hit my head on the bathroom sink. The loud bang awakened Mary, who desperately helped me regain consciousness. Another three hours later, the ambulance finally showed up and, while I sat at A&E waiting for a brain scan, I asked myself, why am I here?

If you pay close attention to your life, you'll notice that it gives you signals about what's most important. The problem is most of us either don't pay attention or we don't look out for the signals. Instead, we're all quietly working ourselves into the ground.

That night and the many hours in A&E would become a point-of-no-return event like many others that I'd experienced before. I took my phone out of my pocket and recorded a video, speaking to the camera to remind myself of how I felt at that moment. I promised myself that I would never be here again and started reassessing my priorities immediately.

I asked myself repeatedly: what do I really want in my life and what does money have to do with it? The answer was simple. I wanted a financial life that we love with the things and experiences that bring us joy at the centre of it. The thing is, although we'd been working hard for years on our journey towards achieving financial independence and living frugally, our overwhelming focus was on trying to achieve our freedom number. The 'financial' element of our money journey dominated our lives with insufficient focus on what brought us joy.

The long hours from my job, coupled with the tiredness that Mary experienced in her job while also looking after our children, meant that on a good day, by the time we sat down to eat dinner and chat after putting our children to bed, we were both worn out. Something had to change – and sooner rather than later. In our quest to find a better balance, we took some time out as a couple to reassess our lives and goals.

At that weekend away, we realized that creating a financial life that we love comprises two areas that you don't typically bring together: what we want vs what we need.

What we want – the 'financial' element – represents our money goals, such as financial freedom, and speaks to the more logical and maths-driven part of our brains.

What we need – the 'joy' element – represents the emotional aspects of our lives, such as the desire to travel and explore the world, the need for a happy family life or the need to do purpose-led fulfilling work that we enjoy.

Breaking things down into these two parts made it clear that it was hard to have one without the other. If we were going to create a wholesome life that was sustainable, and gave us the options to experience life to the fullest many years into the future, without regrets, we needed to design a life of financial joy.

Having lived this balanced life of financial joy for over seven years, since 2017, we'll be sharing with you the trade-offs necessary to achieve this balance and how you can do the same in ten weeks. In addition, we'll be sharing why financial joy is now more important than ever during times of uncertainty.

WHAT IS FINANCIAL JOY?

Imagine a life where your financial situation no longer causes stress, anxiety or sleepless nights; a life where money becomes a tool for empowerment, enabling you to pursue your dreams, support your loved ones and make a positive impact in the world. This is the essence of financial joy.

In other words, financial joy is a mindset and model that anyone who earns or spends money can use to ultimately design a balanced life of wealth and well-being. It's not just about accumulating wealth or achieving financial independence. It's about finding harmony in your relationship with money, aligning your financial goals with your values, and experiencing a deep sense of contentment and peace regarding your finances.

Financial joy is about transcending the traditional notions of success and redefining what wealth truly means to you. It's about cultivating a mindset that allows you to navigate the ever-changing financial landscape with confidence and resilience.

We choose joy because it is a deep and lasting sense of inner contentment and delight. It is a profound emotion that arises from within and is independent of external circumstances. Joy can be present even during challenging times, such as recessions or when the cost of living rises.

WHY ACHIEVING FINANCIAL JOY IS ESSENTIAL FOR PERSONAL WELL-BEING AND HAPPINESS

Achieving financial joy is essential for personal well-being and happiness, because it has a profound impact on various aspects of our lives. Here are several reasons why financial joy is crucial.

Reduced stress and anxiety

Financial stress is a leading cause of anxiety and worry for many individuals. When we are constantly concerned about making ends meet, paying bills or dealing with overwhelming debt, it takes a toll on our mental and emotional well-being. By achieving financial joy you can alleviate this stress and enjoy greater peace of mind.

Example: To help us reduce stress and anxiety in our lives from the long hours at work, we changed jobs and used our transferable skills to start new careers.

Freedom and independence

Financial joy provides us with the freedom and independence to live life on our own terms. It allows us to make choices based on our values and aspirations rather than being limited by financial constraints. You can pursue your passions, take risks and seize opportunities without being bound by financial limitations.

Example: To help us prioritize financial freedom, we started simplifying our lifestyles in order to reduce our monthly costs and remove the pressure on our finances. The expensive car had to go, we bought a house in a cheaper area, we went plant-based, we changed our shopping habits and so on. After a few years, all this gradually increased our savings rate from 10% to 65%. More on this later.

Improved relationships

Money can significantly impact our relationships, whether it's with our partners, family or friends. Financial stress can strain relationships and lead to conflicts. On the other hand, achieving financial joy promotes healthier relationships by reducing money tensions and providing a stable foundation for building strong connections.

Example: To help improve our relationships, we stopped talking to friends and family about money unless it was absolutely necessary. Instead, we created environments in which we could to speak to each other about our finances without blame or judgement and talked more about our family vision.

Enhanced quality of life

Financial joy and stability enables us to improve our overall quality of life. It allows us to meet our basic needs comfortably, enjoy leisure activities and invest in experiences that bring us joy and fulfilment.

Example: We love travelling and plan our adventures 12 to 24 months ahead to get the best deals and save money by collecting loyalty points that we then use for travel. We also create a photo book of each holiday to relive the joyous experience as we look forward to the next one.

Future security and preparedness

Financial joy involves planning for the future and being prepared for unexpected circumstances. It means having savings and investments that can provide a safety net during emergencies or retirement. By achieving financial joy, we can feel secure and confident about our future, knowing that we have taken steps to protect ourselves and our loved ones.

Example: When Covid struck in 2020 it was a true test of preparedness, because we were running our own small business and therefore ineligible for furlough. Thankfully, we'd been saving and investing for years, and having that financial security helped to remove stress and anxiety from our lives.

Pursuit of personal goals and dreams

Financial joy empowers us to pursue our personal goals and dreams without the constraints of financial limitations. Whether it's starting a business, travelling the world, furthering our education or supporting charitable causes, financial stability allows us to align our actions with our aspirations, unlocking a sense of purpose and fulfilment. By achieving financial stability and aligning your finances with your values and aspirations, you can experience a greater sense of joy, contentment and overall well-being.

Example: We'd always dreamed of being our own bosses and doing purpose-led work that gave us fulfilment. Without choosing to design a life of financial joy years ago, we wouldn't have had the option to quit our careers and start our own passion projects, running the Humble Penny and Financial Joy Academy to help others with their finances. In addition, we're able to charitably support causes and projects we love, including a Compassion child in Uganda.

WHAT DOES A LIFE OF FINANCIAL JOY LOOK LIKE FOR YOU?

It's time to get practical and design your life of financial joy. To give you a practical example, here is what our life of financial joy looks like today. Remember, this is personal, and has evolved over time and will continue to do so. It also looked very different a decade ago. Yours will be unique to you, too.

Financial	Joy
1. Remain financially independent by keeping our costs low, reducing waste and ruling out moving to a bigger house.	1. Put God first in our lives, pray daily, read daily, work out in the gym daily (aim for 10,000 steps) and eat well daily (mainly plant-based with lots of water).
2. Invest in our pensions and max out our Individual Savings Account (ISA) allowances each year, investing 100% in globally diversified stocks with a bias for ethical stocks.	2. Spend time daily in our garden with our children and enjoy their formative years. Play table tennis, football and card games listening to music.
3. Use 5% of our income to explore new opportunities and use any gains from that to support our parents or wider family.	3. Ensure 20% of our family income is spent travelling to dream world destinations (for example to Europe and across Africa) to explore local culture and history with our children. Aim to travel two to five times a year on a budget.
4. Co-invest with our children each month in their Junior ISAs and Junior SIPPs.	4. Continue doing work we love that's fulfilling, and enriches our souls and those of others, working six hours a day, four days a week.
5. Give 10% or more of our income and increase this yearly.	5. Each month, give generously, from the heart, our money, time and skills (for example do pro-bono work, and serve in our local church, community or local schools).
6. Pay our bills and taxes on time, and show gratitude for every interaction we have with money.	6. Take three months off work throughout the year to rest, explore hobbies more deeply, spend more time with our children and to spice up our marriage, including weekly date nights on our day off, Friday.
7. Don't ever worry or stress about money, no matter what. Worry does more damage. Instead, focus on living now.	7. Annually, bless others in financial difficulty, starting with ten fully paid scholarships to Financial Joy Academy.

To help guide you, here are some questions to reflect on and answer. By answering these questions honestly and thoughtfully, you can gain a deeper understanding of your financial aspirations, values and priorities. This will guide you in designing a life of financial joy that aligns with your unique circumstances and goals. We'll deep-dive into these various elements in more detail over the next ten weeks. For now, write your answers in the spaces provided below:

1. What does your life of financial joy look like? How would you describe it in your own words? Make sure you balance your desired financial life with what brings joy to your life.

Financial	Joy

2. What are your financial values and priorities? What matters most to you when it comes to money and financial well-being?

3. What lifestyle do you want to lead? How does money play a role in achieving that lifestyle?

4. What are your strengths and weaknesses when it comes to managing money? What areas do you need to improve upon?

Strengths	Weaknesses

Now that you've painted a picture of what financial joy looks like for you, let's talk a little bit about financial stress and why prioritizing a life of financial joy is important during times of uncertainty.

FINANCIAL STRESS AND HOW TO RELIEVE IT

Financial stress refers to the emotional strain and anxiety experienced as a result of financial difficulties or challenges. It could, for example, be caused by recent major events, such as the 2020 pandemic or the recent cost of living crisis, or by more personal events, specific to the individual, such as redundancy or divorce. This stress can lead to anxiety, depression and mental health disorders, sleep problems, relationship strain, reduced quality of life and even physical health implications.

It's important to note that the impact of financial stress on mental health can vary from person to person, and individuals may respond differently based on their coping mechanisms, support systems and other factors. However, it is clear financial stress can have a significant toll on mental well-being.

To mitigate existing challenges, you need to make difficult lifestyle trade-offs, adopt effective budgeting techniques, saving strategies and long-term financial planning. You also need to explore ways to enhance your income, reduce expenses and adapt to the changing financial landscape. These can all seem overwhelming, but having lived through these challenges ourselves, we know that even in financial difficulty you can still take proactive steps and design a life of financial joy.

TEN ACTIONABLE STEPS TO BEAT FINANCIAL STRESS AND ANXIETY

Here are some practical things that you can do to beat financial stress and anxiety.

Step 1: Understand your financial situation

Taking a close look at your finances is like going for a dental checkup. You know it's going to be uncomfortable, but it's necessary to keep things healthy. Understanding your financial situation involves looking at your income, expenses, debts and assets. It literally gives you an idea of what to do next, for example, which debts are most urgent or which expenses you could let go of. We'll cover this in detail in weeks 5 and 6.

Step 2: Talk to someone about your financial anxiety

Consider speaking to a counsellor, trusted friend or a family member about your anxiety. They may be able to provide you with valuable insights, offer support and advice, or simply be a sounding board enabling you to think through your thoughts and feelings. We recently had breakfast with someone who had a lot of anxiety about their financial future. Within 45 minutes of talking through her numbers and her investing, she felt calmer about the future. We looked at a compound interest calculator, for example, and made sensible assumptions about her investing returns. This showed that she would be okay in the future and that gave her some peace of mind.

Step 3: Create a joyful spending plan (aka a budget)

By understanding your financial situation in step 1, you can create a joyful spending plan and identify areas where you can cut expenses, carve out money for fun or see opportunities to increase income. We'll cover this in detail in week 5.

Step 4: Set financial goals

Setting financial goals can help you stay motivated and focused. If you've got £5,000 of credit card debt, you can set a goal that will clear it over the next ten months, for example £500 a month. This creates the motivation to start working towards it. We'll cover this in detail in week 4.

Step 5: Build an emergency fund

Having an emergency fund can help you feel more secure and less anxious about unexpected expenses. A good starting point is having £1,000 set aside. We'll cover how to save your emergency fund faster and where to keep it in week 5.

Step 6: Review your bills and subscriptions

Make a detailed list of your bills and subscriptions to see if there are any you can cancel or reduce. This can free up some cash and reduce financial stress. Keep things that are improving your knowledge or well-being, or helping you to build wealth.

Step 7: Negotiate your bills

You may be able to negotiate better rates on bills such as your phone, internet or insurance. Don't be afraid to ask for a discount or shop around for better deals. We recently called up our car insurance and business insurance companies, and negotiated discounts. Those negotiations were based on loyalty and doing research to show them where we could get things cheaper.

Step 8: Consider debt consolidation

Debt consolidation is like going on a first date – you're nervous, you don't know what to expect and you're hoping for a happy ending. But unlike a first date, with debt consolidation you get to choose your perfect match – a loan with lower interest rates, better terms and more manageable payments. If you have multiple debts, consolidating them into one loan can make them easier to manage and reduce stress. However, make sure you understand the terms and fees before consolidating. We'll cover banishing debt for good in week 6.

Step 9: Create a self-care plan

Taking care of your physical and mental health can help you feel more resilient and better equipped to deal with financial stress. Make time for exercise, relaxation and activities you enjoy.

Step 10: Keep educating yourself

You're already doing this by reading this book. Keep going. There are also lots of great online resources, like our blog and YouTube channel, among others. The most important thing when it comes to learning is acting, which is why this book is very practical. So watch out for the small action steps at the end of each week.

Together, over the next ten weeks, each action step you take will help you prioritize financial joy in your life and put joy at the centre of your finances.

WEEK 1: LESSONS AND ACTION STEPS

Three lessons for week 1

- Financial joy is a mindset for wealth and well-being that's accessible to you now, no matter where you are on your money journey. The life that you want to create for yourself is a design problem that can be solved, even if you have no money right now.

- A well-designed life of financial joy is one that aligns your values, money goals and purpose, and prioritizes the experiences that bring you joy and improved well-being.
- Embracing financial joy is vital during times of uncertainty and will help you to remove financial stress, worry and anxiety, while giving you the tools to adapt, grow and stay resilient.

Three action steps for week 1

Action step 1: Design your life of financial joy (see page 33).

Action step 2: What is your financial joy state? See the exercise below and score yourself. Repeat this exercise again after ten weeks as you take action.

You can download a free and dynamic Excel copy that adds up all your scores automatically at www.thehumblepenny.com/financialjoystate. Feel free to take a photo of your response to this exercise and share your score with us on Instagram – DM us @thehumblepenny or send it via email to Book@thehumblepenny.com and feel free to ask us any questions.

Action step 3: Set one specific goal for the ten-week programme based on something you scored yourself at 1, 2 or 3 on your financial joy state exercise.

Your Financial Joy State

Note: Score yourself once for each line using the key below. Then add up your total score.

# Understanding today	1	2	3	4	5	Total
1 I know and track my monthly expenses and income						
2 I am saving and investing at least 10–20% of my monthly income						
3 I know and track my current net worth						
4 I know how much debt I have and have a debt free plan						

Dealing with storms	1	2	3	4	5	Total
5 I have an emergency fund that covers 3–6 months of expenses						
6 I have adequate state cover for health and/or health insurance						
7 I have life insurance that covers my mortgage and living costs						
8 I have done estate planning and written a will						

Dreams for the future	1	2	3	4	5	Total
9 I have clear and defined goals for my future						
10 I am taking steps to create an additional income stream						
11 I have a plan for my personal growth and development						
12 I have a plan for financial independence & optional retirement						

Thinking of others	1	2	3	4	5	Total
13 I am committed to giving to at least one charity or cause						
14 I am actively volunteering my time to help others						
15 I am part of a small community where we support each other						
16 I am considering what legacy I want to leave one day						

Work, life and joy balance	1	2	3	4	5	Total
17 I see work as purposeful and there's more to life than money						
18 My partner and I are on the same page & planning life together						
19 I am teaching my children all I know about money management						
20 I am spending 5–20% of my income to have fun, play and enjoy my life						

Feeling financially joyful overall?	Out of 100

Key:

1 = I am not doing this at all.

2 = I am barely doing this.

3 = I am kinda doing this but could be a lot better.

4 = I am doing this confidently but with room for improvement.

5 = I am absolutely doing this very well and confidently.

Note: If you're single or don't have children, rate yourself a 5 score for no.18 and/or no.19.

Week 2:
Build a positive relationship with money

A life of financial joy is created by letting go of a scarcity mindset, and adopting an abundance and positive mindset coupled with healthy money habits.

KEN'S MONEY STORY

Have you ever wondered how you met with money? Where did your relationship begin? For us, the true origins of our relationship with money are hard to trace back and are filled with turmoil. As child, I lived in a town called Oguta, in southeastern Nigeria, and in Badagry, in the megacity of Lagos, before moving with my family to the UK at the age of 14, in search of a better life. Oguta was a small place and there was no TV, no internet, no advertising and no credit cards – in fact, none of the usual trappings of a modern existence. I lived in my own world and money lived in its own world.

My world was simple, warm, and filled with mango, coconut and soursop trees. I played games with other children on the sand outside or jumped into the local river, where my grandparents caught fish for lunch, which was often pounded yam and fresh fish soup.

My earliest memory of my relationship with money is when I was about five and at nursery school, and I walked up to the hawkers carrying trays on their heads by the school gates and asked for *kpo-ko-ro-rom*, a snack of plantain crisps with stew on top of it, named after the sound when you ate it. The hawker asked for money, and one of my teachers gave it to me and I paid for it.

That is the first time I met with money. Fast forward a few years to around the age of nine and we'd moved from Oguta (population under 20,000) to Lagos, a bustling city of more than 20 million people. When I wasn't playing football, barefoot, on the street with my friends, I was at a local shop that sold Mars and Snickers chocolate bars from England. Seeing these things I'd never had, but desperately wanted, began to shift my relationship with money. I wanted money badly, so that I could taste the good life. Money became what I needed to buy what other people had.

Fast forward to the age of 14, when we moved to the UK, and it was obvious that the entire country ran on an established monetary system and you needed money to survive. Whether you count your money in dollars, pounds, euros, yen, rupees, yuan or naira, money is an essential requirement in contemporary society and remains a push and pull in all our lives. Seeing money as a requirement for survival is where my fear-based relationship with money began.

A FEAR-BASED RELATIONSHIP WITH MONEY

As immigrants without money, it became clear that we were poor in a rich country. In Nigeria, the poverty wasn't clear, because everyone around us was at the same level. For example, no one had football boots and the only time anyone ate chicken was on Christmas Day. But in the UK, your postcode was the first signal as to how rich or poor you might be. Then there was the question of what your parents did for a living, followed by whether you owned your own home or not.

My parents sacrificed all they had to bring us to the UK, believing everything would be better here, but the best jobs they could get initially were cleaning or working in a supermarket. I dreamed of becoming a 'professional', and many years later I became a chartered accountant and started earning real money. The problem was my relationship with money meant I found myself wanting the finest things.

I started buying what other people either wanted or had, just to show that 'I'd arrived'. I wanted people (especially girls) to see that I was becoming successful. Life was all about fitting into my immediate environment, and keeping up with my friends and the social pressure to buy designer clothes, expensive jewellery and fast cars. I wrapped up so much of my personal worth in the things I owned, but as quickly as I owned those things, I became dissatisfied, because I'd see someone with something better or newer.

Truth be told, as money came into my life, it immediately left it. I was living hand to mouth and didn't have much in the bank. I was afraid that if my lifestyle carried on as it was, I would run out of money. I was afraid that I didn't have enough money, but, of course, my true underlying fear was the fear of being poor again.

I wasn't alone in this fear. Many of us are deeply afraid that we'll never have enough, and accumulating as much money as possible, at all costs, becomes our primary occupation. I've seen multi-millionaires who still obsessively pursue money, driven by a fear of never having enough, so much so that the dynamics of their relationship with money have shifted to the point where they are controlled by money.

In today's comparison culture, contentment and inner abundance are scarce virtues. However, the desire to change my money mindset, and my views on scarcity and abundance, were what moved my life on from a decade of surviving to a decade of thriving and, ultimately, financial independence.

YOUR MONEY STORY

What is your personal money story? Where did you meet money? What experiences or fears have driven your relationship with money so far?

After we met, and started our personal development quest and journey to financial independence, we learned that our money mindset and attitudes towards money are part of a deep-rooted 'money blueprint' that we inherited from our parents.

If your parents were compulsive spenders, then the chances are you, too, will have a bias for spending. If your parents were savers or investors, then you're more likely to have a bias for saving and investing.

The more we watched our parents in our early 20s, the more we realized that we had a lot in common in terms of how we looked at money. It was deep-rooted in survival and borne out of scarcity. We also recognized that there were good things we wanted to keep, such as their work ethic, enterprising natures and their love for us, and things we didn't want to inherit, like the arguments about money when those 'final demand' letters arrived.

We spoke with our parents to better understand our money stories and learned that our money stories were not only connected to our parents, but also to our grandparents. They told us how, in the late 1960s, they survived the Nigerian Civil War, which claimed the lives of between 500,000 and 3 million people, and how they learned to be enterprising by trading yams and other produce to get by. Those experiences and more shaped the actions and life outcomes of our grandparents and their relationships with money. Consequently, their money stories shaped those of our parents, which then shaped our own money stories.

So, to truly understand your relationship with money, if they're around, you should speak with both your parents, or those who raised you, and your grandparents, or those who knew them, to get a fuller picture of your money story. The good news is that you can think of the money blueprint that you inherited from your parents as version 1.0, and you can upgrade that money blueprint, rewrite your money story and change your relationship with money.

MARY'S MONEY STORY

As a young child I have vivid memories of my earliest experiences with money. At the age of nine, I was given daily pocket money of 30p, which I would spend on my way to school. I would buy two packets of Space Raiders snacks, one beef flavour, one pickled onion, from the local newsagents and with the remaining 10p I would indulge in penny sweets. These simple transactions taught me the value of managing my money, a skill that seems to be less prevalent among children today due to the rise of cashless transactions.

I also noticed that some children received 50p as their pocket money, which seemed like a fortune to me at the time. However, I never complained or felt envious, because I had a sense of contentment. Perhaps this was influenced by my awareness that some of my family members back in Nigeria were in need of financial support. It made me appreciate my privileges and be conscious about spending from a young age.

Saving money was ingrained in our family tradition. I remember creating a DIY piggy bank using two-litre soft drink bottles. I would tape the lid shut and carve a hole in it for coins to enter. It was exciting to watch the bank gradually fill up and, once it was full, I would eagerly count the coins before depositing them in my savings account. Any spare change would find its way into the piggy bank. My siblings and I regularly engaged in this savings ritual.

At the age of 12, I had my first job, earning £3 for ordering and collecting a batch of leaflets from a print shop in Hackney for my eldest brother's computer business. I would immediately deposit this money into my DIY piggy bank. Starting to earn money at such a young age taught me valuable lessons, and I quickly realized that some jobs paid more than others and that certain jobs provided more job satisfaction.

I recall a conversation with a friend when I was around 15. I informed her that I intended to quit my retail job at a local store. I had done the maths and realized that I wasn't even earning the minimum wage, which at the time was around £3.20 per hour. This was my Saturday job. After calculating that I made more money from crafting and selling CDs, I decided to focus on that instead. It was a decision based on both financial considerations and personal fulfilment.

Growing up, my family predominantly cooked homemade Nigerian food. Our meals were prepared in large quantities, resulting in surplus food that we stored in our big freezer. Whenever I asked if we could get fast food like McDonald's or KFC, the response was always, 'There is rice at home.' This phrase, which I'm sure many people from certain ethnic backgrounds can relate to, would later make me realize the financial savings and health benefits of avoiding junk food. Now, as a parent myself, I understand and appreciate how much my parents saved by adopting this approach.

While you reflect on your personal money story, let's take a look at different money personas to help you better understand your relationship with money.

YOUR MONEY PERSONA

Money personas refer to different categories that you may fall into based on your attitudes, behaviours and beliefs about money. These personas help you understand how you approach money management, spending habits and overall financial decision-making.

While these personas are not rigid classifications, they provide a framework for identifying common patterns and tendencies. Here are 13 money personas that we've identified in our research and work helping others to improve their relationships with money:

1. The passenger

Known for: Not knowing what's going on with their finances until things go wrong

Personality trait: Passengers usually allow their partner to look after all aspects of their household finances and don't get involved at all. In a lot of cases (although not exclusively), passengers are women who have traditionally seen it as a man's place to look after money. They often see money management either as too complicated or they're too busy raising children or making money as entrepreneurs. As a result, they're usually not well placed to spot the signs of mismanagement of their household finances until problems become obvious.

2. The grinder

Known for: Working hard instead of working smart

Personality trait: Grinders place a strong emphasis on constant work, productivity and a relentless pursuit of success. It is often associated with the idea of 'hustle', where individuals prioritize work above other aspects of life, such as family, leisure, rest or personal relationships. In grind culture, there is a glorification of long hours, burning the midnight oil and sacrificing personal well-being for the sake of career advancement or entrepreneurial goals. It promotes the idea that success is achieved through tireless dedication, hard work and a willingness to go above and beyond what is expected. However, all this can lead to burnout, chronic stress, neglect of self-care and strained relationships.

3. The gambler

Known for: Looking for the next stock or crypto that will go 'to the moon'

Personality trait: Gamblers are all about short-term gratification instead of long-term gain. They have a strong inclination towards taking unusual financial risks and find excitement, thrill and sometimes even addiction in games of chance or speculative investments. They often make impulsive decisions when it comes to their finances. They may act on hunches without considering potential consequences. They often struggle to set limits on their expenditure and when they experience losses may be driven to chase those losses to recoup their money. This can lead to a cycle of further gambling and potential financial instability. Finally, they face significant consequences due to their gambling habits that can lead to debt, strained relationships, financial instability and even addiction-related issues.

4. The soft-lifer

Known for: Trying softer instead of trying harder

Personality trait: Soft-lifers prioritize a comfortable and leisurely lifestyle over financial ambition or material wealth. Achieving a healthy work-life balance is crucial for the soft-lifer. They strive to create a lifestyle where work is not the central focus and they have ample time for travel, hobbies, nature and spending time with loved ones. They value tranquillity and a slower pace of life. The soft-lifer is often content with a modest income that covers their basic needs and provides a comfortable lifestyle. They may prioritize job satisfaction and personal fulfilment over pursuing higher-paying careers. While the soft-lifer may not be driven by financial ambition, they recognize the importance of financial independence as a way of having more control over their time and choices.

5. The dreamer

Known for: Being highly ambitious, driven by big dreams and aspirations

Personality trait: Dreamers may take risks, pursue entrepreneurial ventures and actively seek opportunities to increase their wealth, because they are highly aspirational and have clear financial goals. They tend to have an optimistic and positive outlook, believe in their abilities to achieve their dreams and are not easily discouraged by setbacks or failures. Dreamers look for ways to grow, personally and financially, but they need to be mindful of balancing their dreams with responsible financial management. Taking calculated risks and pursuing big dreams can yield great rewards, but can also lead to losses.

6. The avoider

Known for: Saying 'I'll do it tomorrow'

Personality trait: Avoiders tend to shy away from dealing with financial matters. They may avoid budgeting, ignore financial planning and are likely to be uncomfortable discussing or confronting money-related issues.

7. The investor

Known for: Seeking a return on investment (ROI)

Personality trait: Investors are knowledgeable about investing and are willing to take calculated risks to grow their wealth. They may have a long-term perspective and seek opportunities to maximize their financial returns.

8. The planner

Known for: Geeking out on spreadsheets and creating scenarios

Personality trait: Planners meticulously organize their finances, create budgets and set specific financial goals. They value structure and control in managing their money and prefer to make informed decisions based on careful analysis.

9. The status-seeker

Known for: Wanting to be seen by others

Personality trait: Status-seekers place a high value on material posses-sions, luxury goods and appearances. They may use displays of wealth to signal their social status and spend money on expensive items, such as private schools or luxury holidays, to project a certain image or to fit into a particular social group. Status-seekers use outward displays of wealth to signal their social status. They may frequent upscale establishments or participate in exclusive events to be seen among an elite group. A status-seeker may feel the need to upgrade their home to a larger and more luxurious property after seeing a friend purchase a lavish mansion.

10. The frugal saver

Known for: Looking for discounts or enjoying knowing they paid less

Personality trait: Frugal savers are dedicated to living a minimalist lifestyle. They focus on cutting expenses, avoiding unnecessary purchases and finding creative ways to save money. They are not misers, but only spend when necessary. They create financial security for themselves and are likely to move quickly to being debt free.

11. The carefree optimist

Known for: Taking life easy

Personality trait: Carefree optimists have a relaxed and positive attitude towards money. They prioritize living in the present and savouring life's experiences. They appreciate the joy and pleasure that can be found in everyday moments, which can enhance their overall well-being. However, they may overlook the importance of comprehensive financial planning. They may not pay enough attention to budgeting, retirement saving, or investment strategies, which can lead to financial instability in the long run. Carefree optimists can benefit from incorporating some planning and consideration of potential risks into their approach, while still maintaining their positive and optimistic mindset.

12. The impulsive buyer

Known for: Saying 'if I see a deal, I just get it'

Personality trait: Impulsive buyers make spontaneous purchases without much thought or consideration. They may be easily influenced by sales, marketing tactics or the desire for instant gratification. They're more likely to go online shopping late at night, for example. Impulsive buying can lead to the accumulation of unnecessary possessions. Over time, this can clutter living spaces, create disorganization and result in wasteful consumption. By consistently spending impulsively, they may miss out on opportunities to save or invest their money in ways that could generate long-term financial growth or security.

13. The generous giver

Known for: Giving back and making a positive impact in people's lives

Personality trait: Generous givers find joy in giving and supporting others financially. They prioritize philanthropy, charity work or providing financial assistance to loved ones. Generous givers may sometimes stretch their financial resources beyond their means. Their generosity can lead to financial strain, impacting their own financial stability and ability to meet their personal needs. They may feel obligated to give in every situation, even when it may not be practical or sustainable for them.

WHICH OF THOSE MONEY PERSONAS DO YOU MOST IDENTIFY WITH?

You can have a combination of these money personas to varying degrees. You may primarily identify with one persona while displaying traits of another. The key thing is they're not labels that should define you. Your money persona will shift and change over time as your relationship with money changes.

For example, in the past, we've been the grinder (60%), the status-seeker (20%) and the impulsive buyer (20%). However, as our relationship with money has become healthier, today we identify with the soft-lifer (30%), the dreamer (20%), the generous giver (20%) and the investor (30%).

Understanding your money persona can help you identify your strengths, weaknesses and areas for improvement in managing your personal finances. If you have a partner, it should also help to ignite some fun and honest conversations between yourselves, but without pointing fingers. A great question to ask yourself or each other is: 'What aspects of my finances would I like to improve to align with my desired money persona?' Developing a healthy money mindset, which we'll cover next, will help you to get started.

DEVELOPING A HEALTHY MONEY MINDSET

To understand how to develop a healthy money mindset, it helps to clarify what 'mindset' actually means.

Mindset: Refers to a set of attitudes or beliefs held by someone.

Money mindset: Refers to your unique set of beliefs, attitudes and the thoughts you hold about money.

Money mindset includes your deeply ingrained perceptions and values regarding wealth, abundance, scarcity, success and worthiness. A money mindset can be positive, negative or a combination of both. It influences how you think and feel about money, which, in turn, impacts your financial behaviours and outcomes. A healthy money mindset involves having positive beliefs and attitudes about money, embracing abundance, and cultivating a mindset of growth and opportunity.

How does your money mindset relate to your relationship with money?

Your relationship with money is influenced by your money mindset but is also shaped by external factors such as upbringing, cultural influences and life experiences. Your money mindset is the internal perspective and set of beliefs you hold about money, while the relationship with money represents the external manifestation of those beliefs in your financial behaviours and actions.

Interview: Anna

Anna Williamson (42) is a Brit who lives in London. She's married to Alex, a Sicilian, and they have two children. Her 25-year career spans children's presenting, broadcasting, entertainment reporting and journalism. Today, she's an author of four self-help books, runs a relationship coaching platform and is a presenter of the flagship dating show, Celebs Go Dating. *Here is how she developed a healthy relationship with money.*

In my mid-20s I experienced a mental breakdown and was diagnosed with Generalised Anxiety Disorder, partly due to dysfunctional relationships, people-pleasing and burnout. Going through talking therapies opened my eyes to the world of mental health.

My current relationship with money is healthy. I like money and respect it, but I don't see it as the sole purpose of life. Health and family hold higher value for me. I grew up with parents who had a healthy attitude towards money. They were savers and taught my brothers and I not to rely on credit and only spend what we could afford. This instilled a deep respect for money in us. If you can't afford something, then you're not going to have it. There's no fun in paying for a sofa two years later when it's all stained and crappy.

Financial joy is being able to afford wonderful experiences for my family without constant worries about meeting basic expenses. It's about enjoying the process of earning money, making it not feel like a hardship. Having the privilege of not stressing about whether I can pay the mortgage or meet basic needs is a significant achievement.

Managing money as a couple is crucial, as it's one of the leading causes of relationship problems. My husband and I share similar attitudes towards money, which has been a tremendous advantage. He tends to be more financially cautious, having seen the pitfalls of relying on credit. We manage our money in one joint account, but also maintain individual accounts. About 70% of what we earn goes into a joint account and 30% stays outside. Creating multiple income streams gives me an incredible feeling of empowerment, financial freedom and career freedom. However, it didn't happen overnight.

I'd spent the ten years before my mental breakdown as a freelancer, at the beck and call of whether a TV company hired me or not, and that created a lot of stress. Then I had an epiphany – I was not in control of what I earned and of who was employing me, and I felt very vulnerable financially. So it became a game plan when I realized that I have many different skillsets. If I create many sources of income, then I'm not relying on one more than another. So I set up my own coaching practice (one income source). I got a book deal (another source). I continued with my TV career in broadcasting (another source). I currently have eight sources of income. Some are dormant at times and some are riding higher than others. It's just having that belief and tapping into your skillset. No matter what industry you're in, it's about saying, 'How can I utilize my skills to the best of my ability?'

My journey hasn't been easy. I've spent a few years living hand to mouth and having to seriously economize and do any job I could to earn money. I worked at McDonald's and I cleaned toilets for a while, too – the portaloos at Wimbledon, etc. In creating the life I want, I've learned not to limit my possibilities and to find joy in sharing the fruits of one's labour. Earning money just to keep in the bank doesn't bring me happiness, but being able to take my parents on holiday or support my family brings me joy. And I don't mind the odd handbag.

If you are struggling with your relationship with money, you need to drop the ego and reach out for help. Money is a deeply personal subject, like talking about our feelings. It is steeped in hierarchy, society and sociology, but it can be a wonderful thing as well. Seek your financial educators and put your hand up.

SCARCITY VS ABUNDANCE MINDSET

What's the first thought that usually crosses your mind when you wake up in the morning? If you're like most people, it's probably, 'I didn't get enough sleep.' And throughout your week, you might find yourself saying:

- 'I don't have enough time in the day for everything.'
- 'I don't have enough work-life balance.'
- 'I'm not slim enough or fit enough.'
- 'I don't have enough joy and leisure in my life.'
- 'I don't have enough money to cover my basic needs and enjoy certain experiences.'

That list goes on. Before the week is over, you've talked so much from a place of 'not enough' that it blinds you entirely from what you already do have. Focusing on what you don't have all the time means that you always operate from an empty place deep within. Scarcity in our mindset, which is deep-rooted in fear and manifests as scarcity of resources, becomes the fuel that drives our actions, behaviours and ambitions.

Stephen Covey, in *The 7 habits of Highly Effective People*,[1] writes that 'Most people are deeply scripted in what I call the scarcity mentality. They see life as having only so much, as though there were only one pie out there. And if someone were to get a big piece of the pie, it would mean less for everybody else.'

Here are some examples of a scarcity mindset:

- Your friend or colleague gets a promotion at work and you look happy for them, but deep within it's crushing you.
- You get your self-worth from owning things and comparing yourself to others.
- You don't invest money and like to see your money in your bank account, because you grew up with very little and so seeing your money makes you feel secure or successful.

But where does this deep-rooted scarcity mindset come from? The scarcity mindset related to money does not exist in nature and is not something we were born with. Money was invented thousands of years ago and the scarcity mindset related to money and other resources is programming built into the money system that we all live and breathe daily.

Money is referred to as currency for a reason – because it is like a flow of energy and there is an infinite amount of money in the world, with more and more of it being created daily. In order to re-programme our mindsets from scarcity to abundance, it is important to be clear about the toxic myths of the scarcity mindset:

Toxic myth 1: There's not enough to go around

This myth suggests that resources like money are limited and there's never enough for everyone. It's like thinking there's only one pizza and, if one person takes a big slice, others will get less. In reality, though, an abundance mindset means that more pizzas can be made and we can find fair ways to share them, so everyone gets enough to eat.

Toxic myth 2: More possessions indicate abundance

This myth equates material possessions and the relentless quest for more money with abundance and happiness. It suggests that the more one has, the more abundant one's life is. This is why a lot of us continue to follow the Joneses and suffer lifestyle creep. There is no concept of 'enough' in our vocabularies. Every year, we want to upgrade our lifestyles or level up or want more just for more's sake. Every year, we continue to grind and work long hours at all costs, swapping our life's energy to fill a well that will always need topping up.

Toxic myth 3: Scarcity mindset is inherent

This myth assumes that a scarcity mindset is natural and unavoidable. It suggests that we're hardwired to hoard resources and view the world as a zero-sum game. This mindset produces a culture where we think it's okay for ethnicity and gender wealth gaps to exist or, because we've become so accustomed to systemic racism, we see it as just how the world works. It creates 'them' and 'us', so we think one person or community's gain has to be another's loss.

The truth is, we can choose to radically shift how we look at money and our relationship with it. While scarcity can influence our thinking, it is not an inherent trait. Our beliefs and mindset can be shaped by societal factors, experiences and education. By challenging and shifting our mindset, we can cultivate a sense of abundance and possibility.

True abundance goes beyond material wealth and encompasses various aspects of existence, including personal relationships, well-being and fulfilment. Shifting the focus from material accumulation to holistic measures of abundance can help us promote greater overall well-being and design balanced lives of financial joy.

Here are some simple ways to begin shifting from scarcity to an abundance mindset:

Make gratitude a core value: Recognize and celebrate where you are now and appreciate what you already have. No matter how bad your day is, ask yourself: what am I grateful for? Write it down in a notebook daily. This gives you optimism for what is to come in your life.

Remove negative vocabulary from your day-to-day: Instead say to yourself: I am enough, I have enough time, I am smart enough, I see opportunity all around me, and so on.

Take your thoughts captive: How many times have you said to yourself: I cannot do X because I don't have Y. For example, I cannot increase my income, because I don't have transferable skills. Or you focus on other scarcity-based thoughts, such as: why does this always happen to me?

Taking your thoughts captive simply means pausing to ask yourself why you (in particular) are saying what you're saying. Oftentimes, we say certain things because it's what people around us say, but when you do this you create a new internal culture for yourself, which quickly becomes a cloud over your life.

Choosing an abundant mindset doesn't immediately mean that all resources around you will become abundant. It simply means that you're creating fertile ground on which you'll plant good seeds that will create a more wholesome life of abundance in the near future.

MONEY BLOCKS THAT STOP YOU IMPROVING YOUR RELATIONSHIP WITH MONEY

In addition to having a scarcity mindset, there are many other money blocks that might prevent you improving your relationship with money.

Negative beliefs

Can you think of certain phrases you have heard from your parents or people around you? Here are examples we came across when we were growing up.

'Money is the root of all evil' – this one belief alone still holds back millions of people across the world today and stops them from actively seeking sustainable ways to grow their incomes or build wealth. In our experience, money is not the root of all evil. It is neither good nor bad and takes on its energy from the person handling money. If you're generous and kind with money, then your money will be generous and kind, too. It's the love of money that we should avoid at all costs and our focus should be on the stewardship of money.

Other beliefs that we came across are: 'Money doesn't grow on trees,' 'You have to work hard to make money' and 'Investing is only for rich people.' Holding negative beliefs can create a subconscious block to financial success.

Tip: Challenge these beliefs and reframe your perspective. Recognize that money can be used as a tool for positive impact and contribution.

Fear of failure

This can stop you taking risks, pursuing opportunities and making financial decisions that could potentially lead to success and wealth. One way this manifests itself is in procrastination and indecisiveness. Fear of failure can paralyse people, causing them to delay financial decisions or remain indecisive about investments, career choices or how to manage their money.

Tip: Break tasks and decisions into smaller, manageable steps. Focus on taking action rather than seeking perfection. Set clear deadlines and hold yourself accountable.

Guilt or shame around money

A good example of this is feeling ashamed of past financial mistakes or harbouring guilt for wanting to accumulate wealth.

Tip: Practise self-compassion and forgiveness. Learn from past mistakes and focus on making better financial decisions. Shift your perspective to view money as a tool for personal growth and positive impact.

HOW TO HEAL YOUR MONEY TRAUMAS

We all have money traumas and wounds from our past interactions with money. Examples include: financial infidelity and betrayal by a partner, catastrophic investment or business failure, chronic overspending and debts, complex family dynamics, Black tax (where you feel pressure to support family members financially 'back home'), emotional spending as a coping mechanism, bad divorce, horrible redundancy, the anxiety and insecurity of childhood scarcity, poverty mindset and feeling unworthy of success, or the death of a loved one.

Acknowledging and healing past financial wounds and traumas is crucial for personal growth and creating a healthier relationship with money. Healing money traumas can be a deeply personal and transformative process. Here are some steps you can take to begin the healing journey:

Step 1: Awareness and reflection

Start by becoming aware of your money traumas and how they have affected your relationship with money. Reflect on your past experiences, beliefs and emotions surrounding money. Understanding the root causes of your money traumas is crucial for healing.

Step 2: Seek support

Consider seeking support from a therapist, counsellor or financial coach who specializes in money psychology. They can provide guidance, tools, and a safe space for you to explore and heal your money traumas.

Step 3: Challenge limiting beliefs

Identify the limiting beliefs you hold about money and challenge them. Replace negative and scarcity-based beliefs with positive and empowering ones. Affirmations, visualization exercises and daily reminders can help rewire your mindset.

Step 4: Embrace self-compassion

Practise self-compassion and forgiveness. Be gentle with yourself as you navigate your money traumas. Acknowledge that healing takes time and effort, and it's okay to make mistakes along the way.

Step 5: Educate yourself

Educate yourself about personal finance, money management and investment strategies. Building financial literacy can empower you and increase your confidence handling money, reducing anxiety and fear. You're doing well already by reading this book and following the ten-week programme.

Step 6: Take action

Start taking small steps towards financial empowerment. Create a budget, track your expenses and set achievable financial goals. Celebrate your progress, no matter how small, as it reinforces positive associations with money. Simply follow the small action steps at the end of each week in this book.

Step 7: Create new money habits

Develop healthy money habits that align with your financial goals and values. Cultivate a mindset of abundance and gratitude. Practise mindful spending and saving to foster a healthier relationship with money.

Step 8: Release emotional attachments

Let go of emotional attachments to money. Recognize that money is a tool and your self-worth is not determined solely by your financial status. Focus on cultivating fulfilling relationships, experiences and personal growth.

Step 9: Build a supportive community

Surround yourself with supportive individuals who share positive attitudes towards money. Join financial or personal development groups where you can exchange ideas, learn from others and receive encouragement. Feel free to join our community of people of a similar mindset at www.FinancialJoyAcademy.com.

Step 10: Continual growth and reflection

Healing money traumas is an ongoing process. Regularly assess your progress, reflect on your financial journey and address any new challenges or triggers that arise. Remember, everyone's healing journey is unique and healing takes time, so be patient with yourself.

We're here to support you all the way on this journey.

Does money buy happiness?

In 2010, an influential study by the Nobel Prize-winning economists Daniel Kahneman and Angus Deaton concluded that money only boosts happiness up to annual income of about $75,000 (£60,000).[2] Beyond that amount, they concluded, money had little impact on happiness. However, in 2021, Matthew Killingsworth of the University of Pennsylvania found that happiness increased steadily with income beyond $75,000, with no evidence of a plateau.[3]

To resolve the conflict, Kahneman and Killingsworth joined forces to research a new hypothesis: that both a 'happy majority' and an 'unhappy minority' exist. They found that for an unhappy minority of around 15%, once they reached an annual income of $100,000 (£80,000), additional money failed to improve their overall sense of well-being.[4]

This was consistent with Kahneman and Deaton's original 2010 findings. Beyond $100,000, in the lives of the 15%, heartbreak, bereavement, clinical depression and so on could not be assuaged by higher incomes. In other words, if you're rich and miserable, more money won't help. In sharp contrast, for the happy majority – the happiest 30% in various income categories – happiness increased at an accelerated rate beyond an income of $100,000, right up to at least $500,000 (£407,000). For everyone else in the happiness distribution there are nearly linear gains in happiness with rising income.

So what can we take away from this? It by no means says that money can solve all our problems – as the late Notorious B.I.G. reminded us in his classic 'Mo Money, Mo Problems', 'It's like the more money we come across, the more problems we see.' However, money can probably help, although it's not the secret to happiness and indeed a longitudinal study by Harvard University, drawing on over 80 years of data, found that close relationships, rather than money or fame, are what keep people happy throughout their lives.[5]

So on a personal level, does money buy happiness? Our experience is that money can be a tool to design a beautiful life that brings you good health and buys you time from the pressures of the grind, so that you can focus more on what brings you joy, whether that's family life, friendships, work, travel, hobbies or generous living.

In addition, our experience is that if money is going to play a positive role in designing that beautiful life, you need to know what 'enough' looks like for you, so you can focus on contentment and don't fall into the trap of forever wanting more.

WHAT A LOVING RELATIONSHIP WITH MONEY LOOKS LIKE

Bringing a lot of research together with 15 years of our own money journey and our experience of coaching thousands of individuals and couples who have had varying relationships with money, we've identified eight signs that you have a loving relationship with money:

1. Gratitude

You appreciate the money you have and express gratitude for it. Instead of focusing on what you lack, you acknowledge and are grateful for the resources and financial stability you currently possess. We say 'Mbona', which means thank you from the heart, each time we spend, receive, give or invest money. The energy with which you let money flow out of your life is the same energy with which it will flow back in.

2. Mindful spending

You make conscious decisions about how you spend your money. Instead of impulsive or excessive spending, you align your financial choices with your values and prioritize expenditures that bring you joy, fulfilment and long-term benefits. For example, we've always dreamed of travelling across Africa. So far, we've visited Tanzania, Kenya, Ghana, Nigeria, Egypt, Ethiopia, Morocco and counting. These travel experiences, funded through diligence with our finances, continue to enrich our souls and bring us joy now, not when we're retired.

3. Financial responsibility

You practise responsible money management. This includes budgeting, saving and investing wisely. You make efforts to live within your means and avoid unnecessary debt.

4. Abundance mindset

You believe in the abundance of money and opportunities. Instead of a scarcity mentality, where you feel there is never enough, you cultivate a mindset that attracts and welcomes financial abundance into your life. You focus on abundance, growth and prosperity. In reality, one way we personally maintain this abundance mindset is to speak goodness into our lives. We start off each day and week with prayer, and believe that favour and opportunity will come our way – and it does.

5. Aligning money with purpose

You use money as a tool to support your life goals, passions and purpose. You prioritize spending on experiences, personal development, education and investments that align with your values, and long-term aspirations. One passion of ours is the work that we do with the Humble Penny and Financial Joy Academy to help others with their finances. Back in 2009, if we hadn't aligned money with our desire to achieve financial freedom and pursued that goal diligently, we'd never have been able to quit both our careers a decade later to focus on these passion projects.

6. Generosity

You embrace the power of giving and sharing. You find joy in helping others and making a positive impact with your financial resources. You contribute to charitable causes, support your loved ones, and create a ripple effect of abundance and prosperity. The goal is not just to give, but to become a giver and make giving a part of your lifestyle. Your heart will smile whenever you give.

7. Self-worth independent of money

You recognize that your value and self-worth are not solely determined by your financial status. While money can provide security and comfort, you understand that true happiness and fulfilment come from meaningful relationships, personal growth and inner well-being.

8. Healthy boundaries

You establish healthy boundaries with money. While appreciating its bene-fits, you don't let it consume your life or define your identity. You maintain a balanced perspective and prioritize non-financial aspects of life, such as relationships, health and personal well-being.

Remember, cultivating a loving relationship with money is an ongoing process that requires self-reflection, awareness, taking faith walks and making conscious decisions. It's about adopting a mindset and behaviours that promote financial well-being while recognizing the broader aspects of a fulfilling and joyful life.

FAITH AS A CURRENCY IN OUR FINANCES

In a world of deep uncertainty about the future of our economy, finances, health, relationships, the impact of technology and so on, we believe that the best way to go into such a future is by taking 'faith walks'. This means, particularly during difficult times, putting everything in God's hands, and staying faithful that everything will work out for us, while still taking prac-tical action daily to reach our goals. Money is energy and it is spiritual, so to wrap up on this week, we'd like to share how important having faith as the currency in our finances is for us.

Faith is defined for us as 'the substance of things hoped for, the evidence of things not seen.'[6] This isn't about religious beliefs, though, but about how you take faith walks in situations that are both under or outside your control, and how you trust the process. We cannot see or understand or anticipate everything. For us, on a deeply personal level, trusting the process means trusting God to bless the plans that we've laid out for our lives. It's about being positive and practical about life, being diligent with our finances and taking action, but living that life boldly and prayerfully by faith and without fear.

Making faith a currency in your finances improves your relationship with money and shifts that relationship beyond just the physical and emotional dimension, completing the picture with a spiritual dimension.

Faith walks

WEEK 2: LESSONS AND ACTION STEPS

Three lessons for week 2

* Your relationship with money is complex and deep-rooted in fear and scarcity as a default. To understand and improve your relationship with money, you need to first understand your money story and how that has shaped your mindset, beliefs and behaviours around money.

- A scarcity mindset makes you operate from an empty place with a focus on what you don't have rather than on the abundance of what you already have or what's possible. It is one of the many money blocks and limiting beliefs that hold you back in your finances, but the good news is that you can embrace an abundance mindset, heal your money traumas and create a loving relationship with money.

- Money and happiness are directly linked, with, in some but not all cases, happiness increasing as you earn more money. Designing a life of financial joy gives you access to the best of both wealth and well-being while leaving out the greed.

Three action steps for week 2

Action step 1: What's your personal money story? What were your parents' attitudes to money? Think back to your parents and grandparents, and their money stories. How have these shaped your money beliefs, mindset and relationship with money?

Action step 2: What fears, money blocks and limiting beliefs have shaped your relationship with money so far or held you back?

Action step 3: What could you do more or less of in order to have a more loving relationship with money? If in doubt, look at the learning for this week at our list of eight signs that you have a loving relationship with money. Be specific and discuss these with your partner if you have one.

I could do more...	I could do less...
1.	1.
2.	2.
3.	3.

Week 3:

Overcome behavioural biases: the key to achieving financial joy

A life of financial joy is created by closing the behaviour gap between where you are now and the wholesome life you want to create for yourself.

Let's play a little game.

- Hands up if you've ever sent a friend a text while driving – yes or no?
- Hands up if you've eaten more junk food this week than you know you should – yes or no?
- Hands up if you have more debt than you know you should – yes or no?

If you answered 'yes' to some of those questions, as we have, it tells us something fundamental, which is that there are many things we know we should do in life, but what we actually do in reality is different. Why?

If you think about how to close the gap between what you know you should do and what you actually do, the usual response is to educate people – in other words, give them more information. Take cigarettes. We all know smoking is bad for you and there are billions spent each year trying to educate people about the dangers of smoking, yet people continue to smoke.

The same goes for being in debt. People know they shouldn't get into more debt by spending money they don't have, but does that reduce the number of people in debt? No. Don't get us wrong, financial literacy is necessary and to a certain extent it works. However, other forces are at play that repeatedly keep us shackled to debt, even though we know we shouldn't be.

Everything from the constant barrage of advertising, social media FOMO and the rise in financial abstraction, which means money is becoming more and more digital, and we're not only losing a sense of how much we're spending, but we're also spending more easily.

The sheer volume of decisions that we each have to make, coupled with the pressures of day-to-day life, means that we rely more and more on shortcuts to make those decisions, so it's no wonder we often fall foul of a number of behavioural biases that drive our decision-making and derail us from our progress towards financial joy.

While financial literacy is highly important for the financial well-being and inclusion of people worldwide, it is not enough. A World Bank meta-analysis of more than 200 studies on financial literacy[7] found that when you teach people financial literacy, they learn and remember. However, do they take action and apply the learning? Not really.

HOW TO IMPROVE YOUR FINANCIAL BEHAVIOUR FOR THE BETTER

Social science research tells us that to change behaviour we should focus on changing the environment, not the people, and to improve your environment and change your behaviour, let's use an example given by psychologist Dan Ariely.[8]

He said, think of behavioural change in the same way we think about sending a rocket to space. To change the environment around the rocket, we need to do two things: reduce friction – you want the rocket to have as little friction as possible, so that it is as aerodynamic as possible; inject motivation – you want to load as much fuel as possible, to give it as much energy as possible.

The same idea can be applied to behaviour change when it comes to our finances. Here is an illustration. Imagine that point A in the diagram below represents where you are now, for example living in debt. Point Z represents where you want to get to in your finances, for example becoming 100% debt free. The void between point A (underpinned by your current behaviour) and point Z (your desired behaviour) is the behaviour gap.

The behaviour gap

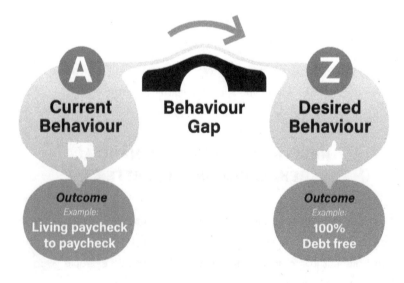

Taking steps to gradually reduce that behaviour gap leads to behaviour change over time, which leads to big outcomes in your financial life. To do this, we have to look at things in two stages. First, to change your behaviour, you need to change your environment. Second, to change your environment, you need to:

- Dial friction up or down
- Inject motivation

Example: Grace is a 35-year-old who earns £40,000 ($51,000) a year, but struggles to save money. She enjoys the good things in life a little too much and has a habit of borrowing on her credit card to book holidays, for example. Grace knows she should avoid debt and save money every month, but somehow she just can't seem to manage to do it. Her current behaviour holds her back from her desired behaviour of becoming a regular saver.

One way we'd help Grace to break this cycle is to change the environment surrounding her circumstances. In this case, we'd increase friction to reduce the chances of her spending and we'd inject motivation to encourage saving.

We might suggest:

- Giving her credit card to someone she trusts to keep for her (this increases friction).
- She calls the credit card company and reduces the credit card limit (this increases friction).
- She uses a budget to help dictate where her money goes (this increases friction).
- She creates a vision board with her boyfriend for what life could look like if they took saving seriously (this injects motivation).
- She prints out a photo of that house she wants to save a deposit for one day (this injects motivation).

Cumulatively, these small changes will help to change the environment surrounding Grace's circumstances. None of this will happen overnight, but as she begins to take these steps over time, she will gradually begin to close that behaviour gap. The same practical ideas can be applied to your finances to gradually move you forwards and closer to your desired life of financial joy.

Although changing our behaviour is critical to improving our financial lives, it is not the only force we must overcome. Let's take a look at behavioural biases.

Interview: Mabel

Mabel Oseghale-Jimawo (59) is a social worker originally from Nigeria who has lived in the UK for 34 years. She lives in Liverpool. Here is how financial joy has changed for her across different stages of life as she prepares for retirement.

My relationship with money has always been positive, thanks to my parents. They taught me how to manage money wisely. I learned valuable lessons from my mum, who was excellent at trading goods and turning a profit, and my dad, who was also skilled with finances. I've always been quite comfortable with money from an early age.

Financial joy for me has evolved over the years. Initially, my focus was on raising my children well and ensuring they could take care of themselves. I also prioritized getting good life insurance in case something happened to me. However, as my children have grown up and become independent, my focus has shifted to ensuring a comfortable retirement. My goal is to maintain the same level of comfort I currently enjoy when I retire.

My husband and I managed our finances differently when we

first moved to the UK. We didn't have joint accounts and I handled most of the financial responsibilities, including paying bills. We had a unique way of working together, respecting each other's roles, even if it wasn't as structured as what younger couples do today.

To gain financial stability, I began to pay more attention to my finances. I learned to budget more intentionally, pay closer attention to my pension pot and avoid spending on unnecessary things. My money journey has had its share of challenges, especially when it came to adjusting to a new country and dealing with financial demands from back home. In response, I established clear boundaries with family members and gradually reduced financial support for extended family.

I've taken some unusual steps to achieve financial stability, including attending a detox program to prioritize my health and downsizing our living space to reduce unnecessary expenses. Throughout my journey, I've learned the importance of valuing my health and enjoying the present moment. I've become more intentional about managing stress and understanding its impact on overall well-being.

If I were to offer advice to anyone seeking to take control of their finances, especially the younger generation, I'd encourage them to start early. From your first job, begin your pension plan right away. Don't worry about feeling it's late, because it's never too late to start. Improve your financial literacy and be mindful of your spending.

There's a lot of financial noise out there, so don't get overwhelmed. Start with what you think you can manage and gradually build from there. Looking to the future, I feel very positive about my financial prospects. I'm confident that my retirement will be comfortable, and I'm continuing to focus on my financial goals. What brings me contentment is knowing that I'll maintain my current lifestyle in retirement and live without financial stress.

THE COMMON FINANCIAL BIASES THAT CAN DERAIL YOUR PROGRESS

To achieve financial joy there are several biases that you need to overcome. To help you understand the most common behavioural biases and what to do about them, we'll use practical examples that we and others have struggled with.

Confirmation bias

You seek out information that confirms pre-existing beliefs and ignore information that contradicts those beliefs.

Example: Your friend made quick money from trading on the stock market and you want to do the same. As a result, you only read articles that support that investment strategy.

To overcome this bias: Seek out diverse perspectives and sources of information. This could include reading content that challenges your beliefs, consulting with financial advisers who have different viewpoints or seeking out feedback from trusted friends and family.

Anchoring bias

You rely too heavily on an initial piece of information (the 'anchor') when making decisions or judgements.

Example: You are trying to get on the property ladder and see a house you love. The price is higher than what the house is worth, but because you've fallen in love with it, you make an inflated offer without doing further research to see if it is worth the price tag.

To overcome this bias: Conduct thorough research on recent compa-rable sales in the area, run numbers on affordability, and consult with property professionals to determine a fair and reasonable offer.

Loss aversion bias

You are more motivated to avoid losses than to achieve gains.

Example: You are hesitant to invest in the stock market, because you are afraid of losing money, even though historical data shows that over the long term, the stock market has provided strong returns.

To overcome this bias: Focus on the potential gains rather than the potential losses. Take a long-term perspective and remember that short-term losses are often temporary.

Sunk cost fallacy

You continue to invest time, money or other resources, because you have already invested so much, even if it no longer makes sense to do so.

Example: You started a side hustle with £500 ($630), but after two years of running it you've lost £5,000 ($6,300), but you just can't and won't give up and continue to hope it turns around.

To overcome this bias: Evaluate decisions based on their current and future potential, rather than past investments. Don't throw good money after bad just because you've already invested a lot.

Herd mentality bias and social proof bias

You follow the crowd – for example, friends in a WhatsApp group or an influencer and their community on social media – even if it's not in your best interest.

Example: You might invest in a popular stock just because everyone else is talking about it and without doing your own research.

To overcome this bias: Do your own research, and consider your own needs and goals before making decisions. In addition, make it a rule to wait 24 hours from when you first felt compelled to buy something.

Overconfidence bias

You overestimate your abilities and underestimate your risks.

Example: You bought one stock that gave you unusually high returns, so you believe you're a great stock-picker and start looking for the next Amazon or Apple to beat the market.

To overcome this bias: Seek out objective data on what percentage of investment professionals actually beat the market when they invest. Consider a range of potential outcomes for your money, for example could you diversify and still get good returns?

Status quo bias

You prefer things to stay the same rather than making changes.

Example: You may stick with the same expensive investment account charging high pension fees, even though better options are available.

To overcome this bias: Regularly review your finances and seek out better deals.

Present bias

You prioritize short-term gratification over long-term goals.

Example: Times are hard for you financially, but you're also getting older. Instead of saving for your retirement, you say, you only live once (YOLO) and book a holiday.

To overcome this bias: You need to achieve a balance. Set clear long-term goals, such as making automatic savings or investment contributions, and develop a plan to achieve them. Then create a separate pot for your holidays.

These are the most common biases to be aware of and how to overcome them as you work towards your life of financial joy. Remember, the more conscious you become of these biases and how they affect your decision-making, the more you'll make smarter decisions about your money and beat the advertisers who spend billions persuading you to spend on things you don't need.

HOW SOCIAL MEDIA IMPACTS YOUR BEHAVIOUR AND MAKES YOU SPEND

By far the biggest influence on the spending habits of Gen Zs and Millennials is the degree to which they use and engage with social media. Take Instagram, for example. According to 2019 research by Meta involving 21,000 people aged 13–64 in 13 countries (including the UK, US and Australia), who used Instagram at least once a week, 80% used it to make purchase decisions and 54% said they made a purchase immediately after seeing a product or service on Instagram.[9]

The rise of mobile usage and social media integration has contributed to increased mobile shopping. Statista reported that about 90% of social media users in the UK accessed social platforms via mobile devices, making it easier for them to make purchases on the go.[10]

Being mindful of the effects of social media and practicing responsible online behaviours can help you mitigate negative impacts on your personal finances and overall well-being. Here are some quick tips to help you reduce impulse buying on social media:

Set a budget: Determine a monthly or weekly budget for discretionary spending, including purchases influenced by social media. This will help you allocate your money wisely and prevent impulsive purchases that might exceed your financial means. We'll cover how to create a joyful spending plan in week 5.

Pause before purchasing: When you come across a product or offer on social media that catches your attention, avoid making an immediate purchase. Instead, step back and give yourself some time to think it over to reduce the chances of impulse buying.

Unfollow or mute tempting accounts: If certain social media accounts or influencers consistently trigger your impulse-buying tendencies, consider unfollowing or muting them.

Create a wish list: Instead of making immediate purchases, create a wish list for the products or items you find interesting on social media. Make a note of these items and revisit your wish list after a few days or weeks to assess if you still desire the item.

Disable or limit notifications: Social media platforms often send notifications about sales, promotions or limited-time offers. Consider disabling or limiting these notifications to reduce the constant bombardment of tempting offers, which can trigger impulse-buying behaviour.

Comparison-shop and research: Before making a purchase, take the time to research and compare prices, read reviews and explore alternative options. This helps ensure you make an informed decision and avoid making impulsive purchases that you may regret later.

Practise self-reflection: Take a moment to reflect on your values, priorities and long-term financial goals. Consider whether a purchase truly aligns with these goals or if it's driven purely by impulse.

Seek support and accountability: Share your goal to reduce impulse buying with a trusted friend, family member or even your partner (if you have one), so they can provide support, remind you of your intentions and help hold you accountable.

Overall, being mindful and intentional with your purchases can help you avoid impulsive buying on social media and contribute to healthier financial habits.

SHOW ME YOUR HABITS

Show me your habits and I'll show you your financial future. You see, becoming that person who eventually becomes good at consistent budgeting and so on really begins with putting in place the right habits and routines.

According to James Clear, author of *Atomic Habits*, 'Habits are the compound interest of self-improvement. The same way that money multiplies through compound interest, the effects of your habit multiply as you repeat them.'[11]

We've adopted his 'habit-stacking formula' to great effect in our lives. It's a powerful hack for establishing good habits or routines. You start with one small habit and gradually stack other habits on top of it.

For example, if you want to review your bank balance daily and never get around to doing it, stack that new habit around an already established habit, such as brushing your teeth. You could say, 'Whenever I brush my teeth, I could check my online bank statement on my phone straight after.' Over time, that habit would stick.

Small task: Diarizing

To establish habits and routines that will be helpful for managing your finances later, in week 5, let's focus on an area we can all relate to: your calendar. Think of the calendar as the new focal point of all your life's activities. If you give it some respect, you'll get some results. We personally use Google Calendar and highly recommend it.

Diarize key recurring events and activities in your life – birthdays, holidays, dinners with friends, paying your mortgage or rent, your net worth monthly review and so on – with reminders. We'd even suggest diarizing this ten-week programme by setting reminders.

Why does this diarizing activity matter? It is helping you operate from the future. When you plan ahead and anticipate what's coming, you're more prepared. The same goes for your finances. More importantly, what we're really trying to help you achieve here is a routine of relying on your calendar as part of your toolset for success. Remember, this calendar has become your life's new personal assistant, so make it a thing to check this calendar ahead of each day's activity.

The goal is to run your daily life from your calendar for the next 25 to 30 days. Do this and it will become a habit. Diarize today's date so that you can track how long you've done this challenge for. Remember, trust the process, because it works. Soon you will find yourself establishing new healthy money habits and stacking those habits on already established habits in your life.

WEEK 3: LESSONS AND ACTION STEPS

Three lessons for week 3

• Financial literacy is critical for creating a life of Financial Joy; however, it is not enough. You need to focus on not just your learning but, more importantly, changing your habits and behaviours.

• The most effective way to change behaviour is not to change who you are but to change the environment around your circumstances. You do this by introducing friction and motivation.

• Many forces exist to stop you from adopting healthy money habits and moving forwards with your goals. These include behavioural biases that drive your decision-making, the allure of advertisers with big budgets to make you spend unnecessarily and the pull of social media. The more you're aware of these forces and take action to adopt healthy money habits, the more you'll make decisions that move you forwards with your finances weekly.

Three action steps for week 3

Action step 1: Which behavioural biases do you think you have in your finances? Refer back to our list of eight examples (see page 80) and write down an example of when you believe you've made a decision driven by a behavioural bias.

Action step 2: Do a habit audit by reflecting on your current money habits and writing down three habits that are holding you back in your finances. Then write down how you could introduce friction or motivation to change your environment and gradually change your behaviour. Here is an example:

Which unhealthy money habits are currently holding you back in your finances?	How could you introduce friction or motivation to gradually change your behaviour?
I spend too much time on Instagram every week and make impulsive purchases using my credit card.	I could introduce friction by unfollowing certain accounts that encourage my unhealthy money habit.

Now write down your own habits and how you could introduce friction or motivation:

Which unhealthy money habits are currently holding you back in your finances?	How could you introduce friction or motivation to gradually change your behaviour?
1.	
2.	
3.	

Action step 3: Decide on one new healthy money habit to track daily and what you'd stack it on to ensure you gradually form that habit. Examples of money habits to consider tracking include:

Review your money goals: This could be stacked on your lunch break or your daily walks, so during your lunch break or after your daily walks you'd review your money or life goals.

Review your online banking transactions: This could be stacked on having your breakfast, so you'd review your online banking on your phone after you've eaten.

New habit to track	I will stack this on...

Week 4:
Begin with the humble penny: from small beginnings to financial freedom

A life of financial joy starts with humble beginnings tied to a vision for a better life.

WRITE YOUR VISION AND MAKE IT PLAIN

One of the most powerful ways to start any journey is to first dream and visualize the destination. To show you how powerful this exercise is, let's take a journey back to January 2011. That year mattered, because it was the year that I had full clarity on my dream financial life. I was 27 years old and had proposed to Mary, and she said yes! I was on cloud nine and soon to be married to my beautiful fiancée. Life felt so good, but as exciting as this was, life was about to get very serious, too. Yikes!

Getting married and starting a family is no small undertaking. I'd spent many years before that year desiring a better life financially. I had a job as a management accountant, but my financial life was nothing to write home about. I was spending emotionally to feel better about myself. On the outside, I looked like I was doing well. I had a really nice Mercedes Coupé (bought with part of my savings and lots of debt), but not a lot left in the bank. As an immigrant, success was defined back then by what people saw, hence the nice car. This turned out to be one of my biggest money mistakes.

I needed a radical mindset shift and deep down I knew that I wanted a very different life for myself. I wanted a simpler life with no money worries; a more intentional and organized life where I didn't live waiting for payday. But I also wanted to travel. Sometimes I'd sit in the park, look up at the skies and wonder where everyone in those planes were going.

It was bitterly cold and wet in the UK that January. Having dreamed of doing this for so long, we both put some money together and booked a holiday to our dream destination, Zanzibar in Tanzania. We booked transit flights to keep costs lower. On arrival in Zanzibar, it was stunningly beautiful and 35°C (95°F).

It was my second holiday ever, but this holiday would be different. We were there to not only have fun, but also to plan our lives. We played Scrabble, picked beautiful shells along the crystal-white sandy beach and felt truly free. As we sat by the beach with our books and a notepad for planning our wedding, we asked ourselves, 'What do we want out of our lives as a married couple?' Although we both wanted different things, we were united on a number of very important things.

Our dreams were:

- One day to buy a house with its own front door, so we could walk up to the door and just open it without climbing stairs. Mary wanted a kitchen with an island and I wanted off-road parking.
- One day to have children. I wanted two and Mary wanted three.
- We wanted to travel and see the world together each year.
- We wanted to pay off our house mortgage earlier than our parents.
- We wanted to become financially independent, but didn't know how we'd do it.

We looked at each other and said, 'Let's call it our ten-year plan.' Then, we discussed why we really wanted to achieve these dreams.

Again, our motivations were very similar. Our immigrant roots meant that we wanted more out of life. We'd seen our parents sacrifice so much and work too hard just for our families to survive. We both wanted to create a life that gave us the freedoms that our parents never had.

Our 'why' gave us a deep sense of purpose. Note that at this point we didn't own a house or have children or anything. Even more crucially, we didn't have the money for any of them. We just dreamed about them together and believed we'd do it one day.

This act of dreaming and painting a vision for our lives set in motion everything else that would gradually follow. It gave us something to work towards, with financial independence as the pivotal North Star goal that united all the other goals. This act of dreaming at the beach was our humble beginning and the great thing about starting off with so little is that there is nothing to lose. The only direction things could go was up.

Even though 2011 was challenging economically – we'd not too long emerged from the global financial crisis of 2008 and the global economy still felt fragile – having a vision still felt like we had a secret no one else had.

Another factor that helped us feel deeply excited about the future was that we believed in the power of taking faith walks. As far as we were concerned, if we had faith that we'd achieve financial freedom one day, and backed it with a plan and consistent action, we'd get there. In our minds, everything aligned and we could see it vividly. Very crucially, we not only painted a picture of the vision, but we wrote the vision and made it plain.

Ten years later, in January 2021, we'd not only achieved the vision we painted in 2011, but far exceeded it, even with the ups and downs in that decade, including the pandemic. Yes, of course timing helped in some ways. However, we believe that the significantly biggest driver for what we achieved in that decade was the result of who we became in that decade, driven by our clear life vision.

Life can get very busy. Before you know it, days turn into weeks, weeks into months and months into years, but we can remember ten years ago like it was yesterday and we bet it's probably the same for you. We say that to remind you that, although the future might seem far away, it will come by quickly.

One thing you can control is how you arrive at that future and what you'd like to see. And one way of beginning that journey from your humble beginning is to write your vision and make it plain. We've created a practical framework that will help you do just that.

Tip: It's easier to write your life's vision if you change your environment and your routine, so you could do this in a café, in your garden or in another space that isn't where you usually hang out.

THE POST FRAMEWORK

The POST framework is what you should use to write out your vision. It stands for purpose, objectives, strategy and tactics.

Purpose: This is your why. It is the fundamental and deeply meaningful reason or intention that drives your actions, goals and choices. It is the underlying motivation that provides a sense of significance, fulfilment and meaning in your life.

> **Example:** You want to live a stress-free life of financial freedom, while doing work you find fulfilling and enjoying your life.

Objectives: This is your what. It's the goals you're working towards, which can be your North Star goal or can be broken down into smaller goals.

Objectives must be SMART – specific, measurable, achievable, relevant and timebound.

SMART goals allow you to prioritize your goals so you can allocate your resources and efforts accordingly. They also help you clearly articulate what you want to achieve, such as saving for a deposit on a house, paying off debt or building an emergency fund. This clarity enables you to concentrate your efforts.

> **Example:** You want to build an investment portfolio worth £600,000 ($765,000) 15 years from today, plus own a mortgage-free house in 15 years' time, when you're 55.

Strategy: This is your how and who. It's the high-level plan you'll follow to achieve your specific goals and clarity on who you'll need to achieve your goals. Getting someone else involved gets you results faster, removes guesswork and reduces chances of mistakes. It also makes you fully committed and removes the limitations you put on yourself, while introducing other people's ideas and connections.

> **Example:** Your how could be investing monthly in the stock market with a 100% focus on low-cost globally diversified index funds and exchange-traded funds (ETFs), coupled with career maximization and starting an online side hustle. Your who could be your employer, partner, coach or mentor.

Tactics: This is the detail of your how. Tactics are specific actions you'll follow to achieve short-term objectives within the broader picture of your strategy. Unlike strategy, which focuses on the overall plan and who you need, tactics are more focused on the execution and implementation of specific actions on a daily basis.

> **Example:** Get guidance from your 'who' on the best approach, open a tax-efficient investing account, start investing 40% of your take-home

pay and supplement that with side hustle income, automate your investing and move jobs every two years to earn more.

Now that you have a framework for how to write your vision and make it plain, it's important to acknowledge where you are right now, because that is where you're going to build from.

YOUR MONEY SELFIE

Your money selfie is a snapshot of where you are right now in your financial life. One of the easiest ways of working this out is to calculate your financial net worth. This is similar to how the financial position of a business is determined by looking at the balance sheet.

Here is a simple calculation: your financial net worth = sum of all your assets minus the sum of all your liabilities.

An asset is something you own or control – a source of future economic benefit or something that adds money into your pocket. Examples of things to include are: property (including your residential property), cash, savings in your bank accounts, stocks and shares, a business and its assets, digital assets, trademarks, patents, music rights and so on. Examples of things to exclude are: your income (this goes in your budget) and you may also want to exclude your residential property in order to work out your accessible net worth.

A liability is an obligation to pay something to someone. In simple terms, it's anything that takes money away from your pocket. Examples include: credit card debt, overdrafts, loans and mortgages, buy now pay later (BNPL), car loans, unpaid rent, student loans (although this depends on where you are – in the UK, this is more of a tax) and so on.

Your financial net worth

Assets		Liabilities	
Stocks:	£10,000	Credit cards:	£17,000
Savings:	£5,000	Overdraft:	£1,000
House:	£350,000	Mortgage:	£250,000
Car:	£10,000	Car loan:	£5,000
Emergency fund:	£3,000	Buy now pay later:	£750
Total assets:	**£378,000**	**Total liabilities:**	**£273,750**

Net worth: (total assets − total liabilities) = £378,000 − £273,750 = £104,250

Net worth: *without* principal residence = £104,250 − (£350,000 − £250,000) = £4,250

We've excluded the principal residence (home equity) so that you can see your accessible net worth. Of course, if you downsize one day, this will become accessible. We'd also exclude the transfer value of any defined benefit (DB) or final salary pension, but keep in the value of your defined contribution (DC) pension. This will be important later, in week 9, when we look at retirement and work out your financial independence number.

Working out your net-worth has important advantages:

Tracking: What gets measured, gets improved, so the more regularly you work out your net worth, the more you'll be motivated to make it grow to achieve your goals.

Patterns: Seeing your net worth on one page helps you to spot patterns. For example, in the net worth illustration above, it makes no sense having expensive credit card debt charging, say, 35% APR, while also having savings generating, say, 4% interest. It would make sense to use the savings to pay off the expensive credit card debt.

Clarity: Our finances can become very overwhelming. Seeing it all on one page helps to reduce that overwhelm.

Reflection: If you have a zero or negative net worth, that should encourage you to reflect on why you are where you are and encourage action. If you're in a relationship, this is a good opportunity to talk about money, your goals and dreams.

You'll get to work out your net worth as part of the actions steps for week 4. For now, feel free to download our dynamic Excel net worth tracker here: www.thehumblepenny.com/networthcalculator

THE MONEY JOURNEY

Everyone is on a money journey right now, but not everyone realizes it. Understanding where you are in your finances will help you understand where you are on the money journey and you can start to paint a picture of how far away you are from where you want to be. The fundamental thing to note is that no matter where you are on the money journey, you can experience financial joy now.

This is about gratitude for where you are now, the peace that comes from knowing you have a plan that you're working towards, while putting the small experiences that bring you joy at the centre of your finances. Here is what the money journey looks like.

The money journey

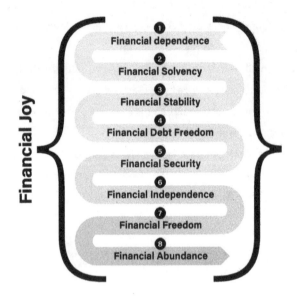

The one thing that unites all the stages is that you can experience financial joy at them all. Your life of financial joy is unique to you, and aligns with your values and purpose. This mindset gives you a sense of contentment, of knowing that you're on your unique journey of measured progress that has an end destination. No matter where you are on that journey, you have peace and experience joy, and won't feel like you can't be happy just because you've not achieved financial freedom yet.

Let's explain what each of these stages means so that you have an idea of where you might be right now on the 'financial' half of your journey.

Stage 1: Financial dependence (foundation)

This is the stage of the money journey where you're either still living at home with your parents or someone you completely depend on for your livelihood. People at this stage usually have no assets and might not even have an income source.

Stage 2: Financial solvency (survival)

This is where you're living paycheque to paycheque and typically above your means, or you spend most of what you earn on your lifestyle and paying down debts. You struggle to save due to cost of living and lifestyle choices, even though you have a relatively decent income. People at this stage usually rely on one income source and may have no investments. Most adults, unfortunately, remain at this stage throughout their working lives and accept it as their reality.

Stage 3: Financial stability (peace)

At this stage, you have some stability as you've managed to save an emergency fund, which implies that you're living below your means and you're developing healthy money habits.

Stage 4: Financial debt freedom (flexibility and growth)

Beyond stability, debt becomes the next target for you at this stage, with a focus on the expensive bad debts (credit cards, overdrafts, personal loans and so on) that risk pushing you back into the phase where you didn't have breathing room. At this stage, you focus on how to become debt free (week 6) and you'll likely be exploring alternative sources of income (week 8). As you gradually banish your debt, you start to sense freedom is not too far in the distance.

Stage 5: Financial security (protection)

Congratulations, you've gotten rid of all your expensive debts, and you've now joined a small group of people who are not only debt-free but have between one year and three years' worth of living expenses saved. This creates a great deal of security and you can even afford to take a sabbatical if you want or quit your job if it is not serving you. This stage of the money journey is well on the road to financial independence, but it will require diligence, consistency, creativity, growth and risk-taking to get there.

Stage 6: Financial independence (freedom and generational wealth)

This is the stage of the money journey where working for money becomes optional. You've either paid off your mortgage in full and built up a significant stash of savings (in the UK received wisdom says this should be 28.5 times your annual expenses or 25 times in the US) and/or you've invested in assets with enough income to cover your essential monthly living expenses. See week 9 for how to reach financial independence.

Stage 7: Financial freedom (independence and generational wealth)

This stage is the same as stage 6 except the income coming from your assets can also cover more of your lifestyle expenses beyond your essentials. Once you're at stage 6 or 7, you have the option for early retirement or if you want to (you don't have to, though) you can leave your career to focus on passion projects or simply supplement your lifestyle with part-time work.

Stage 8: Financial abundance (legacy)

This final stage is reserved for the likes of Warren Buffett, Elon Musk, Rihanna, Taylor Swift, Tyler Perry, Jay-Z and Beyoncé, and Jeff Bezos. These are the people you see on lists of the highest-earning or wealthiest people in the world. In our view, financial abundance begins in the heart and mind. You could have £1,000 in the bank and have a life of abundance in many ways, beyond money.

Wherever you are on this journey, remember that you don't need to have achieved financial freedom or abundance to create a life of financial joy for yourself.

The peace and joy that people look forward to when they're financially free should be something that we all experience now in our own individual ways. It all starts with a mindset of appreciating where you are and choosing to put joy at the centre of your finances today, while intentionally working towards tomorrow.

So let's say that you have decided you want to get to a particular stage of the money journey. It can seem pretty overwhelming and most people simply don't know where to start.

Interview: Felicia

Felicia Ogedengbe is married to Michael and they're both 40 years old and they have three children. They live in Kent and they're of Nigerian heritage. Today she works as a brand strategist. Here is how she improved her poor relationship with money and took control of her finances.

I worked as a social worker from 2009 until 2022, when I decided to quit. Initially, I got into social work just to find a job after university and I didn't enjoy it at all. As I approached my 40s, I realized I didn't want to spend my life in a job I didn't enjoy. I retrained as a brand strategist after starting a small business during the Covid-19 pandemic.

I used to have a poor relationship with money. I often spent money on things to make myself happy, especially on flashy bags, cars, makeup, etc. I used to think that having expensive possessions would make me happy, but I eventually realized that true happiness comes from within. My focus on materialism was impacting my relationship with Mike, who is much better with money. Over the years, I recognized that this behaviour was an issue and I didn't want our kids to inherit it. I had to learn how to manage money effectively and curb my spending habits.

Previously, we'd set budgets, but had not reviewed them regularly. Our financial situation felt unfocused and we'd often let things spiral out of control. To gain financial stability, I started by writing down our financial obligations and addressing them bit by bit. I tackled the smallest debts and made a plan to pay them off. Reviewing our financial situation on a monthly basis has helped us stay on track.

One unusual step we took to achieve financial stability was going without a car for a few months. This was challenging, but made us realize how many expenses are associated with owning a car. It helped us see that we could manage without a car and that there are more cost-effective ways to get around. Although it's not a long-term solution, it gave us a fresh perspective on our expenses and allowed us to save some money.

My credit score had dropped to 550 due to unpaid bills and

accumulated debt. You guys inspired us, because I was like, they haven't got two heads. These guys have paid off their mortgage and I'm still here chasing small things. There's something about approaching your 40s that makes you think that if you don't sort these issues now, it will be a big regret. I took steps to improve the situation by focusing on paying off the small debts first and this made a significant difference. My score has improved significantly and reached 999 for the first time [see page 130 for more on how to get your credit score to 999], although I still feel we're a work in progress. We're also more aware of how our financial decisions can impact our credit scores.

My advice to others trying to achieve financial stability is to get organized. Create a clear financial plan, list your obligations and set financial goals. Prioritize your high-interest debts and work on paying them off. Lastly, be open and honest with your partner about finances.

HOW TO BREAK DOWN LARGER GOALS INTO MANAGEABLE STEPS

We found the POST framework (see page 93) actually helps us to achieve our goals. You can use this method whether you're single or a couple working towards the same goal. For example, let's assume your goal is as follows.

Objectives: You want to buy a house in 24 months and you want to save up a deposit of £60,000. This could seem overwhelming given the large amount and the long-time horizon, but here is how we suggest breaking the large goal into manageable steps that will help you take action to achieve your goal.

Step 1: Define the goal by making it SMART.

We've already done this above.

Step 2: Break the time horizon and amount into quarterly goals.

Most people view their goals annually and spend most of that year procrastinating and never actually achieving their goals. However, if you view the time you have in 12-week chunks rather than as a two-year block, it forces you to take action. We like the 12-week year system.[12]

If you give yourself a generous deadline or a large amount of time to complete a task, the work will tend to stretch and fill up that entire time-frame, even if it could have been completed in a shorter period.

You can apply this idea to how you approach and achieve goals by breaking the amount and time horizon into 12-week intervals. For the above goal of saving £60,000 in 24 months, it would be equivalent to saving £7,500 over eight intervals of 12 weeks each.

If you earn an income monthly, this is equivalent to £2,500 per month.

Strategy: Decide how you're going to achieve this goal in 12 weeks.

Step 3: Your strategy here could be to focus on saving more while also earning more. In addition, be clear on who you need around you to stay committed and increase the likelihood of achieving this goal. For example, it could be your employer or a partner.

Step 4: Decide on up to five tactics you'll focus on for 12 weeks. Tactics are the actual actions you'll take to achieve your goal.

Tactic 1: Make a list of all your non-recurring and recurring expenses and make changes to your lifestyle to increase how much you save from your salary from 15% to 30%, so you save £1,500 a month.

Tactic 2: Get a part-time Saturday job to make an extra £750 a month.

Tactic 3: Make a list of items you don't use at home that can be sold to raise £1,000 in 12 weeks.

Tactic 4: Explore a side hustle buying and reselling items on eBay or Etsy to generate profits after tax of £1,000 in 12 weeks.

This plan will lead to you saving £8,750 in 12 weeks if you execute it well. Although the amount is above your intended £7,500, it gives you a steep target to aim for and if you don't quite get there, you'll still come as close as possible to £7,500.

Step 5: Put dates next to each tactic and diarize them using a calendar system.

Your tactics only become real if you make an appointment with yourself to achieve each one. Block out time in your calendar and set weekly reminders for what's coming up. Make sure you leave spaces in your diary so you can make adjustments if things don't go to plan, which they probably won't!

Step 6: Review your results weekly.

Each week on the same day, review how you got on and even score yourself out of ten for each tactic that week. Don't beat yourself up for not achieving all or most of your goals in any specific week. What's most important is following the process and staying consistent until you see results.

Step 7: Assess where you are after 12 weeks and start the next interval of 12 weeks.

Do a full review of how things went in the last period, tweak your tactics if necessary and begin the process again from the beginning for another 12 weeks.

This method has been tried and tested by us in our personal finances and business, and we consistently see good results.

CELEBRATE WINS ALONG THE WAY

As we've said, working towards achieving your money goals can feel pretty overwhelming. However, attaching a weekly budget-friendly reward to specific milestones is one way of ensuring that you celebrate your wins on the journey.

Examples of ways that we celebrate our wins each week include:

- Ordering our favourite meal as a takeaway (we love jollof rice and pepper soup or Italian pasta with king prawns).
- Going to the cinema or theatre.
- Booking a weekend away once at least every three months if not more often.
- Going out with friends.

It doesn't have to be expensive or elaborate. The key thing is to do what brings you joy within your budget.

CREATE A TRACKING SYSTEM

A tracking system is important for measuring your progress. We track our progress using Excel (or Google Sheets) and Google Calendar. The spreadsheet keeps track of your progress and the calendar helps you show up and be held accountable. You can use the same or simply use a physical or digital planner coupled with a calendar system.

Below is an example of how simple your tracking system could look by week over the next 12 weeks.

Goal 1:			
Tactics	**Week due**	**Date due**	**Owner**
1.			
2.			
3.			
4.			
5.			

As we mentioned earlier, what gets measured, gets improved. So the effort that you put into making this system work for you will pay off. You can extend the above table if you have more than one goal over 12 weeks.

WEEK 4: LESSONS AND ACTION STEPS

Three lessons for week 4

- Having dreams about where you want to get to in your finances is not enough. You need to write your vision and make it plain.
- The POST framework will help you turn your vision into a plan of action led by why you want to achieve your goal, followed by how you're going to achieve it and who you need around you for guidance, ideas and connections.
- Celebrating your wins along the way provides the necessary motivation to keep going. Don't see your journey as a sprint, but a marathon.

Three action steps for week 4

Action step 1: Write down the vision you currently have for your financial life.

Use the POST framework to structure your vision above into a plan.

Purpose	
Objectives	
Strategy	
Tactics	

Aim for a maximum of three SMART objectives every 12 weeks. For each objective you need a strategy and up to five tactics.

Action step 2: Based on the eight stages of the money journey (see page 98), what stage are you at right now?

What stage are you at now?	What stage are you trying to reach next?

Action step 3: Take a money selfie (see page 95) by working out your financial net worth. Complete the template below and add more assets and liabilities as appropriate. This exercise will take some time as you speak with your partner (if you have one), make calls to banks or log into online accounts, but it will be worth it.

Assets	Liabilities
Pension (DC):	Credit cards:
Pension (DB):	Overdraft:
ISA or savings:	Mortgage:
House value:	Car loan:
Car value:	Buy now pay later:
Emergency fund:	Unpaid rent:
Buy-to-let (house value):	Buy-to-let (mortgage):
Total assets:	Total liabilities:

Net worth (total assets – total liabilities) =

Net worth *without* your principal residence and DB pension =

Remember, you can download our dynamic Excel net worth tracker here: www.thehumblepenny.com/networthcalculator

PART 2

Building financial joy

Goal: Become braver and grow your money after mastering your day-to-day finances.

Week 5:
Master your day-to-day finances

A life of financial joy is created through stewardship, diligence and creativity.

In 2019, Nims Purja, a Nepali-British mountaineer, achieved a remarkable mountaineering feat by successfully summiting all 14 of the world's 8,000-metre peaks (including Mount Everest) in just seven months. This incredible accomplishment, known as Project Possible, shattered the previous record of climbing all 14 peaks in seven years. This story inspired us deeply, because Nims is our age and, faced with the many challenges (including financial) of life in the UK, he quit his military career and took up this challenge, not only to prove that nothing is impossible, but also to bring more recognition to his community of Nepali Sherpas.

Nims had a clear why, which created a burning desire, determination and perseverance to achieve his goal. When many of us look at our goals and day-to-day finances, it can all seem like an impossible mountain to climb. Where do you start and how do you get the motivation to keep going?

The average weekly household expenditure in the UK is £528.80[13] (circa £27,500 a year) and rising, with the main areas of expenditure being housing, transport, food and energy. For some people there are also spiralling childcare costs and it's no wonder many people feel like giving up even before their day has started. It's a daily battle for survival while costs rise and economic circumstances change. It can feel like the rug is being pulled from under your feet every time you try to stand still. Today, most people, including many with relatively high incomes, are living month to month and struggling to find a way out of this cycle. The number one reason why most people live paycheque to paycheque is because of their inability to manage cashflow – the flow of money in and out of their lives.

This same inability to manage cashflow is why you see high-earning footballers, boxers, musicians or celebrities more generally go from making lots of money to becoming declared bankrupt. Why? Outside of unforeseen or tragic life circumstances, the biggest drivers of people's inability to manage their cashflow is a combination of the lifestyle they choose to adopt, their lack of financial literacy and their choice of poor money habits and behaviours.

Every hour of the day, we all make choices, consciously or unconsciously, that will either move us closer or further away from our goals. Given we all have the power to choose, it is never too late to begin making the choices that will help to turn our lives around. The good news is that it is possible and you can start making those choices today.

UNDERSTANDING STEWARDSHIP

Stewardship is an ethical value, and refers to the concept of managing and taking care of something that belongs to someone else, for example the responsibility and accountability for money, resources, skills, gifts and blessings that God has entrusted to us. In the Parable of the Talents,[14] a master entrusts different bags of gold to his servants before going on a journey. To one servant he gives five bags of gold, to another servant two bags and to the third one bag, each according to their ability. The servant with the five bags immediately puts his five bags to work and doubles them to ten bags. The one with two bags also gains two more bags. The one who receives one bag digs a hole in the ground and hides his master's money – out of fear. When the master returns after a long time, he commends the faithful servants for their stewardship and rewards them, but he rebukes the unfaithful servant who hid his money rather than investing it wisely.

This example demonstrates different aspects of stewardship, including managing resources wisely, investing and multiplying what we have been given. It serves as a valuable lesson and inspires us to be faithful and accountable stewards of the blessings, resources and opportunities entrusted to us. When you're a responsible steward of money, it creates more flow and abundance, and enhances your life of financial joy.

In part one of this book, you laid the foundations for a life of financial joy. In part two you're going to take the practical steps to help you to master your finances, become braver and grow your money. To start, let's create a plan for where your money should go when you get paid. Remember, it's not just the existence of a plan that's important, but the habits and behaviours that you cultivate in order to implement that plan.

CREATE A JOYFUL SPENDING PLAN

A budget is a plan for where your money should go each month. We like to think of it as a compass that guides you and your money in the right direction, towards achieving your goals. A joyful spending plan puts joy at the centre of your finances. By this we're not just referring to the things and experiences that bring you joy in the moment, but, in addition, the joy that comes from knowing that you're putting money aside for your medium- and long-term goals.

In our experience, a joyful spending plan brings together the 'financial' and 'joy' elements of your life into a plan that aligns fully with your values, lifestyle and goals, while also being realistic. It's a plan for both your income and expenses, although, typically, most people only focus on their expenses when they think about budgeting. Let's look at each one in turn.

Part A – income

Imagine that it's the start of a new month and you want to budget your income. You start by writing down, as accurately as you can, how much you expect to make and from what sources.

Income source (A)	Net amount expected (B)	Net amount received (C)	Difference (D)
Salary			
Side hustle			
Total			

You add up the amounts in column B to figure out how much money you expect will hit your bank account in the coming month. Keep this as realistic as possible. If you earn an irregular amount of money each month, use the average of the last three months. The importance of starting your joyful spending plan with your income is that you give focus to the area of your plan that has the potential to grow over time. It also gives you time to consider your income goals (week 8 – see page 227) as part of the process. At the end of the month, you complete column C with what you actually received as income and column D is the difference between what you expected and what you actually received.

Part B – expenses

You might have heard of the popular 50/30/20 rule for budgeting that allocates 50% of your after-tax income to your 'needs', 30% to your 'wants' and 20% to your 'savings and financial goals'. While we think this method is good as a starting point, we prefer to get a bit more detailed in our joyful spending plan. In order to build wealth over time, here are eight places your money should go when you get paid.

Place	Percentage	Reason
1. Workplace or private pension[15]	10% of gross income	Pay yourself first and invest for the future then deal with household expenses (week 7 – see page 182)
You then pay tax on the remaining 90% of your gross income – what is left is your net income We'll now allocate 100% of the net income that hits your bank account to seven places		
2. Emergency fund	5% of net income	Create a safety net and pay yourself first before household expenses
3. Debt pay-off	10% of net income	Pay expensive bad debts to create flexibility to build wealth

4. Stocks and shares ISA and lifetime ISA[16]	15% of net income	Invest monthly to get compounding working for you early (week 7 – see page 182)
5. Needs	50% of net income	Pay for your necessities, including protection
6. Fun and wants	5% of net income	Give priority to experiences that bring you joy and enjoy yourself guilt free!
7. Giving	10% of net income	Generous living and a heart for others
8. Growth and risk fund	5% of net income	To seek opportunity, increase what you have and learn (week 8 – see page 227)
	Total 100% of net income	

Note that this is not a rigid guide and you can tweak it as you see fit, depending on your personal circumstances. For example, if you already have an emergency fund or have no debts, then the allocation to those areas can go towards more savings, investments or more needs. One of the biggest pushbacks we get with this plan is that people argue, why would you only have 5% for fun and wants, and 10% for giving? Or why should I give if I'm in debt? Truth be told, the 5% for fun and wants is already a part of the 90% that you're allocating fully to yourself as either an expenditure or an investment. Plus, it can be increased over time. We started at 5% and currently spend around 20% of our net income on experiences that bring us joy, but this came after debt freedom.

About giving 10%, we believe that a life of financial joy should involve giving generously from our hearts, and out of that flow and generosity, which is an act of love, comes a flow of more abundance into our lives.

Here we're talking about, for example, giving to social or environmental causes or charities you're passionate about, giving back to communities that have served you, paying a tithe, giving to strangers who need it and so on. We give because we're blessed to be a blessing to other people and don't give in order to receive.

However, 10% is a guide. Some will give less and some will give more. There is no compulsion to give. What is most important is the heart with which you're giving and seeing giving as an integral part of your lifestyle – a form of mini philanthropy. If you give £1 or £10 from the heart it's better than giving £100 begrudgingly. Once you become good at giving by starting small, it further removes your scarcity mindset and helps you to operate more abundantly from a place of love. Other ways to give include offering your time and skills.

Daniel works in marketing and earns £35,000 a year. Here is a suggested allocation of his income to eight different places in his joyful spending plan.

Place	Percentage	Amount
	Gross income	£35,000
1. Workplace or private pension	Less 10% of gross income	(£3,500)
	Gross after pension	£31,500
	Less personal allowance	(£12,570)
	Taxable income	£18,930
	Less tax	(£3,786)
	Less National Insurance	(£2,692)
	Add personal allowance	£12,570
	Net annual income	£25,022
	Net monthly income	£2,085
2. Emergency fund	Less 5% of net income	(£104)

3. Debt pay-off	Less 10% of net income	(£209)
4. Stocks and shares ISA and lifetime ISA	Less 15% of net income	(£313)
5. Needs	Less 50% of net income	(£1,042)
6. Fun and wants	Less 5% of net income	(£104)
7. Giving	Less 10% of net income	(£209)
8. Growth and risk fund	Less 5% of net income	(£104)
	Total 100% of net income	0

Please note: Tax rates, National Insurance rates and personal allowances will change over time and differ if you're outside the UK, but the overall percentages are relevant as a guide.

What if you can't make the allocations above work for you?

If you live in a major city like London, you may struggle to allocate 50% of your net income to your needs, because rent and mortgage costs, let alone other living costs, tend to be high. In addition, due to the rising cost of living and high interest rates, it is difficult to save more generally. This is where you need to make some hard decisions.

For example, given that property costs (rents or mortgages) make up a significant portion of people's disposable incomes, a reconsideration of where you choose to live is important. We deliberately chose to move out of London to a cheaper commuter town in Kent so that we could borrow significantly less in order to make our budget work for us. That's because we were being driven by a bigger North Star goal – to achieve financial independence.

The question for you is, what hard sacrifices are you making right now to achieve your financial goals? If you can't make the allocations work, you need to earn more (week 8 – see page 227) or reduce allocations in one or two of the eight areas.

STRATEGIES FOR STAYING ON TRACK AND ADJUSTING YOUR PLAN AS NEEDED

Here are some practical strategies for staying on track and adjusting your budget as needed.

Decide on a home CFO

Staying on track with your joyful spending plan requires discipline and communication. In order to create discipline in a household, it needs to become someone's responsibility and that's where the home CFO comes into the picture. Having worked as a CFO for many years, managing the finances of companies worth many millions, one of my main areas of responsibility was to make sure that we never ran out of cash. We applied the same idea to our home personal finances.

Just as at work I had to report to my CEO as a form of accountability, at home I had to report to Mary on our family finances. We even established a threshold for communication. Any expense of £50 or above by either one of us had to be brought up in communication before it happened. This worked for us as a couple and may work for you if you're in a relationship. However, what if you're single? If that's the case you have to wear the home CFO hat yourself and may need someone else to hold you accountable.

Of course, the home CFO doesn't need to be the man in a relationship. It should be the person who is willing and capable of taking on responsibility for stewarding the household finances.

Simplify your accounts

A simple tip for staying on top of things and tracking your joyful spending plan is to simplify your bank accounts and savings accounts, so you only have a few. That way, you can easily keep an eye on the inflow and out-flow of money.

Decide on a money day

A money day is a day when you choose to review your finances in detail, either by yourself or with your partner. This is important because, first, it creates a habit of keeping track of your finances and, second, it acts as an effective communication tool. Our money day is Friday morning each week, but it can be weekly, biweekly or monthly. Then diarize it as a recurring event. If you have a partner, ensure this is a non-judgemental meeting and ideally have the chat in a different environment to keep things relaxed. We even have a cup of tea, biscuits and a mini agenda. Although this section is focused on staying on track with your joyful spending plan, here are the general things to consider discussing on your money day.

- Personal reflection: How are you feeling about life? What are you excited about right now? What are you grateful for?
- A review of your vision and the POST that you created in week 4.
- Your joyful spending plan: Did you stick to your plan? If not, what issues arose?
- Your financial net worth: Any changes? How have you progressed?
- What's coming up: Discuss key expenses or events that may involve money, for example holidays, rising rent or mortgage costs, back-to-school expenses and so on.

We've summarized these for you in a monthly master day-to-day finances checklist at the end of this week's learning.

Use a budgeting tool

There are various ways in which you can keep track of your finances.

Manually or digitally on paper
Some people prefer the old-school way of budgeting by keeping track in a notepad or planner, or even using the notes app on their phones or computer.

Use a budgeting spreadsheet
You can create a simple budgeting spreadsheet yourself on Excel or Google Sheets or find one online. Alternatively, get our Simple Budget spreadsheet at: www.thehumblepenny.com/SimpleBudget

Use a budgeting app
Thanks to open banking, there is a rise in apps that help you not only budget and track your money, but also save small amounts with each transaction. Apps to consider include Moneyhub, Emma and YNAB. These pull your bank accounts and transactions into one place.

Budget through your bank
Banks or investment apps that offer budgeting features or saving pots include Starling Bank, Monzo, Revolut, Chip and Moneybox.

Key things to watch out for overall:

• Ensure they're regulated by the Financial Conduct Authority (FCA) and covered by the Financial Services Compensation Scheme (FSCS).

- Be wary of privacy and check that apps are not selling your data to make money.
- Some are free and some are paid-for, so try a few out to see what works best for you.

Having tried all four methods above, we have a personal preference for using a spreadsheet, because it helps you roll your sleeves up and get to understand your numbers better. In addition, you also have no privacy issues.

Interview: Nathan and Sabrina

Nathan and Sabrina Dennis are 42 and 39. They've been married for 17 years and have four daughters. They're of Jamaican heritage and live in the West Midlands. Here is how they improved their relationship with money and took control of their finances using a jar system.

Nathan: Our financial journey began when I faced a significant overdraft of £15,000. I was stressed out, thinking my life was over, and I had to break the news to Sabrina about the mess I'd gotten myself into. We realized we needed to work together.

Sabrina: Our relationship with money has evolved significantly. Before, we'd get money and spend it. We weren't transparent about our finances. Today, we feel we're doing a phenomenal job. We've learned to respect money and realize that it can be a powerful tool for solving problems. We see it as a currency meant to serve a purpose.

Nathan: Financial joy is about having a sense of freedom and not worrying about finances. It's about taking trips and providing experiences for our family, which we couldn't have done earlier. For example, we took our children to Jamaica, which was a significant achievement for me as a father. Additionally, we find joy in giving back to the community, like organizing food drives in the area where I grew up. It's all about making a positive impact.

Sabrina: It's also about having mental freedom and not constantly worrying about how to make ends meet. We've been in a situation where we couldn't afford basic things like baby milk, and it's empowering to be in a position where we can provide for our family and help the community.

Nathan: We've developed a structured approach to managing our finances as a couple. Every Friday we have Finance Fridays. We have an agenda meeting, which goes like this: i) prayer, ii) check the balances of all the accounts, iii) a reconciliation of those accounts, iv) look at the income that came in and what we need to do with that income in terms of actions, v) look at things we need to send out (e.g. invoices for the business) and open up letters and action them, vi) we pray about giving, and vii) close with any matters arising.

Sabrina: Our financial system evolved from the need to resolve issues with our joint account where payments kept bouncing. To resolve this, we established a structured approach to our finances, created separate accounts for specific purposes and signed agreements to adhere to these rules. While it may seem extreme, this system brought order and structure to our finances, allowing us to effectively manage personal and joint finances, even with our businesses.

Nathan: Initially, we used the 'jar system' to divide cash into five jars for various expenses: 10% tithe, 10% investment, 5% fun, 5% safe to spend and 70% debt and bills. This system helped us build discipline and stewardship skills. Later, we converted the jars into bank accounts, which allowed us to fund various endeavours while maintaining the same level of discipline.

My advice for someone trying to take control of their finances is to get help and not bury your head in the sand. If you're struggling, reach out to organizations like the Citizens Advice Bureau. You're not alone.

Sabrina: Start somewhere, even if it's a small step. Opening one letter or addressing one financial issue can make a significant difference.

TIPS FOR CUTTING COSTS AND REDUCING UNNECESSARY EXPENSES

With some strategies in place for tracking your income and expenses, here are some tips to help you cut costs or reduce unnecessary expenses.

Essential vs non-essential

Make a list of your essential vs non-essential expenses, and make a call on what should stay or go and why. This is a difficult conversation, because what might seem non-essential to one person may be essential to someone else.

For us, a holiday is essential, because it is a big part of what brings us joy. However, if things became tight, we'd find a much cheaper alternative, but still enjoy our holidays in a low-cost way. For you, getting a coffee in the morning might be your thing. Although it might seem non-essential to others, it might be just what you need for your mental health.

Essential expenses might include food, gas and electricity, rent or a mortgage, insurance and an inexpensive car (depending on where you live). Non-essential expenses might include multiple TV packages, takeaway food and a nice car. Again, although the above is a guide, you might think of them differently, depending on what brings joy to your life.

Lifestyle changes

Choosing to adopt a healthier and simpler lifestyle also saves money. We, for example, chose to go from eating red meat to eating around 90% plant-based food. This was a health and environmentally led decision, but one that helped to massively cut our food budget. In addition, we don't drink alcohol and we don't smoke. Not everyone can implement these changes. However, any steps you can take towards a healthier and simpler lifestyle will also be better for your pocket. You don't have to have massive lifestyle changes to see a change in your finances, because small changes add up over time.

HOW MUCH EMERGENCY FUND TO SAVE AND WHERE TO KEEP IT

A good place to start with an emergency fund is to aim to save your first £1,000 or $1,000. Beyond that, we suggest aiming to have between three and six months of your essential expenses as an emergency fund. In terms of where to keep your emergency fund, there are three things you ideally want: easy access, low market risk and interest- or dividend-bearing. Here are five options to consider for your emergency fund:

Easy access savings accounts

These accounts work a lot like an ordinary bank account – they let you make withdrawals whenever and wherever you want. Interest rates that you should expect will be fairly low, so your savings won't grow as fast as a result. According to the Personal Savings Allowance (PSA), basic rate taxpayers can earn £1,000 without paying tax on the interest and higher rate taxpayers can earn £500.

NS&I Premium Bonds

This is an opportunity for you to save and potentially win tax-free prizes of up to £1 million each month. It differs from the lottery, because you never lose your money. We use premium bonds ourselves and find that the biggest benefit is that it creates more friction and psychologically makes it harder for us to spend our emergency fund. Benefits include: easy access – you can withdraw your money whenever you want; all prizes are free from UK income tax and capital gains tax; and you can buy Premium Bonds for children under the age of 16.

Regular savings accounts

They are similar to normal savings accounts, but they require you to save a fixed amount each year for a higher interest rate than other savings accounts offer. Currently, you can get up to 7% AER with some banks.[17] However, note that this rate will decrease or increase over time as economic circumstances change, so you might not get this rate at a later date. A con of using a regular savings account is that there are limitations on withdrawals and you need to be an existing customer to access the top rates.

Cash ISA

An individual savings account or ISA is a flexible savings account where you never pay tax on the interest. In the UK, everyone over 16 gets an annual allowance, which is currently £20,000.

Globally diversified index funds or exchange-traded funds (ETFs)

This option will not be suitable to everyone and we would not suggest putting all your emergency funds here. If you have insurance for major cost areas in your life, you could invest a portion of your emergency fund if you have the risk appetite, but your capital will be at risk. Only do this if you will not need your money for the next 24 months at least. This is the only option that is likely to beat inflation (more on this in week 7 – see page 182).

STRATEGIES FOR GROWING YOUR EMERGENCY FUND FASTER

You've spent time understanding where your money should go when you get paid and you've figured out how much of an emergency fund you need. Now let's look at practical tips for how to grow your emergency fund, assuming you've got little to no emergency fund right now.

Start selling things: Look around your home for items you might not have used in the last six months and sell them online on platforms like eBay or, if you have clothes to sell, Depop or Vinted. Doing this could raise you that first £1,000 fast.

Get a tax rebate: If you're a higher rate or additional rate taxpayer and make contributions into a self-invested personal pension (SIPP), claim an additional 20% or 25% rebate, beyond the automatic 20%. Contact the tax office for a rebate and opt for a cheque instead of adjusting your tax code.

Move back in with your parents or family: This will not appeal to everybody (especially those with children), but it will help you build up your savings very quickly.

Do a spend freeze: Practise a spending pause on non-essential items, turning it into a game or challenge with friends. Discovering what you can live without may lead to lasting savings in that area.

Start meal planning: Plan your entire week's meals, including breakfast, lunch and dinner, and shop accordingly to avoid unnecessary purchases and reduce wastage.

Freelance or start a service-based side hustle: Explore an immediate side income by offering your existing skills. For example, if you're an accountant, offer bookkeeping for small businesses on platforms like Upwork or PeoplePerHour.

Lower necessary expenses: Review all your necessary expenses and ask yourself whether you really need them all. You might find that by reviewing those expenses, you have one or two that are due for renewal and you could find better deals, especially if you've been using a particular provider for years.

Rent out a spare room: This will only apply if you own your home and have a spare room, but if you do you can make up to £7,500 in a year tax-free.

Now that you have practical strategies to help you build an emergency fund, once you've built one up the next focus should be to tackle your expensive bad debts. You might also have other goals, such as obtaining a mortgage to buy a house. This is where having a good credit score comes into the picture.

HOW TO GET YOUR CREDIT SCORE TO 999

A credit score is a tool used by lenders to work out to what extent you qualify for loans, credit cards, mortgages, etc. A good credit score (881–960) or excellent credit score (961–999) opens doors to favourable offers, while bad credit leads to limited options and higher costs. Your credit report and score are like a financial X-ray, reflecting your financial health. Having a good credit score is crucial, especially in the Western financial system, where your credit file is accessible to relevant authorities such as lenders, utility providers, landlords, employers, government agencies, etc. The good news is that you can influence what is documented about you. Here is how to improve your credit score to 999 and keep it high:

Check for errors in your report

Credit reference agencies can get things wrong. I (Ken) recall once checking my credit report (i.e. a record of your history of managing and repaying debts) years ago and seeing a County Court judgement. This is possibly the worst thing you can have on a report. It had an adverse effect on my credit score, but fortunately I got the error corrected and my report was updated. However, while it was being fixed, it was very stressful for me. Had I not checked it and applied for a mortgage, I would have been refused and it would have compounded my problems.

Pay bills on time without fail

Some people avoid paying their phone or utility bills and assume that small amounts won't be chased. Utilities are by far the worst kind of bills to ever ignore. The consequences will persist for a long time. A simple review of your credit score and the related report will immediately show you where you're going wrong.

Ensure your credit balances are low

In order to be approved for debt, you usually have to show that you're able to manage debt, so it's no surprise that one way to improve your credit score is to manage your existing debt well. Credit cards are a good way of doing this. If you already have credit card debts, then ensuring your balances are low – around 30% or below the credit limit – improves your score. For example, if you have a credit card with a £3,000 credit limit, you should aim to have a balance of £900 or less.

Consider your length of credit history

The length of time you've had a bank account for matters. If you're like us, you've probably got accounts with at least three to five banks. If you ever want to close an account, try to keep the accounts you've had the longest as they demonstrate trust and your ability to maintain an account for a long time.

Keep things diverse naturally

Lenders like to see that you're able to manage a variety of credit types. This is because in life you're expected to demonstrate balance. So rather than have five store cards, it's ironically better to have a credit card, a car loan and so on. The best outcome is to demonstrate your responsibility for them.

Register on the electoral register

Having your name on the electoral register is one important way of demonstrating stability. This is partly because you have to go through certain checks in order to add your name to the register and the penalty for incorrect information is very high.

Turning a low credit score into a high credit score demonstrates growth and responsibility with money, but don't take on debt unless you must and, even then, ensure you have the discipline to pay it back. Borrowing money isn't free, of course, and if you go into it with that mindset you'll remain a good steward of money and be rewarded with a high credit score. Finally, be patient and don't get frustrated. Improving your credit score will typically take one to three months.

A life of financial joy awaits as you implement all these tips, but let's shift gears and focus on one reason that people like to get a good credit score, which is usually because they want to buy a car on finance.

WHY CARS KEEP YOU POOR

Cars are huge status symbols in our Nigerian culture and many other cultures, too. People love their cars and we're not exempt from the car craze. When we met, I (Ken) drove a beautiful Mercedes Coupé with stunning 19-inch alloy wheels that I'd bought almost brand new for around £21,000 with most of my savings and partly on finance. On top of that, I hadn't planned for the insane maintenance costs.

Mary, on the other hand, had a banged-up Vauxhall Corsa that was a few years old. It had a door that barely closed properly, but it worked fine. She also had a low five-figure savings pot that she'd been building up with the aim of owning a property one day.

It was clear that one of us had made good decisions about money and the other hadn't. Not only did the car keep me poor, I ended up selling the Mercedes six years later for just over £2,000.

Today, we drive an electric car, a used 2013 Nissan Leaf that we bought outright for £9,000. So far we've used it for seven years and it has brought us enormous peace, as well as allowing us to save and invest our money. With our lived experiences, here's why cars keep you poor.

Maintenance costs

According to Kwik Fit,[18] before factoring in the actual cost of the car, the average cost of maintaining a car is £162 a month or almost £2,000 a year of net income. Here is a full breakdown.

Item	Average monthly spend
Fuel	£67.63
Car insurance	£31.64
Routine maintenance and servicing	£15.96
Unexpected repairs and breakdowns	£13.26
Vehicle excise duty (road tax)	£12.16
Breakdown cover	£6.96
Parking permits and tickets	£6.89
Cleaning	£4.15
Fines	£3.69
Monthly average total (excluding finance)	£162.33
Finance	£226.12
Monthly average total (including finance payments)	£388.45

When finance costs are included, it brings the total average monthly cost of running a car to £388. These numbers will no doubt be a lot higher by the time you're reading this book, driven by rising inflation and the cost of living, but people's incomes are not rising as much.

What is your car truly costing you?

To understand what your car is truly costing you, it's helpful to understand the opportunity cost of what you're spending – or what else you could have achieved with that money.

Let's assume that rather than paying £226.12 a month over five years, the typical average duration of financing a car, you invested that money in the stock market (assume the S&P 500 for illustration purposes only and assume an average 8% return per year). Using a compound interest calculator, this will result in a total value of £16,725.35, with a return of £3,158.

Since we're looking at opportunity cost, if you extrapolate this calculation over 25 years, the results are astonishing. The same £226.12 invested and assuming an 8% average annual return would result in an investment portfolio worth £215,951,[19] with total deposits of £67,836 and compounded returns of £148,115. Our point here is that when you think about whether you can afford a car, don't just say to yourself, 'I can afford £226.12 a month.' Instead, ask yourself, 'What big opportunity am I missing out on by doing that?'

Opportunity cost of owning a car

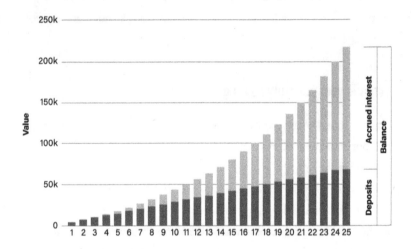

There is a time value to money, and money put into appreciating assets has the potential to create wealth rather than keeping us poorer.

Tips for winning the car game:

- If you can, don't borrow from your future to buy a car now. Save and buy a car with cash because it stops you from overpaying on average.
- If you must buy a car, buy a good quality secondhand car with a service history. Strongly consider an electric car. In our experience, it saves you a lot of money. We went from paying £40 per week for diesel to paying £28 a month for an electric car doing the same average monthly travel. It's also better for the environment.
- Invest what you would have spent on financing a car (we'll show you how in week 7 – see page 182).

- Drive your car for as long as possible (aim for ten years), maintain it and get the most value out of it.
- If you're a family with two cars, make a case for one car. It will help your wealth-building potential. If you're a family with one car, do everything to avoid upgrading to two cars.

Finally, if you insist on spending lots of money on a car – because it brings you joy or because you're already in a good place in your finances – that's fine so long as you're happy to accept the trade-off with the true opportunity cost of owning a car.

RENTING VS BUYING A HOME

The topic of buying a home vs renting is emotional and complex. Most people have been programmed to see buying a home as the default option. Shows on daytime TV like *Homes Under the Hammer, Escape to the Country* and *A Place in the Sun* sell us the dream of home ownership, and you can even feel you're not successful enough if you don't own a property. In fact, some people feel attacked if you tell them that buying a house at all costs might not be the smartest thing to do with their money and energy.

We've personally had a good experience with buying a house as a family with two children and we advocate that, if you can, you should buy a house as early as you can, in a good location, for the long term, without too much debt, and look to pay off your mortgage as quickly as possible. However, we also understand that renting is a better or even smarter option for some people, depending on their personal circumstances.

Renting should not be frowned upon as an option and we should all question our deep-rooted programming around home ownership. Some people even consider renting 'dead money', because they're supposedly paying off someone else's mortgage. Although far from perfect, renting, when done well, is the provision of suitable accommodation with the option of regular maintenance at the expense of the landlord. Given that buying and renting have their varying pros and cons, let's consider why you should – and why you shouldn't – buy a house.

Why you should buy a house

Here are the key reasons why we suggest that, if you can, you should buy a house.

Stability and security: Homeownership provides a sense of stability and security. Owning a property offers greater control over your living arrangements, allowing you to customize and make changes to your home as you desire. It also provides a sense of belonging and can create a strong community connection, especially if you have good neighbours or buy close to family members.

Retirement: Owning your own home reduces your lifestyle costs in retirement, giving you the opportunity to live more comfortably and without worry. Yes, you'll still have maintenance costs and council tax, but these will be insignificant relative to the cost burden of renting in retirement.

Income source: In our experience, your home could become one of your greatest wealth-building tools. For example, you may be able to rent out rooms in your home to international students or lodgers (see page 313 for a real-life example).

Equity and wealth accumulation: Buying a house allows you to build equity over time. As mortgage payments are made and the property potentially appreciates, you can accumulate wealth that can be tapped into through equity loans, refinancing or selling the property in the future. It also offers the opportunity to pass down the property to future generations, ensuring a legacy.

Long-term cost savings: In some cases, owning a house can be more cost-effective in the long run than renting. While monthly mortgage payments may sometimes be higher than rent payments (especially with rising interest rates, if you're not on a fixed rate), homeownership eliminates the uncertainty of uncontrollable rent increases and provides an opportunity to build more equity with each payment.

Why you should not buy a house

Here are reasons why it might make sense for you to rent instead of buying a home, and you can then reassess your personal circumstances over time.

Affordability: Aim for your mortgage expense to be a maximum of 25% of your after-tax income before any overpayments. This makes up half of the 50% that we allocated to your needs as part of your joyful spending plan earlier on. If you find yourself materially exceeding 25% in your plans to buy a house, it might make more sense for you to rent until you're ready. In addition, if you can avoid it, don't buy a house by extending the term of the mortgage to 35 years or more just so that you can make the maths work. It piles on tens or hundreds of thousands more in interest. Here is an example:

The true cost of buying a house as a first-time buyer over 25 years vs 35 years

	25-year mortgage	35-year mortgage
Average UK house price[20]	£286,000	£286,000
Deposit paid (10%)	£28,600	£28,600
Stamp duty[21]	0	0
Legal, arrangement and other purchase fees (2%)	£5,720	£5,720
Mortgage interest (5% a year)[22]	£196,056	£273,703
Annual maintenance[23] (1% or £2,860)	£71,500	£100,100
Home insurance[24] (£216 a year)	£5,400	£7,560
Major home improvements[25]	£107,350	£118,085
Life insurance[26] (£38 a month)	£11,400	£15,960
Council Tax[27] (£2,065 a year)	£51,625	£72,275
Total cost	£763,651	£908,003

Please note: This is a simple illustration and does not factor in inflation. Stamp duty depends on the property price. Mortgage interest is based on a 25-year average and will increase or decrease over time. To run these numbers yourself with your own mortgage rate, find a suitable mortgage calculator online or download our free spreadsheet at: thehumblepenny. com/mortgagecalculator

The above numbers don't even factor in other certain costs such as removal and moving costs, or new furniture and white goods, and if you live anywhere near a major city, you can expect these numbers to be significantly higher. In addition, there is the opportunity cost of the money you spend on a house to factor in as well.

Unforeseen maintenance: If you're renting, when the boiler breaks or the washing machine or other appliances stop working you call the landlord to fix it at their expense. When you buy a house, you have to pay for all unforeseen expenses, including the uncontrollable costs of service charges if you buy a flat.

Small deposit: Although in the UK you can buy a property for a 0% or 5% deposit, we recommend saving to put down at least a 10% deposit. For the first time since 2008, the UK has introduced 100% mortgages that don't require a guarantor. While this is aimed at helping renters get on the property ladder and will appeal to some people, we suggest building up a bit of deposit, because this helps you not only take on less debt, but also gives you a better choice of mortgage rates to choose from.

Flexibility: Having the option to move home to another area for a job opportunity or even to move country should not be underestimated. It might even be that you want the flexibility to travel across the country or the world, while still being able to work online, independent of location. If these are priorities for you, then renting might make more sense.

Not settling down: If you're not ready to settle down, it might make more sense to rent until you are. In our experience, having two people to bear the costs of homeownership makes it financially easier. Of course, if you're single and can comfortably afford to own your home, then that's great. Alternatively, consider finding others who you might be able to share your property with as a way of spreading the cost and earning income quicker to pay off the mortgage faster.

Overall, if you can afford to buy a house for the long term without too much debt, do so as early as possible, try to pay off the mortgage ASAP and avoid moving. We suggest not buying the biggest house that you can based on your salary multiples. If you have children, consider that your children might end up living with you for longer into adulthood, so buy what works for your household, but be led by the numbers and don't overborrow, even if it means moving further out to buy cheaper and borrow less.

However, as we've made clear, buying is not the default for everyone and, depending on their personal circumstances, some people will be better off renting and could then reassess their needs over time. If you choose to buy or aspire to get on the property ladder, we'll show you how we paid off our mortgage in seven years in week 6.

THE REAL COST OF RAISING A CHILD

The decision to have a child is one of the most expensive life decisions you can ever make and it's no wonder there is a growing child-free movement. When people think of having a child, the focus is often on the costs of childcare during the early years, which have been astronomical, with the average annual cost of a full-time nursery place for a child under two in Great Britain costing £14,836[28] ($19,287). Many parents have had to cut their hours or give up work as it doesn't make economic sense for them and others have chosen to either delay having children or not bother at all.

In our experience of raising two children for more than a decade so far, we've learned that there are many costs (cost of opportunity, energy, emotion) beyond money that are often overlooked when considering having a child. Then there's the quality of lifestyle that you want to give that child.

The average cost of raising a child to the age of 21 in the UK is estimated to be £230,000[29] ($299,000), which you can then scale up if you're having two or more children, with some savings expected if you have children of the same gender. To make the monetary costs more real, we've estimated the cost ourselves, based on our lived experience coupled with detailed research, and split the costs assuming four different lifestyle options.

Four lifestyle levels for raising a child

Lifestyle	Assumptions
Basic life	You rely on the state for education (primary and secondary), healthcare and your child doesn't go to university.
Basic life+	Same as basic life except your child goes to university for three years.
Mid life	Your child is educated privately at primary level and goes to university. You also pay for private health insurance to add to your state benefits and you have life insurance that also covers your child.
Rich life	Your child is exclusively privately educated and then goes to university. You also pay for private health and have life insurance that also covers your child. In addition, everything else is expensive, from extracurricular activities to holidays and car costs, as you likely drive brand new cars.

Please note: For all categories above, we've assumed that childcare provision is full-time to the age of four, and other forms of after-school and holiday care carry on until the age of 12.

Here is our estimated cost of raising a child to the age of 21. Note that the numbers are inflated by 2% every year, so the totals are the sum of future costs. You would have to discount backwards to see the present value, although, to be honest, that won't be that different:

Cost of raising a child to age 21

	Estimated Costs Per Month (£)				BASIC LIFE	BASIC LIFE+	MID LIFE	RICH LIFE
	Basic	Basic+	Mid	Rich				
Food	60	60	80	240	18,564	18,564	24,752	74,256
Clothing	30	40	50	150	9,282	12,376	15,470	46,410
Nursery and Other Childcare	1,052	1,052	1,284	3,016	63,759	63,759	77,821	182,793
Private Primary education	-	-	1,505	1,505	-	-	113,887	113,887
Private Secondary education	-	-	-	1,624	-	-	-	122,914
Private Sixth form education	-	-	-	1,706	-	-	-	41,360
University education	-	1,063	1,063	1,271	-	39,801	39,020	46,671
Private health insurance	-	-	33	56	-	-	10,313	17,189
Toys	20	20	30	50	5,139	6,188	9,282	15,470
Holidays	42	42	100	250	12,892	12,892	30,940	77,350
School trips	25	25	67	125	3,285	3,285	8,760	16,425
Extra curricular activities/fun	100	100	150	250	19,169	19,169	28,753	47,922
Housing	200	200	600	1,200	61,880	61,880	185,640	371,280
Car	129	129	129	185	40,062	40,062	40,062	57,296
Term Life Insurance	-	-	10	33	-	-	3,094	10,313
Miscellaneous	20	20	30	40	6,188	6,188	9,282	12,376
Total in GBP					£ 240,220	£ 284,163	£ 597,076	£1,253,911
					or	or	or	or
Total in USD					$ 312,286	$ 369,412	$ 776,198	$ 1,630,084

The immediate reaction to these numbers is likely one of shock. We've kept them as realistic as possible and probably missed out on a few cost categories, but these numbers essentially tell us that the cost of raising a child over time is not insignificant, no matter what path you choose. Note that a huge factor here is location. We've assumed that you're raising a child in the UK or a similar country near a major city. Someone raising a child in a remote town or village will, of course, do it a lot cheaper due to a lower average cost of living. In any case, there is money to be spent. Here are more tips to help you reduce the cost of raising a child:

Tips to reduce cost of childcare

SECONDHAND

Ask family and friends for secondhand clothing and toys or use charity shops.

GOVERNMENT HELP

Get tax-free help from the government depending on the age of your child at: www.Childcarechoices.gov.uk

MEAL PLANNING

Budget, plan your meals in advance, make a shopping list and stick to it.

START A BUSINESS

Consider re-training and starting a childcare business to reduce your costs and help others.

COMMUNITY GARDEN

Join or start a community garden where you can grow fruits, vegetables and herbs collectively. Sharing the cost of seeds, tools and maintenance can help reduce your grocery expenses.

Reduce the cost of raising children

INVEST EARLY

Consider saving and investing 50% of all cash gifts and child benefit, plus other savings early in a Junior ISA.

BUY PRE-LOVED

Consider borrowing or buying pre-loved equipment, high chairs, strollers, etc.

EMBRACE DIY

Make homemade baby food, sew and mend clothes and craft toys.

BABYSITTING CO-OP

Create a community of trusted friends, family or neighbours who offer and receive childcare for free.

CARPOOLING

Coordinate with other parents in your area to establish a carpooling system for school drop-offs, extracurricular activities and play dates.

Note that the government's tax-free provision of childcare in England is increasing and it's expected that most working families with children under the age of five will be entitled to 30 hours a week of free childcare support. This will help parents with childcare responsibilities move into or take on more paid work. For the latest information on your entitlement to tax-free childcare from the UK government, visit www.childcarechoices.gov.uk and use the childcare calculator to see what help you could get with child-care costs.[30] You may also be eligible for more cost-of-living help under the Help For Households scheme.[31]

The natural response from reading the above is that having children is a disaster financially. However, we think what is worth considering deeply is the real joy of raising a child. Parenting brings with it joys that are hard to put into words.

All that said, although having children has been a blessing and a big part of doing life well for us, it is not for everyone as some people can either not have children or simply choose not to have them and we fully respect that. Don't feel pressured by society, cultural norms, parents or friends to have a child (or more children) if you don't want to. Live your best life and do whatever works for you having considered the costs and joys of raising a child.

MANAGING MONEY AS A COUPLE

Should you completely combine your finances in a joint account or manage them separately? There isn't a right or wrong answer to this. However, in our experience, prioritizing communication, trust and transparency in your finances as a couple will not only make things easier for you and keep you together, but it will also take you further.

We see all the money that comes into our household as the family money and not his or her money. This way, it removes the pressure that one person earns more than the other or contributes more. Our incomes go into our joint account for full transparency and out of that we have automated payments that go to our investment accounts equally, as well as payments for various household expenses. We also have individual accounts where we transfer money for each of us to spend on whatever we want. However, if we're spending money above a certain amount from our joint account, we have to talk to each other about it before we do so. This way, we're not only transparent, but we hold each other accountable to make sure that we're meeting our savings and other financial goals, and not spending on things we hadn't planned for.

We understand that this is an unusual approach, but we've learned the hard way from watching our parents, who have completely separate finances, and one big regret they have is that they feel they could have gone so much further in life (for example, made more investments) if they had worked better together and overcome their trust issues. This is quite common for their generation where one person typically has no idea what the other person earns.

New research, the first longitudinal study to look at the way couples structure their bank account and how it influences the quality of their relationship over time, found that a joint bank account can help couples align their financial goals and adhere to communal norms, rather than behaving in a more transactional way. If all money is everyone's money, then the individual partners don't need to keep score.[32]

You should do what works for you, but we've never regretted combining all our finances as a couple. In fact, we'd argue that it has improved our marriage and gives us a unique advantage.

To bring week 5 to an end, creating a life of financial joy rests on mastering your day-to-day finances and living within your means, which will create a life where you sleep better and enjoy freedom, calm and peace. Outside of uncontrollable life events and circumstances, this will depend on the lifestyle choices that you make around key areas such as housing, food, cars, children and non-essentials. It will also depend on the degree to which you're able to manage the inflow and outflow of money through your life to not only pay for those expenses monthly, but also to create enough of a buffer to save and invest for the future. Given our world works hard to encourage us to outspend our means and rely on debt, achieving debt freedom is key to a life of financial joy and we'll be tackling that in week 6.

WEEK 5: LESSONS AND ACTION STEPS

Three lessons for week 5

- Your day-to-day lifestyle choices and the habits you develop will be the biggest determinants of your ability to live below your means, save money and invest in assets that help you build wealth. The simpler and more intentional your lifestyle choices are, the easier the wealth-building journey will be for you. Consider strongly the costs and benefits of your big decisions about housing, getting married, having children, buying a nice car and so on, but don't let over-analysis paralyse you from living your best life.

- Creating a joyful spending plan will help you to tell your money where to go each month and provided you allocate money to your savings and investments first, spending your money on experiences that bring you joy (even as your income rises) should be guilt free, because you've intentionally planned for it.

- Building wealth begins with mastering the minute inflows and outflows of cash through your life. If you gamify it by using tools such as the monthly master day-to-day finances checklist and resist the urge of lifestyle creep that often comes with comparing yourself to others, you'll design a well-intentioned life where you're a confident steward of money.

Three action steps for week 5

Action step 1: Create a joyful spending plan, aka budget, for your income and expenses and use the suggested percentages below to decide on eight places your money should go each month when you get paid. Adjust the second column of our suggested plan to reflect your personal circumstances and write your plan to move forwards with in the third column.

Place	Our suggested percentage	Your percentage
Workplace or private pension	10% of gross income	
You then pay tax on the remaining 90% of your gross income – what is left is your net income Now allocate 100% of that net income that hits your bank account to seven places		
1. Emergency fund	5% of net income	
2. Debt pay-off	10% of net income	
3. Stocks and shares ISA and lifetime ISA	15% of net income	
4. Needs	50% of net income	
5. Fun and wants	5% of net income	
6. Giving	10% of net income	
7. Growth and risk fund	5% of net income	
	Total 100% of net income	

Action step 2: Decide on a home CFO and money day.

The Home CFO (and it could be you) will be in charge of staying on top of the admin necessary to manage your monthly finances and build wealth over time. The money day could, for example, be the first Saturday of each month as you're usually working retrospectively. Choose a date that works for you and remember to keep it light-hearted and fun.

Action step 3: Use the monthly master day-to-day finances checklist (or something similar) to stay on top of your finances each month.

Monthly master day-to-day finances checklist

No.	Activities	☑
1	Diarize a money day weekly, bi-weekly or monthly. Make it recurring.	
2	Review your POST (Purpose, Objectives, Strategy and Tactics) for your vision and goals. Are you making progress? Discuss.	
3	Calculate your financial networth (i.e where you are now). Any progress?	
4	Discuss your debts and the progress you're making. Make sure you're clear on the one debt that you're paying off right now.	
5	Check your investments. Are they performing well over the last 12–24 months? (Remember, investments go up and down, so think long term.)	
6	Review your Joyful Spending Plan. Did you stick to your planned allocations of your income? If not, why not? Discuss.	
7	Review the details of your expenses over the last 30 days by comparing the actual numbers on your bank statement to your expected budget. Did you stick to your plan?	
8	If you have a mortgage, is there any room for overpayments? If so, make the overpayment. See page 173 for why overpayments matter.	
9	Check all monthly standing orders or direct debits. Can you stop or renegotiate anything?	
10	Check your credit report and score. Anything unusual? Discuss what you need to improve using the tips we shared above.	

Week 6:
Debt reduction strategies:
banishing debt for good

A life of financial joy declares war on bad debt,
but uses good debt responsibly to build wealth.

Debt is a double-edged sword, and the system of debt that the UK and global economy is built on discriminates. On the one hand, poorer households borrow for survival and, because they typically have lower credit scores and are without the security of assets, the cost of borrowing is usually significantly higher, with a greater reliance on expensive credit cards, overdrafts, payday loans and personal loans. Due to the higher interest rates, that debt compounds more quickly and becomes harder to pay back, as poorer households struggle to manage on typically lower levels of income and usually focus on paying back just the minimums.

Richer households, on the other hand, borrow to invest in assets that make them richer, because they're able to borrow relatively cheaply through mortgages, thanks to typically better credit scores and ownership of assets that can be offered as security. Since 2008, the wealth divide has grown more than ever, driven by asset inflation caused by over a decade of record low interest rates and billions in money printing, aka quantitative easing. In simple terms, if you own assets then you're laughing and will likely carry on doing well in a world of high inflation. If you own expensive liabilities, you may struggle as interest rates rise.

How do you turn things around from a world where it feels like you're constantly working to pay off debts, to a world where you become debt free and start putting aside some money to invest in assets?

We'll be covering exactly that in this section of the book and sharing the strategies that will help you to pay off expensive so-called 'bad debt', such as credit cards, and develop the habits that could help you to consider using cheaper so-called 'good debt', such as mortgages, responsibly, as a tool, to build wealth one day if you want to. The latter part on using mortgage debt to build wealth by investing in property will be covered extensively in week 9, when we look at how to be braver with money.

HOW DEEP IN DEBT ARE WE?

Money borrowed by individuals is referred to as household debt and this is made up of financial debt (credit cards, loans and other non-mortgage debt) and property debt (mortgages and equity release secured on properties). Total household debt in Great Britain is about £1.28 trillion,[33] of which £1.16 trillion (91%) is property debt and £119 billion (9%) is financial debt. Both types of debt continue to rise, with the biggest increases in financial debt being driven by increases in student loans, hire purchase and credit card debt. To understand who is holding all this debt and how it relates to their wealth positions, let's take a look at three important charts. Imagine the population divided into ten groups called deciles. The 10% of households with the most total wealth are the tenth (highest) decile and the 10% with the least total wealth are in the first (lowest) decile. The first chart below reveals one of the reasons why we have a growing wealth gap. It shows us that poorer households are more likely to have financial debt compared to middle to high wealth households, who are more likely to have property debt.

Percentage of households with household debt by type

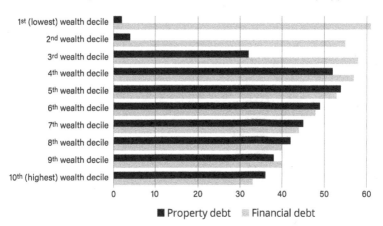

In the first decile (poorest households), around 61% of households have financial debt compared to 2% with property debt as fewer people earn enough to get a mortgage. However, from the fifth decile (middle class) to tenth decile (wealthiest households), those with property debt exceed those with financial debts. The tenth decile households have around 36% property debt compared to 33% financial debt. But what about total debt? The wealthiest 50% of households hold around 64% of total household debt and the least wealthy 50% of households hold 36% of total household debt.[34]

ARE DEBT AND WEALTH RELATED?

The short answer is, yes. The fact that the wealthiest households have more debt and a higher proportion of cheaper property debt leads to a positive correlation to their wealth outcomes. One way to see this is to look at the ratio of total household debt to total household wealth by decile.

Ratio of total debt to total wealth

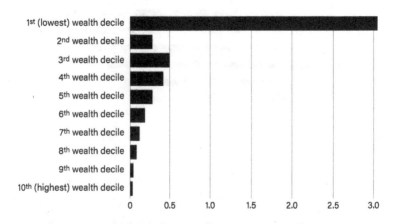

This tells us that while the least wealthy households had a lower total debt compared to wealthier households, their total debt was three times larger than their total wealth compared to the wealthiest households, with zero debt-to-wealth ratio. Below is a full picture of household wealth by asset type, with property wealth representing the second largest proportion of wealth for the wealthiest households, after pensions. This pattern has been growing for years and similar patterns exist in the US and other debt-based economies around the world.

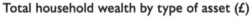

Total household wealth by type of asset (£)

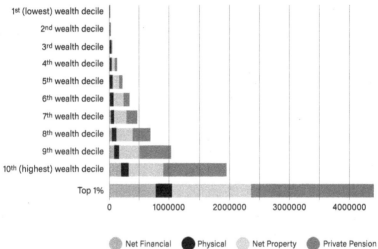

Why does all this matter for you? The type of debt that you hold matters. Of all households in the first decile, 15% hold what's known as problem debt, meaning such households have difficulty repaying their debts, especially as interest rates rise, and this could affect a family's living standards, stability and financial inclusion. Comparable numbers for the middle class and wealthiest households are 5% and 2% respectively. Getting rid of financial or 'bad' debts is critical to building long-term wealth. In order for us to figure out how to banish such debts, it's important to understand how we got there in the first place.

22 REASONS WHY REAL PEOPLE GET INTO DEBT

As we covered in week 3 (see page 74), having the knowledge that you should not be in debt is not enough to ensure you avoid debt. It comes back to managing the things you can control (behaviours, money mindset and the choices you make) and creating a plan to cope with the things you can't control (unexpected life events and circumstances). Given money remains a taboo subject culturally and we usually don't want to talk about it, because we want to avoid judgement or shame, creating an environment where people can talk about their debt situations is important. We asked people in the Humble Penny communities how they actually got into debt. The answers were both shocking and revealing, and there were common noteworthy trends. Here are the real responses from people who got into debt.

22 reasons real people get into debt

	Reason	Real words
1	Expensive weddings	'Wedding. Had to take a 6k loan days before to pay off vendors.'
2	Big mortgage after kids	'Never got into debt, but have a big mortgage bcos I underestimated the effect on my salary after kids.'
3	Emotional buying	'I like to buy when I'm sad and when I'm happy, so I'm screwed.'
4	Living above your means	'Thinking I would earn enough to pay it back and then things changed.'
5	Holidays	'Went on holiday and then had unexpected expenses.'
6	Borrowing money to invest	'I used debt to buy index funds!'

7	Not having insurance	'My father got into debt treating cancer because of NHS waiting lists.'
8	Borrowing money for others	'Ex-husband asked me to get a loan for him. I stupidly agreed. He refused to pay it back.'
9	Mismatch between expenses and income	'Overspending and not checking how much I have coming in to ensure I can clear it.'
10	Keeping up with appearances	'I kept borrowing to maintain my lifestyle even though my real situation was getting worse.'
11	Trying to have kids (IVF)	'IVF and don't regret it one bit.'
12	Bad business advice	'Bad advice from an ex-business partner/manager... Like, terrible advice.'
13	Luxury living	'Too many luxury direct debits. They soon add up and ended up being more than I earned.'
14	Buying car on overdraft	'Buying a car on overdraft thinking I could pay it off easily, but couldn't.'
15	Pleasing others	'Trying to please others by buying and wanting to always give people the best.'
16	Unexpected life events	'My parent died and I took over household bills while on a doo-doo wage.'
17	University	'Decided to go back to uni later in life, but loans and grants aren't available for mature students so I used credit cards.'
18	Parental debt	'My father got into debt and faced civil imprisonment. My mum and his family pressured me to take out a loan to pay his creditors.'

19	Using debt to improve credit score	'Being a first-time immigrant, I'm trying to get in debt using credit cards for credit score.'
20	Ignorance	'I honestly didn't realize there was an alternative.'
21	House renovation	'House renovation. Will hopefully add higher value.'
22	Lack of financial literacy	'Lack of education while young. I had the attitude where I would never check my bank balance.'

Did any of the reasons for getting into debt resonate with you? They certainly resonated with us. Unemployment is another major reason why people get into debt. This isn't a complete list, of course, but it highlights to us that the routes to getting into debt are diverse. However, the good news is that there are things we can do to get rid of and avoid getting back into debt.

Bringing this closer to home, how did you get into debt? Pause for a moment and reflect on that. If you have a partner, discuss it with them, but without blaming each other. You'll need to be clear on this before using the Debtonator® Method later on. If you're unsure how it happened, a review of your bank statements to figure out exactly when you got into debt and where your money went is a good exercise to do.

HOW TO DEAL WITH NEGATIVE EMOTIONS ABOUT DEBT

When we think of our journey of being in debt and eventually becoming debt free, the range of emotions began with stress, frustration, anxiety, fear and shame, and over many years, as we gradually made progress towards becoming debt free, the emotions were excitement, empowerment, freedom, contentment and joy. Dealing with negative emotions about debt can be challenging as your emotions are a part of who you are. However, there are several practical tips that can help you manage those emotions and use them to your advantage in creating a more positive mindset.

Talk about how you feel: It can be liberating to talk about how you feel, because you'll find that you're not in a deep dark hole that you genuinely can't get out of. Other people have either been there or are currently in the same situation as you and there is a way out. Speak with a trusted friend or family member or join a community where others are also on a debt-free journey and are happy to talk about it without comparison. See the resources section of the book for debt charities to speak to.

Find healthy outlets for stress: Engage in activities that help reduce stress and anxiety, such as exercise, meditation, deep breathing, journalling or spending time with loved ones.

Use the power of auto-suggestion: This is a psychological technique that involves repeating positive affirmations or statements to yourself in order to influence your subconscious mind. For example:

- 'I am worthy of a debt-free life and I am taking the necessary steps to achieve it.'
- 'I am attracting abundance and financial freedom into my life by managing my debts responsibly.'
- 'I am committed to living a debt-free life. I can absolutely do it!'

You can write these on affirmation cards that you repeat daily or simply memorize and repeat them when you feel down about your debts. When combined with taking action, this can be a powerful tool to change your mindset and behaviours, which in turn can help you gradually become debt free.

Visualize a debt-free future: Imagine how your life will improve once you're debt free. Visualizing the positive outcomes can motivate you to stay on track and also help you to re-write the negative inner beliefs you might have about who you are as someone in debt. Believing that you will become debt free is half the battle won.

Face your debt head-on: If you fit the avoider persona (see page 51), it's easier to say 'I'll do it tomorrow' when it comes to facing your debts. However, one thing we know is that avoiding or ignoring debt can increase negative emotions. Doing things, like actually opening letters that you might have been ignoring, is a big win. Such small steps will help you to create a plan, which we'll cover next.

BECOME DEBT FREE: THE DEBTONATOR® METHOD

We created the Debtonator® Method to help you destroy your debts faster. However, before we can get into the practical details, a mindset shift is required. One of the most powerful ways to solve a design problem such as being in debt is to reframe how you think about it. So, rather than thinking 'I'm paying off debt,' think 'I'm building wealth.' You can make becoming debt free joyful by thinking about it as 'wealth in progress'. Whenever you pay off £1 or $1 of your debt, it should make your heart sing, because you're moving forwards on the money journey and building wealth. The success of The Debtonator® Method, a step-by-step system that we created having become 100% debt free, is based on this reframe and mindset. Here are the ten action steps of the Debtonator® Method.

The Debtonator® Method

Step	Action
Step 1	Stop spending more money
Step 2	Make a list of what you own (your assets)
Step 3	Make a list of what you owe (your liabilities)
Step 4	Work out how much you can afford to repay
Step 5	Create a debt-free plan
Step 6	Prepare for the unexpected
Step 7	Focus on one thing per week
Step 8	Make your debt goal visible
Step 9	Get an accountability partner
Step 10	Make extra money

Let's now explore these in detail, one at a time.

Step 1: Stop spending more money

It sounds really obvious, but the first step to becoming debt free is to stop digging a bigger hole for yourself by accumulating more debt. Given this requires behavioural change, you need to create more friction around your money and debts. There are two options for achieving this.

Option 1 – cash only: This is old-school, but it works. Start using cash! You'll find it much harder to spend £500 or $500 in cash compared to spending the same amount on a credit card. Psychologists call this the pain of paying, which refers to the negative emotions we feel when we make a purchase.[35] This happens because, as human beings, we want to avoid losses, which we perceive to carry more weight than equal gains. The psychological effect of using cash gets even deeper with the denomination effect,[36] a cognitive bias which says that people are less likely to spend currency in larger denominations – a £50 note or $100 bill – compared to their equivalent value in smaller denominations. Budgeting systems such as the envelope system, where you save in different envelopes for different expenses, only work because they're cash based and ultimately help you to change your spending behaviour.

Option 2 – debit only: This is a similar idea to the cash system, but with a focus on spending only what you have budgeted for on your debit card, although you need to make sure that you stop any access to an overdraft facility. A lot of banks now offer 'pots' that allow you to stash money for specific purposes away from your main bank balance.

Step 2: Make a list of what you own (your assets)

Without seeing it all on one page, it is easy to overlook certain obvious things. For example, we once reviewed someone's finances with them and found out that they had around £10,000 in their current account earning nothing in interest, but also had around £30,000 of credit card debts costing around them 22% APR. However, they preferred not to look at the credit card balance, because there was too much going on in life. Burying your head in the sand when things get too much is a common and relatable experience, and we get it. Making a list of everything of value that you own starts to give you clarity. You have already done this in week 4, so refer back to that list.

Step 3: Make a list of what you owe (your liabilities)

Although you wrote down your liabilities in week 4, we need a bit more information for this section. Here is a template to use:

Creditor	Debt type	Amount	Interest rate	Terms or due date	Priority vs non-priority
Total					

Here is an example:

Creditor	Debt type	Amount	Interest rate	Terms or due date	Priority vs non-priority
AMEX	Credit card	£3,000	22.9%	Minimum	Non-priority
HSBC	Mortgage	£250,000	3.99%	25 years	Priority
Barclays	Overdraft	£500	31.9%	£250 at 0%	Non-priority
Student Loans Company	Student loan	£25,000	6%	Linked to salary	Non-priority
Sainsbury's Bank	Car loan	£7,500	7.5%	2 years	Non-priority
	Total	£286,000			

Although it will come as a shock, try not to worry when you see your debts all in one place. This gives you a clear and concise picture, and the most important thing is that you're sorting things out.

In the last column in the table above, you need to state whether your debts are priority or non-priority debts. We need this to decide which debts to pay off first.

Priority debts are debts that are considered to be important due to the potentially severe consequences of non-payment. If you don't address priority debts, you may face serious consequences, such as legal action, loss of important assets or disruption of essential services. For example, mortgage arrears is a priority debt, because your bank could evict you if you don't pay your mortgage.

Non-priority debts are debts that are generally considered to be of lower severity in terms of consequences for non-repayment. While these debts still need to be repaid, creditors have fewer immediate legal powers to enforce repayment compared to priority debts. Below are examples of priority and non-priority debts.

Priority debts	Non-priority debts
Mortgage arrears, rent arrears, council tax arrears, gas or electricity bills, phone or internet bills, TV licence payments, court fines, overpaid tax credits, payment of goods bought on hire purchase, unpaid income tax or VAT, unpaid child maintenance	Credit card debts, store card debts, catalogue debts, unsecured loans, including payday loans, overdrafts, student loans, unpaid water bills, overpayment of benefits, unpaid parking tickets, money owed to friends and family

Step 4: Work out how much you can afford to repay

Working out how much you can afford to repay requires making hard decisions about your existing lifestyle. This is where our recommended eight places your money should go in your joyful spending plan (week 5 – see page 117) will pay off massively. Our suggestion was that 10% of your after-tax income should go towards paying off your priority and expensive debts each month. If this is not enough to meet your debt goals, your other allocations require reconsideration. Review the list of essential vs non-essential costs that you made in week 5 and ask yourself the hard questions. For example, do we really need a car costing us £400 a month? Can we avoid spending £150 a month on takeaways by cooking at home? Focus on eliminating the odd one-off transactions and reducing the recurring payments. This exercise alone will help you free up more money to throw at your debts and will put the spotlight on spending habits that you need to let go of.

If, after reviewing your outgoings and the 50% allocation to your needs, you find that you still require more money to meet your debt goals, we suggest temporarily pausing the 5% allocation to emergency funds, 5% to growth/risk and the 15% allocation to stock and shares until you pay off your priority and expensive debts. You should keep the 10% allocation to your pension and the 5% allocation for fun, because this is necessary to keep you motivated and still enjoying life a little while you're working on becoming debt free. The remaining 10% allocation to giving is too personal and sacred for us to comment on, but remember that giving from the heart is ultimately what matters.

Step 5: Create a debt-free plan

Use the POST framework that we covered in week 4 (see page 93).

Purpose: Why exactly do you want to become debt free? What's your core motivation for debt freedom? Write your answers below.

```
┌─────────────────────────────────────────────┐
│                                             │
│                                             │
│                                             │
│                                             │
│                                             │
└─────────────────────────────────────────────┘
```

Objectives: Exactly how much debt do you want to pay off and by when? Write your answers below.

Debt amount	Your desired debt-free date

If you don't set goals around your debts, chances are you'll just carry on paying off the minimums on autopilot.

Strategy: How are you going to approach paying off your debts? Who do you need to be fully committed? Which debt should you pay off first? Write your answers below

```
┌─────────────────────────────────────────────┐
│                                             │
│                                             │
│                                             │
│                                             │
│                                             │
└─────────────────────────────────────────────┘
```

There are two things to consider in order to decide which debt to pay off first.

Priority debts vs non-priority debts: You should pay off your priority debts first to avoid losing your home, utility services or facing legal penalties. Interest and charges on priority debts can continue to accumulate and worsen your debt position, whereas, although they might still accrue, for non-priority debts they can be negotiated.[37]

Debt snowball vs debt avalanche: The debt snowball is the idea of building momentum and motivation by focusing on the smallest debts first. The debt avalanche is about minimizing interest costs by targeting the highest-interest debts first. Here is a summary of their pros and cons.

	Debt snowball	**Debt avalanche**
Pros	Psychological boost	Interest savings
	Simplicity	Faster debt elimination
	Early wins	Financial efficiency
Cons	Higher interest costs	Psychological challenge
	Longer overall timeline	Longer time to first success

Although research[38] suggests starting with the debt snowball method for the motivation of seeing your small debts paid off quicker, we personally prefer to focus on the debt avalanche and pay off expensive debts, first to save the most on interest, while paying the minimums on other debts. However, the approach you choose will depend on your personality.

Here is a summary of debt priority vs how expensive your debts are:

	Expensive debts	**Not expensive debts**
Priority debts	Mortgage arrears, court fines, child support arrears, income tax and VAT arrears, child maintenance arrears	Council tax arrears, TV licence arrears, benefit overpayments
Non-priority debts	Credit card debts, Store card debts, payday loans, overdrafts	Personal loans, catalogue debts, student loans (repayments), unsecured lines of credit

Our preferred order of debt pay-off is:

1. Priority debts and expensive debts
2. Priority debts and not expensive debts
3. Expensive debts and non-priority debts
4. Not expensive debts and non-priority debts

Note that you can still use the debt snowball method within these categories, so, for example, within 'priority debts and expensive debts' we have debts such as mortgage arrears, court fines, income tax arrears and so on. You could choose to pay off the smallest of these amounts first for the motivational boost it gives. However, you would need to consider the urgency of these debts first to make sure that you're paying off the most time-sensitive debts first.

Tactics: What other smaller steps should you take to become debt free? See below.

Step 6: Prepare for the unexpected

Although it's tempting to throw every £1 or $1 you have into paying off your debts, it's important to prepare for that unexpected flat tyre, broken boiler or even an unanticipated bill. You'll remember from your joyful spending plan in week 5 that we suggested an allocation of 5% of your after-tax income should go towards an emergency fund. An emergency fund of £1,000 or $1,000 is a good starting point if you're in a lot of debt. Beyond that, we'd throw everything else at the priority and expensive debts first.

Step 7: Focus on 'one thing' per week

When you're on a debt-free journey, it is quite easy to get overwhelmed, so our approach is to keep things simple and focus on only one thing at a time. For example, we have already established that you should focus on one debt at a time and we've shown you how to decide on which debt to pay off first. However, from a day-to-day perspective, there are other small activities that you should focus on one at a time in order to progress faster towards your debt-free goals. For example, we recommend focusing on one bank account if you're using a debit card in step one rather than multiple bank accounts, simply because it's easier to see your income and outgoings in one place. Aim for up to five of these 'one thing' activities per week. Here is a summary of our suggestions:

Our suggestion	Your one thing
One debt	For example, 'I'm currently working on paying off my mortgage arrears of £5,500'

One bank account	For example, 'I'll receive my income and incur expenses through my Barclays debit card'
One habit	For example, 'I'll review my online banking statement after breakfast daily to check my outgoings'
One No Spend Day a Week	For example, 'I'll avoid spending any money at all on Wednesdays each week'
One additional income source	For example, 'I'll focus trying to use my existing skill to earn more money'

Step 8: Make your debt goal visible

Making your debt goals visible is a great strategy to stay motivated and focused on your journey to becoming debt free. Here are some of our favourite ways to make your debt goals visible.

Visual tracker: Design a visual representation of your debt pay-off progress. This could be a simple graph, chart or thermometer-style tracker that you can update regularly. Ensure that it has your debt-free date on it and place it somewhere prominent.

Debt-free vision board: Create a vision board with images that represent your financial goals and the things you want to achieve once you're debt free. Include pictures of your dream holiday, a debt-free celebration, any other motivators or even simple messages like 'Stay debt-free' to keep you focused.

Calendar reminders: Schedule regular check-ins with yourself (or your partner) on your calendar as part of your money day. Treat these check-ins as mini milestones where you review your progress, adjust your strategy if needed and celebrate your successes.

Remember, the key is to find methods that resonate with you and will consistently keep your debt goals at the forefront of your mind. Regularly engaging with these visual reminders will help you stay motivated and focused on your path to financial freedom.

Step 9: Get an accountability partner

An accountability partner is someone who you share your debt-free goals with, and they encourage you and keep you accountable to achieve them. You can check in with that person weekly to share progress on your debt-free journey and even share your struggles if you're having any. An accountability partner could be your spouse, a family member or a friend.

Step 10: Make extra money

If you really want to achieve debt freedom faster, simplifying your lifestyle has to be combined with making extra money. In our experience, money making begins in the mind. Gamifying it makes it fun. We'll show you how to make extra money in week 8 (see page 227).

We've now covered the tried and tested ten steps of the Debtonator® Method to help you become debt free. For help with other debt solutions speak with reputable debt charities or see the bonus content at www.thehumblepenny.com/debtsolutions.

HOW WE PAID OFF OUR MORTGAGE
IN SEVEN YEARS

We achieved something that no one in our family history or even our circle of friends had ever done: we paid off our 25-year mortgage in just over seven years while still in our 30s. In total, we paid off around £380,000 ($494,000), including mortgage interest, without inheriting money or winning the lottery, and we did it from 2012 onwards, during times of the lowest interest rates.

Many people thought we were crazy, because why would you be paying off a mortgage at all? It is cheap debt! On top of that, why would you pay it off when interest rates were so low? Why don't you just invest that money in stocks or borrow even more on your house to invest? You see, on your journey to financial freedom you'll need to make many decisions that are counter-cultural and, to some people, do not make sense logically. However, you'll need to be brave and stand by your conviction, even if others don't see the vision that you have for your life. At the time of writing, interest rates are rising significantly and people have started to see why we were paying off our mortgage early. Here is how we did it.

Strategy 1: Make it a goal first

In an environment of rising interest rates, being able to pay the mortgage is more of a priority for a lot of people. To pay off your mortgage early (and this won't be for everyone), it needs to be a goal. Give priority to paying off expensive debts first, for example, credit cards, and have an emergency fund. Your goal doesn't need to be paying it off in seven years either. We started with a 25-year repayment mortgage and initially aimed for around 20 years. Then, as we built momentum, our goal changed to 15 years, then ten years and, eventually, seven years. Do what works for you and focus on your why.

Strategy 2: Choose where you live carefully

Where you choose to live dictates how much of a mortgage you borrow and how much longer into the future you'll be working to pay it off. Even though we could afford to borrow and live in London, we chose to move just outside the capital to a commuter town, where we bought a forever house for around £340,000 ($442,000) that suited our plans to have and raise two children. Doing this meant that we gave ourselves the possibility of paying off our mortgage early.

Strategy 3: Make overpayments

We overpaid monthly to beat the effects of compound interest. Every £1 or $1 matters. Here is an example for illustration only. Imagine you're paying an average interest rate of 5% on a £250,000 ($325,000) mortgage over 25 years:

£100 ($130) per month overpaid: Saves around £26,000 ($34,000) interest and wipes three years off the mortgage.

£500 ($650) per month overpaid: Saves £83,000 ($108,000) interest and wipes ten years off the mortgage.

£1,000 ($1,300) per month overpaid: Saves £112,000 ($146,000) interest and wipes 14 years off the mortgage.

We started small, but at some point we were overpaying by well over £1,000 a month. You'll see how below. The three scenarios above show that there is a saving to be made at any level of overpayment and starting small is worth your while. In case you're wondering how we were able to overpay so much given the 10% overpayment cap that triggers an early repayment charge, we'll share how we overcame this in the next section.

Strategy 4: Live on one income

We adjusted our lifestyles to rely on mainly one income and used the other to invest and overpay our mortgage. This was hard, because Mary's income dropped when she took maternity leave. We had to give up on the nice car and frequent takeaways, and plan our family holiday 12 months ahead to save money. We also started living on a £50 ($65) per week food budget and went on a mainly vegetarian diet for health reasons, as well as to save money. Our food budget is currently around £70 ($91) per week for a family of four. Your choice of lifestyle is everything and the simpler it is, the better. We still had fun, but we found free or cheap activities and planned more intentionally to avoid overspending.

Strategy 5: Start a side hustle

We put a lot of our time and energy into earning more from side hustles like tutoring, creating party templates, starting a nursery business, having a lodger and so on. The more we earned after tax, the more we paid off our mortgage and invested in the stock market.

Strategy 6: Use bonus and redundancy money

As our careers improved, we earned bonuses for hard work and we used some of that money to enjoy our lives, but we threw most of it into investing and mortgage overpayments. Another key source of money is redundancy payments. One thing that helped us pay off our mortgage early was negotiating decent redundancy packages and, rather than living on that money, we found new jobs quickly and used that money to overpay lump sums on our mortgage instead.

Strategy 7: Make two payments per month

If you make two payments a month – for example, an extra one from a side hustle or other means – you end up making 26 half-payments each year, which is equivalent to 13 full monthly payments, instead of the 12 full monthly payments that most people make on their mortgages. This helped to reduce the effect of compounding interest. Ask your bank for a sort code, account number and your mortgage reference number, and use these to either make bank transfers that get applied to your mortgage or set up an automatic standing order.

Strategy 8: Career growth

We focused on career development and did new qualifications that helped us to earn more. Mary retrained by doing a childcare qualification that enabled her to run a family nursery business we'd started as a joint venture and Ken completed his Executive MBA (we also managed to get 70% of the £75,000 MBA tuition fee plus a bursary with living costs paid for by a former employer). These qualifications led to promotions – Ken became a CFO and Mary a manager – pay rises and bonuses that were mostly invested in the stock market, but also went towards mortgage overpayments.

Paying off our mortgage early has been lifechanging for us and we have zero regrets. We highly recommend it as it has allowed us to be braver and pursue new careers and passions doing what we love, and it has given us more financial freedom. However, it won't be for everyone and we appreciate that. Some will argue that the money used to pay off a mortgage could be better invested in stocks or that inflation will reduce the value of the debt over time, so why pay if off? Those are valid arguments, but the mental freedom and guaranteed returns trumped that logic for us.

SHOULD YOU PAY OFF YOUR MORTGAGE
EARLY OR INVEST IN STOCKS?

Although investing in stocks will likely deliver a better financial return, the decision to overpay a mortgage vs invest in stocks will depend on both your immediate personal circumstances and long-term goals. Here is an example.

Imagine a couple with two children. They are both 35, healthy, have decent salaries, own a home with a mortgage. In addition, they're at the financial stability stage on the money journey where they have three to six months of living expenses saved. Should they be paying off their mortgage early or investing in stocks? In our view, they should keep investing their money in stocks to try to get to the next stage of the money journey, financial security, where they have at least one year of living expenses saved. This would provide them with more security and liquidity (how easily an asset can be converted into cash), because they have children and need security beyond just having an emergency fund.

Now imagine that they're at the financial security stage and are ultimately aiming for financial independence. Should they carry on investing in stocks or overpay their mortgage? Let's assume that at this stage they now hate their jobs and don't see a lot of future prospects. They'd love the opportunity for one of them to run their own business. In this scenario, it makes more sense for them to start overpaying their mortgage a little bit to reduce the debt burden and provide more flexibility for a future of entrepreneurship, which doesn't offer a regular paycheque. They can do this while still investing some of their money in stocks.

The point here is that investing in stocks is not a clearcut decision, even if it makes logical sense. Your current personal circumstance could be different. For example, you may have poor health, which would immediately change your priorities and you might focus more on the security that a mortgage-free home offers. We did both and changed the proportions over time. Sometimes we invested 50:50 in stocks vs mortgage over-payments, other times it was 70:30, and as we got closer to the end we swapped to 30:70 with priority given to mortgage overpayments, but we still invested every single month in stocks, even if it meant investing only the regular amount through our workplace pensions.

WISH WE KNEW THIS BEFORE GETTING A MORTGAGE

Here are some things that we figured out along the way to mortgage freedom and that we wish we knew before we got a mortgage to buy a home.

The impact of 25-year vs 35-year mortgage

As property prices rise, more people are getting 35-year (or longer) mort-gages in order to afford their payments, which we understand. However, the implications for such a move aren't always spelt out. Did you know that if you borrow, say, £300,000 at 5% interest and opt for a 35-year mortgage instead of a 25-year mortgage on a repayment basis, you pay over £100,000 more interest for those extra ten years? In other words, that's the difference between £226,000 and £328,000 – just in interest! Although banks make it easier for you to extend your term, you have to remember that it's good business for them. If your goal is to become financially free sooner rather than later, we suggest avoiding extending the term. Although some people extend the term and then, for example, invest what they would have paid on their mortgage into stocks, not everyone is that disciplined.

No-cap mortgages

To become mortgage free sooner, you can get mortgages without a 10% overpayment cap via mortgage brokers. This means that if your budget allows it, you can overpay whatever you want without an early repayment charge.

You can get a consent to let

If you have a property now and want to move and let the existing property out, you can get a consent to let from your bank. This allows you to keep the existing property without getting a buy-to-let mortgage. Banks typically give you a consent to let every 12 to 36 months and you renew it when you need to.

Some banks are easier than others

If you're getting a new mortgage or remortgage, some banks are way easier than others. Knowing this gives you a better chance of success of getting a mortgage. A bit of research in online communities and forums or speaking with a mortgage broker will reveal which banks are worth approaching for a mortgage.

Using a broker is worth it

We prefer to use a broker who doesn't charge an upfront fee and has access to the full market of mortgages. Overall, we value the relationship aspect of dealing with a broker, because they have insights that you won't easily find online. Plus, you are likely to get a great mortgage deal.

You can overpay your mortgage at intervals

Here are the three intervals when you can overpay a mortgage:

- The gap between when your current deal ends and your new deal starts.
- Using the 10% overpayment allowance you get when you start a new mortgage deal.
- When the mortgage year starts, typically every January, your 10% overpayment allowance resets.

This means that if you have more than your 10% overpayment allowance saved, you can carefully time when you make these overpayments without incurring an early repayment charge. Do make sure that you call your bank, though, to make sure that you're within the limits for overpayments and won't incur a penalty.

To bring this week to an end, it's worth zooming out to remind yourself that a debt-free life can become your reality if you choose it. Yes, it will take some time, even years in some cases, but if you shift how you see debt and see it as a tool on your journey to building wealth, you'll not only get rid of 'bad' financial debts in your life, but you'll gradually turn your life around to create the possibility of using more productive 'good' debts responsibly to invest in property or even start a business. In week 7, we'll shift the focus to investing for the future and we'll show you how to invest in the stock market to achieve your long-term goals.

WEEK 6: LESSONS AND ACTION STEPS

Three lessons for week 6

- Debt is a double-edged sword and it discriminates. Expensive financial debts keep poorer households poorer and blind them to opportunities, whereas wealthier households use cheaper property debt to build more wealth. Our goal is to aggressively get rid of all those financial debts, starting with priority and expensive debts first so we can live below our means sufficiently to build a buffer to invest in assets. It's okay to have property debts as a way to get onto the property ladder, but ultimately, mortgage freedom sooner rather than later should be the destination for your primary residence.

- The UK and global economy is built on debt and the psychology of borrowing is all around us with unseen forces always trying to push us towards debt and keep us indebted by normalizing it. You have the power to choose not being in debt as your reality. Words carry power and auto-suggestion among other tools is one way that you can deal with your negative emotions about debt, by using words of affirmation such as 'I am worthy of a debt-free life, and I am taking the necessary steps to achieve it.'

- It is possible to banish 'bad' debts for good and become debt free yourself, but it requires being disciplined, facing the facts of your situation, creating healthy money habits, subscribing to a simpler lifestyle and reframing your view of 'paying off debt' as 'wealth in progress'. In addition, The Debtonator® Method is a tried and tested ten-step framework that will help you to destroy your debts faster.

Three action steps for week 6

Action step 1: Use the Debtonator® Method (see page 160) to create your debt-free plan, referring to the details of each step from earlier in this week's learning.

Action step 2: If you already have a mortgage (and no other expensive or priority debts), consider how much you can free up in your budget every month for mortgage overpayments. Write down a number below – for example £100 or $100 per month – as a starting point.

Action step 3: Don't be afraid to talk about how you feel about your debts. It can be liberating and you'll find you're not in a deep, dark hole that you genuinely can't get out of. If you feel you need to, write down which trusted friend, family member or organization you would talk to about your debts. Remember, this is a step closer to your debt-free future.

Week 7:

Investing for your future: the path to financial freedom

A life of financial joy is created by making your money work for you while keeping things super simple.

The most common myths about investing in the stock market are that you need to be an expert to invest, you need lots of money so it's only for the rich, and investing is just like gambling. Such myths keep many people away from investing to the point where 49% of the thousands of people that we surveyed in our YouTube community identified 'not starting to invest early enough' as their biggest financial mistake.

Once upon a time, we too believed those myths simply because no one in our family had ever invested money in the stock market. After seeing people who we *could* relate to doing it, in 2010 we took that first leap to start investing a small amount of money in stocks. However, with that one leap gradually came the confidence to start learning more by researching stocks and funds that we wanted to invest in for our long-term goal of financial freedom.

Starting investing wasn't all plain sailing, because the buzz and excitement of making money was followed by the agony of losing money on certain individuals stocks. It took a while for us to come to some simple truths about investing that have helped us to grow our wealth considerably and we're going to share these with you to help you get rich slowly but surely, over time, driven by the power of compounding.

Thanks to the smartphone and index fund innovations, you can be in your living room and within minutes have your money invested across the world – and you can do this all by yourself. In this section of the book, we want to help you answer questions such as where on earth do you start when it comes to investing? How do you choose what types of stocks or funds to invest in? How do you avoid losing your money? And so much more. Overall, we want to remove the complex jargon and keep things super simple, so that you can take action to either start investing, if you're a complete beginner, or invest more smartly if you're not.

WHY BOTHER INVESTING?

There are people who have achieved financial security in their lives without investing in the stock market, so why should you bother? We can think of three compelling reasons:

- If you have financial goals and want to achieve them sooner rather than later, investing your money in the stock market buys you ownership in companies, making your money work harder 24 hours a day, seven days a week.
- Investing your money in stocks gives you one of the best chances of beating inflation and building real wealth.
- The stock market has provided a higher average return on investment compared to many other assets over the long term (20+ years) and

it offers diversification, which reduces the overall risk of your invest-ment portfolio.

For these reasons and more, we believe investing in the stock market is critical to building wealth.

WHY INVEST IN STOCKS?

Investing in stocks (also referred to as shares) is at the extreme end of the investment spectrum and that's because it comes with a lot of risks, but also the possibility of a lot of returns. We invested in Apple stock in 2015 and we've seen our money grow by 644% in eight years. In fact, over a ten-year period, to August 2023, Apple shares returned around 1,030%. This is highly unusual, though, as the money we invested could also have disappeared due to the exposure to a single company, which isn't always guaranteed to do well.

Contrast this with our other investment in the S&P 500 index funds (more on this shortly), which over the same ten-year period returned around 217%. Exposing yourself to risk is necessary for high returns, but the key is to understand that investing in stocks should only be done if you have a long-term horizon. First, you must have financial goals. Then you must have a decent time horizon and you must be okay with being exposed to risk.

HOW DO STOCK MARKETS ACTUALLY WORK?

Think of the stock market as a marketplace where buyers and sellers meet. In today's world, this happens online, and the thing being bought and sold is company stocks and shares. Every time you buy a stock, someone somewhere is selling that stock. Why do company stocks and shares exist at all? Because companies are trying to raise money in order to expand their operations. The money they raise is then invested in areas such as marketing, staff, products, tech and so on.

When you invest in stocks and shares, you own a slice of an actual company. It's easy to forget that that company is made up of hard-working employees, many of whom have families, so whenever you own a piece of a company, it means that potentially, thousands of people are working for you.

When you start investing in the stock market, you allocate your money across three main areas:

Stocks: These are high risk with potential for the high returns that are necessary for your wealth to grow. You tend to have more stocks in your portfolio if you're in the wealth accumulation phase of your life and are working towards financial freedom.

Bonds: These are low risk and low return. They provide an income and act as a hedge for deflation (the opposite of inflation). They also help to make the bumpy ride of investing in stocks smoother. You tend to have more bonds in your portfolio if you're in the wealth preservation stage of your life and are nearing retirement.

Cash: Cash has no risk apart from inflation eroding your purchasing power. It is there to act as an emergency buffer and also enables you to take advantage of opportunities when markets fall. You'll find ideas on where to keep your emergency cash in week 5 (see page 127).

How much you allocate to each of these three areas will depend on your risk appetite, time horizon and goals. We, for example, although financially independent, still have almost 100% of our investable assets (excluding property) in stocks with a small allocation to cash. We don't have any bonds. That's because we're 40 and have decades ahead of us before we choose to stop working, so we're happy with our money being exposed to the risk that comes with investing in stocks. This will change over time.

Broadly speaking, if you're in the wealth accumulation phase of your life, it makes sense to go fully aggressive into stocks with few or no bonds. As you seek to preserve more wealth, you can introduce more bonds. You can also allocate money to commodities, such as gold, which act as an inflation hedge or a doomsday investment. We'll touch on this later on, but for now, let's focus on stocks, bonds and cash.

HOW DO YOU START INVESTING IN STOCKS?

To begin investing in stocks, you first need a clear why, followed by an objective. Then you need a specific strategy, followed by tactics. Using our POST framework, here is an example.

Purpose: For example, 'I want to have a worry-free retirement' or 'I want to invest for my children's education.'

Objective: For example, 'I want to build an investment portfolio of £1 million ($1.3 million) in 20 years, when I'm 60, to provide me with an income of £40,000 ($52,000) a year before tax for a comfortable retirement.' Your goal doesn't need to be £1 million as most people will have a good retirement on much less. If you have more than one goal, split them into different groups, such as retirement and financial freedom, schooling and so on. Keep it all in hard numbers and be absolutely clear on your time horizon about each goal as this is an important driver of how much you will need to invest each month in order to achieve each goal, assuming a sensible expected return. We'll be covering how to work out how much you need to invest to reach your retirement goals in week 9 (see page 269).

Strategy: This is the approach you'll follow to invest your money and who you'll learn the most effective approaches from in order to invest wisely.

Tactics: These are the small things you'll do to avoid losing money with your investments, for example, don't look at your investments too often, especially when people are panicking.

Once you're clear on your purpose and objectives for investing, there are two ways to invest in the ownership of a company through the stock market.

Investing in **stocks** means that you buy the shares of a company directly in exchange for cash. You do this via a broker (more on this below) and you pay transaction fees as a result.

Investing in **funds** means that you're spreading your money (via a pool with others) across many companies, which means you get diversification. Each fund that you invest in comes in units, so when you invest, you get units that are priced daily. The fund (a company that pools funds from many people) then makes the investment into companies. By owning units in the fund, you also own small bits of the underlying companies the fund has invested in. The value of each unit you own can rise and fall in the same way as owning shares directly. Investing in funds has the advantage of reducing your specific risk, tied to companies, but you still have general market risk. Given this is a less risky investment, your potential returns are also reduced.

WHAT'S AN INVESTMENT STRATEGY?

An investment strategy is what guides your actions with regards to allocating your assets. Factors that determine what type of strategy you might want to use to invest your money include your risk tolerance and your future need for your money.

Your investment strategy can help you either seek rapid growth in your capital, which is important if you're in the wealth accumulation phase of life, or it can help you focus on wealth protection, which is important if you're in the wealth preservation stage of your life. Strategies for investing in the stock market include:

Trading: This is the type of noisy activity you might hear your friends or random people on social media talk about. Some see it as a way of making quick money. Here, you try to 'time the market' i.e. choosing an ideal time to pick stocks that you expect will do well in the market over the short term, for example, 12 months or less. We say you should completely avoid this strategy.

Buying cheap and selling high: This is also a buy-to-hold strategy where you try timing the market. You pick stocks by buying cheap and selling high, but you typically hold them for longer than 12 months.

Value investing: These are bargain purchases where you essentially pick stocks that are priced below their true value. This type of investing is what Warren Buffett, one of the world's most successful investors, does as he has a skill for valuing companies and enough money to exert significant influence on any company that he invests in.

What all these investing strategies have in common is that you have to either pick stocks or delegate that decision to an investment manager. This type of investing is known as active investing. The time, intellectual know-how and expertise that is put into stock picking come at a big price most of the time. Worst still, a large body of research shows that active investment managers do not outperform the market.

So why pick stocks or hire an expensive investment manager? There are, of course, exceptions, like Warren Buffett, who plays a totally different game as an active manager, but he is the most famous supporter of the investment strategy you should be giving all your attention to – passive investing.

In fact, to prove the point, in 2008 he made a $1 million bet against a hedge fund (a type of active manager) that his passive investment in an index fund would do better than the outperformance promised by the hedge fund and, ten years later, he won the bet.[39] There is an important lesson to be learned from this fun bet and another reason why you should pay attention.

Passive investing

Passive investing is a type of investment strategy that aims to maximize your returns over a long period of time by keeping the buying and selling to a minimum. This is important, because it avoids fees and drags on your future returns from frequent trading. Essentially, it's a buy-to-hold strategy that's at the other end of the scale to what traders do.

Investors using this strategy by investing in index funds and exchange-traded funds (ETFs) are not interested in short-term market movements and most certainly are not timing the market. A key assumption of passive investing is that, given enough time, the market generates positive returns. Passive investing is all about getting rich slowly, steadily and certainly over time.

Our preference for long-term investing is to follow this passive investing strategy as it gives you the best chance of making money while still protecting your money from loss. We do allocate some of our money to individual stocks that we believe in and have done the research on. However, we wouldn't recommend this to complete beginners if you're not prepared to do the work of researching company balance sheets, and profit and loss, and making a case for buying a company. In our opinion, you should only buy individual stocks if:

- You understand how to research or value companies.
- You're a sophisticated or rich investor.

To keep things super simple and stress free it's best to invest consistently via an index fund or ETF and forget your investments, only dipping in once in a while to track your wealth and rebalance if you need to.

GREAT! BUT WHAT IS AN INDEX?

An index is a list, similar to a shopping list. However, rather than groceries, an index is a list of companies in the stock market that you can invest in. Examples of such lists include the S&P 500, FTSE 100, FTSE 250 and so on. The list is usually put together by a committee, based on set criteria. The S&P 500 is one of the most prestigious indexes, because it is a list of the top 500 companies in the US equities market. It's also a prestigious list because of the reputation of the company that maintains the S&P 500 list – S&P Dow Jones Indices. That list is made up of some of the largest tech companies in the world and, hence, it has performed well historically.

ALRIGHT, WHAT IS AN INDEX FUND?

An index fund is a passive fund that tracks the performance of an index. It is the original and simpler of the two main types of trackers, the other being the ETF. It is suitable for newbie and ongoing investors, especially if you do your investing via monthly direct debits. These funds are mostly structured as companies called open-ended investment companies (OEICs), a UK term for money pooled in a pot to be invested across various types of stocks and other types of investments. Other index funds in the UK are structured as unit trusts (in the US these are referred to as mutual funds). Both OEIC and unit trusts are 'open-ended', which means that you can freely buy and sell shares in the fund. Note that index funds don't attract a trading or dealing cost. All you pay is an annual fee, usually zero point something per cent, making them a cheaper way to invest.

When you invest your money in an index fund, you invest it in a fund that then invests your money across the various companies on an index. Using a football analogy, it's like buying the entire Premier League (an index fund) rather than a star club (a single stock). If you invest £1,000 in the S&P 500, that £1,000 is spread across the 500 companies on the index, weighted by their market capitalizations (the total value of a company's stock currently held by all its shareholders). By tracking the index, the index fund aims to deliver the same performance as the index itself. For example, if the S&P 500 index returns 9% in a year, then you'd expect the index fund tracking the index to return around 9% if the fund tracks it closely.

Advantages of index fund investing

Category	Advantages of index funds
Cost	Low costs compared to active funds (typically 0.04%–0.25% vs. 1%–2% annually)
Diversification	Broad diversification reduces specific risks associated with individual stocks
Self-cleansing	Index funds automatically include well-performing companies while dropping underperformers
Emotional stability	Minimizes emotional reactions to short-term market fluctuations, promoting long-term focus
Accessibility	Open to anyone regardless of financial expertise, making investing more approachable
Good returns	Historically yields around 7% average returns over time, contributing to wealth accumulation
Financial freedom	Index funds play a crucial role in cost-effective wealth accumulation and preservation

There are some disadvantages to index fund investing:

Market risk: Although index fund investing removes the 'specific risk' associated with picking individual stocks, you're inevitably exposed to market risk, which is the risk that the market as a whole may go up or down over time. This is inherent and there is no escaping it.

Tracking error: While index funds aim to match the index, they can have a tracking error, which is the difference between the fund's performance and the index's performance. This can be caused by fees, taxes and other factors.

Sector and industry bias: Most index funds are not intelligently representative of different sectors and industries. Indexes such as the S&P 500 could be argued to be heavily weighted towards financial and tech companies. As such, money invested will be mainly allocated to a handful of industries.

Lack of flexibility: The inability to customize the fund's holdings might limit your ability to align your investments with specific values, preferences or risk considerations.

Market returns: This is a fundamental characteristic of index funds. While they provide market-matching returns, they might not deliver significant outperformance, which could be a concern for investors seeking higher returns. However, if you're happy to get rich slowly but surely, this shouldn't bother you so much.

WHAT ABOUT ETFS?

An ETF is similar to an index fund, except it behaves like a share, so you buy and sell it on the stock market. As a result, you pay trading costs (typically around £10 or so per trade). An ETF is the newer kid on the block and offers us, as investors, a ton more choice. There are more than 1,500 listed ETFs on the London Stock Exchange[40] and due to their popularity this will continue to grow for the foreseeable future.

An ETF is simply a way to invest in the entire market (or an index) through buying a unit that behaves like a company share. As it's a tracker, you can buy an ETF that tracks pretty much any index. Examples include ETFs tracking the FTSE 100, S&P 500, MSCI All Country World Index and so on. You can even buy ETFs tracking commodities like gold, silver, cocoa and oil, and ETFs that track companies involved in crypto and blockchain innovations.

Summary comparison of index funds vs ETFs

	Index fund	Exchange-traded fund (ETF)
Structure	Mutual fund (US) or OEIC and unit trust (UK) tracking specific indexes	Investment funds trading on stock exchanges
Trading	Traded at the end of the trading day at the net asset value (NAV)	Traded throughout the trading day on exchanges
Price	Priced once a day after the market closes	Prices change intraday (within a day) in sync with market moves
Cost	Generally have slightly higher annual ongoing charges	Often have lower annual ongoing charges due to structure
Minimum investment	Can have higher minimum investment requirements	Generally have lower minimum investment amounts
Transparency	Holdings disclosed quarterly or semi-annually (twice a year)	Holdings disclosed daily due to intraday trading
Tax efficiency	Typically more tax-efficient due to structure	Can be tax-efficient, if you don't trade frequently
Liquidity (how easily an asset can be converted into cash)	May be slightly less liquid due to end-of-day trades	Highly liquid due to intraday trading
Diversification	Offers diversification across a specific index	Offers diversification across various indexes
Buying/selling	Bought/sold directly through fund management companies	Bought/sold through brokers like individual stocks

| Investor base | Often favoured by long-term, buy-and-hold investors | Suited for both long-term and short-term traders |
| Market tracking | Aims to replicate index performance closely | Aims to replicate index performance closely |

Some products will only be available as index funds and some only as ETFs. The key is to understand the differences and invest confidently, knowing that they're both ultimately doing the same things, which is helping you track an index and giving you the performance of that index.

HOW INDEX TRACKERS WORK TO MAKE YOU RICH

Index trackers essentially help many investors come together and invest in a pool (pot of money). That pool is then used (via index fund and ETF trackers) to buy bits of every company in an index. Some trackers fully replicate the holdings in the index, while some do it partially. As an example of full replication, an S&P 500 index tracker would also mirror and invest in all 500 companies on the S&P 500 index.

Note that the tracker is not focused on picking winning stocks, so it is not timing the market. The tracker simply focuses on its primary job of tracking the index and earning the returns from the related securities. It's through this pooling that you can, in effect, have holdings in potentially hundreds of companies globally, because doing this on your own would be expensive and impractical.

The broader the base of the index being tracked, the better. Examples such as the FTSE Global All Cap Index, FTSE Developed ex-UK Index, FTSE All-Share and S&P 500 Index are the types to focus on. These give as much diversification as possible and remove specific risk tied to individual companies. It's even better if the index being tracked has companies with operations not just tied to one country. This way you're also diversifying away specific risks tied to individual nations. Such global trackers are now available, and cheaply too. The key is to invest as broadly as possible.

> ### Let's talk investing jargon
>
> As previously mentioned, jargon is one of the reasons many people get put off even starting investing. Say you want to buy an ETF that tracks an index – what do you search for and where? We will get to platforms later. For now, let's tackle the 'what do you search for' bit.
>
> All funds have a unique international securities identification number (ISIN) for identifying them. It's 12 digits and alphanumeric.
>
> Below are some random examples of funds (they're for illustration only, not recommendations).
>
> | | Fund name | ISIN |
> |---|---|---|
> | **A** | Vanguard FTSE Global All Cap Index Fund | GB00BD3RZ582 |
> | **B** | iShares FTSE 100 UCITS ETF (Dist) | IE0005042456 |
>
> Let's dive into what the various components in each fund name actually mean.
>
> ### A: Vanguard FTSE Global All Cap Index Fund
>
> | Name component | Meaning |
> |---|---|
> | Vanguard | Name of the fund provider |
> | FTSE Global All Cap | The index (list) that this fund is tracking or copying |
> | Index Fund | The type of structure, which is also referred to as an OEIC in the UK or mutual fund in the US |

B: iShares FTSE 100 UCITS ETF (Dist)

Name component	Meaning
iShares	Name of the fund provider. iShares is from BlackRock
UCITS	Stands for 'undertakings for collective investments In transferable securities' – it's essentially a badge of approval from the European regulator that makes it easier for people to invest their money in funds across different European countries
ETF	Exchange-traded fund structure
Dist	Stands for 'distribution' and means that you get dividends distributed to you, typically quarterly, which you need to reinvest The alternative to a distribution fund is an 'accumulation' fund, which means that it will automatically reinvest any dividends for you over time with the aim of growth

Apart from searching for a fund by its ISIN, you can also search for most index funds or ETFs by a short ticker code that uniquely identifies a specific fund or security. These symbols are used on stock exchanges and financial platforms to facilitate the trading and tracking of these funds.

For example, Vanguard FTSE All-World UCITS ETF in the UK is identified as 'VWRL' and Vanguard Total Stock Market Index Fund Admiral Shares in the US is identified as 'VTSAX'. Where a fund has a ticker code like this, you usually see it next to the fund name, whereas you usually see the ISIN in the overview of the fund, key investor information documentation (KIID) or prospectus.

GETTING STARTED WITH INDEX FUNDS AND ETFS

Given there are thousands of index funds and ETFs out there, it can seem overwhelming to choose a few to create a portfolio with. Before you can decide which index fund or ETF tracker you want to pick, there are several steps you need to take first.

Step 1: Decide on your investment focus and asset allocation

You decide on your asset class (stocks, bonds, cash) and your asset allocation to each of these areas. Focusing mainly on stocks and bonds, one useful rule of thumb is to use 120 minus your age to determine what percentage to invest in stocks and the remainder in bonds.

For example, if you're 30 years old, the rule suggests investing 90% (120 − 30) in stocks and the remaining 10% in bonds. The rule is based on the idea that young investors have more financial capital in the market relative to their human capital − their capacity to work and earn many years into the future. The rule also factors in people's increasing life expectancy.

However, remember that this is a rule of thumb. Nothing stops you investing 100% in stocks or introducing bonds as you wish. If you're interested in investing in property (via real estate investment trusts − REITs) or other broad commodities (excluding gold), you could allocate to this from your stock or equities allocation above, but we suggest limiting this to between 5% to 10% for each.

If you're interested in digital assets like crypto, this should come out of your stock allocation and we suggest limiting this to a maximum of 1% of your investable portfolio, if at all. Investments in gold and cash should come out of your bond allocation. Again, aim to limit these to between

5% and 10%. We'll summarize later in this week's learning what role these assets play in a portfolio.

Step 2: Decide on your diversification strategy

For stocks, you can either invest across the entire world or pick specific markets. If you choose to invest across the entire world by choosing a global fund, your wealth would be allocated with around 60.5% to the US, 3.9% to the UK, 14.1% to Europe ex-UK and around 21.5% to the rest of the world.[41]

How your money is diversified when you invest globally in equities

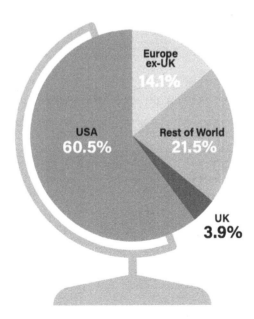

Step 3: What exact markets are you interested in tracking?

For example, it could be the UK equity or US equity and so on. This will depend on where you think will perform well in the time horizon you want to invest in or could be driven by choosing a marketplace that diversifies you away from your home bias. For example, we're already quite heavily invested in the UK through property ownership and the fact that most of our livelihood is here. As such, our preference over the last decade was to focus on the US equity market and that paid off massively. Going forwards, our focus is global, but with a bias for the US as global funds allocate over 60% to the US anyway. Once you're clear on what markets you want to track, you then need to decide what indexes cover those markets.

Step 4: Which indexes (lists) cover those markets?

If you're based in the UK, here is a table of the major markets by indexes and suggested funds to guide your research. It's worth stressing that this is not financial advice or a personal recommendation for you. Do your research thoroughly and seek financial advice if you need to.

Market	Proxy index	Description	Funds examples available to UK investors
Global equities (developed markets)	MSCI World Index	Represents large and mid-cap stocks across 23 developed markets.	iShares Core MSCI World UCITS ETF (SWDA), Vanguard FTSE All-World UCITS ETF (VWRL)

Global equities (developed and emerging markets) – all cap	FTSE Global All Cap Index, MSCI All Country World Index (ACWI)	Covers global equities across large, mid and small cap stocks in developed and emerging markets	FTSE Global All Cap Index Fund – Accumulation, iShares Core MSCI ACWI ETF
UK equities	FTSE All Share Index	FTSE All-Share Index covers 98–99% of the UK Market Cap – it is made up of the FTSE 100, FTSE 250 and FTSE Small Cap Indexes	FTSE UK All Share Index Unit Trust, iShares FTSE 100 UCITS ETF, Vanguard FTSE 100 UCITS ETF (VUKE)
US equities	S&P 500	Tracks the 500 largest publicly traded companies in the US	iShares S&P 500 UCITS ETF, Vanguard S&P 500 UCITS ETF (VUSA or VUAG), Vanguard US Equity Index Fund Accumulation
World ex-UK equities	MSCI World ex-UK Index	Covers large and mid-cap stocks across developed markets excluding the UK	iShares MSCI World ex-UK UCITS ETF, Vanguard FTSE All-World ex-UK UCITS ETF, FTSE Developed World ex-U.K. Equity Index Fund – Accumulation
Emerging markets	MSCI Emerging Markets Index	Covers large and mid-cap stocks from 27 emerging markets	iShares Emerging Markets Equity Index Fund, Vanguard Emerging Markets Stock Index Fund

Global bonds	Bloomberg Barclays Global Aggregate Bond Index	Represents global investment-grade fixed-income securities	iShares Global Aggregate Bond UCITS ETF, Vanguard Global Bond Index Fund
UK government bonds	FTSE UK Gilts Index	Measures the performance of UK government bonds	iShares UK Gilts UCITS ETF, Vanguard UK Government Bond Index Fund
US government bonds	Bloomberg Barclays US Treasury Bond Index	Measures the performance of US government bonds	iShares $ Treasury Bond 7–10yr UCITS ETF, Vanguard US Treasury Bond UCITS ETF

If you're based in the US, here are some starting points for tracking the US equities market.

Equities:

Vanguard Total Stock Market Index Fund Admiral Shares (VTSAX): a mutual fund that tracks the Total Market Index and offers broader market coverage, including large-cap, mid-cap, small-cap and micro-cap stocks

Vanguard Total Stock Market ETF (VTI): an ETF equivalent that has the same coverage as VTSAX above – VTI generally has a lower expense ratio compared to VTSAX due to the cost-efficient structure of ETFs

Vanguard S&P 500 Index ETF (VOO): an ETF that seeks to track the S&P 500 Index – it generally has a lower expense ratio compared to VTSAX due to its focus on large-cap stocks and the cost-efficient structure of ETFs

The choice between them may depend on your investment goals, risk tolerance and preferences for fund structure (mutual fund vs. ETF).

Bonds:

Vanguard Total Bond Market Index Fund (VBTLX): a popular choice for US investors who want exposure to the US investment-grade bond market with the benefits of diversification and a low-cost structure

A popular portfolio pair is VTSAX (or VTI) and VBTLX. You then dial up or down on both, depending on whether you're focused on wealth accumulation or preservation.

If you're not in the UK or US, you should be able to find equivalent funds locally. Please speak with your platform provider or broker.

Step 5: Choose index funds or ETFs that track the indexes covering the markets you want to invest in

As we explained earlier, the broader and cheaper the index fund or ETF, the better. See the table above for a starting point on funds if you're based in the UK. We've also included some fund ideas for the US below the table. You can find these funds on the investment platform provided by your broker (more on this below).

HOW TO CREATE A SIMPLE GLOBAL PORTFOLIO

The main goal when it comes to creating a portfolio is to invest in a diversified way across different asset classes (for example, stocks and bonds) and markets, so you're effectively creating a mix of risks that will not only help you to generate the returns you need for growth, but will also help to protect your wealth from loss as much as possible. If you want a no-fuss portfolio without worry about whether the US will continue to do well in the future or not, then you want to invest globally in a fund that spreads its holdings across the major investable countries in the world.

The good news is that you can achieve this with just one index fund or ETF and pay one low fee. You aren't tied to one country, so you can say bye-bye to the impact of Brexit and other adverse economic scenarios in other countries. In addition, there is no investing FOMO. If people are worrying about moving money out of the UK or the US, you won't care because you're global. Here are two indexes offering global cover,

FTSE All World Index: This covers about 90% of the world's market capitalization across developed and emerging markets, and invests in large, mid-cap and small companies. A popular fund that tracks this index is the Vanguard FTSE Global All Cap Index Fund, which invests in around 7,156 stocks and has an annual ongoing charge (OCF) of 0.23%.[42]

MSCI All Country World Index (MSCI ACWI): This covers about 85% of the world's market capitalization and invests in large, mid-cap and small companies; 89% of it covers 23 developed markets and 11% covers 24 emerging markets. A popular fund that tracks this index is the iShares MSCI ACWI UCITS ETF, which invests in around 1,720 stocks and has an annual total expense ratio (TER) of 0.2%.[43]

An alternative to this one index fund or ETF approach is to construct a simple portfolio of two or three funds, using the approach that we outlined in steps 4 and 5 in the earlier section, by identifying funds that track specific markets that you want exposure to.

Beyond investing in stocks and bonds, over time you may want to introduce other assets into your portfolio. Here is a summary of the different asset classes and the primary roles they play in a portfolio.

Roles played by different assets in a portfolio

Asset class	Capital appreciation	Capital preservation	Diversifi- cation	Inflation hedge	Deflation hedge
Stocks	✓				
Bonds		✓			✓
Real estate (REITs)	✓		✓		
Commodities			✓	✓	
Index funds	✓		✓		
ETFs	✓		✓		
Precious metals (for example, gold)		✓	✓	✓	

Overall, the simpler your portfolio is, the better. If you have a long-term horizon for wealth accumulation, don't be afraid to dial up on the proportion that you have allocated to stocks using the right index funds or ETFs.

HOW TO INVEST YOUR MONEY BY AGE

Here are some general tips for determining what asset allocation is best for you depending on where you are on your wealth accumulation journey. We've used age groups as proxies for simplicity.

Early savers (typically in their teens, 20s and early 30s)

• Expose your money to as much risk as possible (for example, invest mainly in stocks) as you have decades ahead of you to generate big returns thanks to compounding. Invest in index funds and ETFs for peace of mind, but if you have the risk appetite, consider allocating a small amount (maximum 10% of the amount you have to invest) to individual stocks for fun and learning how to research companies. Be prepared to lose some of it, but your long-term horizon leaves room for things to recover.

- Do keep some money in cash or near-cash assets – typically enough for three to six months of expenses.

- Work hard on learning how all the various assets and accounts (ISAs, pensions and so on) work and their tax benefits. This will matter in the next ten years.

- Build the habit of saving and investing, and start with at least 15%–20% of your net income, increasing that savings rate as your career improves.

- A sensible allocation is 80% stocks and 20% bonds, but nothing stops you going to 100% stocks like we did.

Mid-life accumulators (typically mid 30s to early 50s)

- This is the prime of your career and you're making the most money you'll ever make, so the focus for you should be minimizing taxes. More on this in week 9.

- If you're a higher rate tax payer, it will be in your best interest to put a lot of your money into pensions as they're most tax efficient. However, this is not a one-size-fits-all as you might want to retire early.

- Consider increasing your allocation to bonds in your 50s. However, this will depend on your risk tolerance and how far away you are – or not – from your financial goals. Use the 120 minus your age rule of thumb to guide you, but, again, the more allocation to stocks the better.

- Be clear on how many more income-generating working years you have ahead of you. This is especially important if you're working towards financial independence or early retirement. If you think you have 15 years ahead, be prudent and assume it is ten years, which will force you to invest even more of your income now to achieve your goal faster.

Traditional retirees (typically aged 55 and above)

- If you don't have enough invested to retire yet, you'll have a lower tolerance to risk. As such, you'll likely have a bigger focus on your pensions (private, work and state) and ISA, and working out what your shortfall is relative to your needs. It makes sense to introduce a higher bond and cash allocation. A good starting point would be 70% stocks, 20% bonds and 10% cash. This allocation gives you a balance of the need to still generate returns from stocks, while factoring in the need to de-risk a bit. You can adjust these percentages depending on your willingness to take risks.
- If you have more than enough invested to retire on, which is a very small group of people, your focus will likely be on estate planning and how to pass on your wealth. Your focus won't be risk-averse as you already have more than enough, so exposure to some risks via stocks would make sense as that money will still potentially have decades to work for your loved ones.

THINGS TO KNOW BEFORE INVESTING IN INDEX FUNDS AND ETFS

It's important to know that although index funds and ETFs are lower risk investments relative to individual stocks, they're still risky. Your investments can go down as well as up. In addition, not all index funds are equal. Some are good at tracking the index accurately while some are not. Below is a checklist of things to check before investing in index funds and ETFs. You can find all this information on the overview of the fund or by reading the key investor information documentation (KIID) or prospectus.

Index funds and ETFs investing checklist

- ☐ Focus on investing in low cost, ideally globally diversified, index funds and ETFs.

- ☐ Read the Key Investor Information Document (KIID) or Summary of Prospectus.

- ☐ Index being tracked – ensure it tracks total returns i.e. capital & income.

- ☐ Ongoing charge or Total Expense Ratio (TER) – ensure this is below 0.5%.

- ☐ Fund size (over £100m as a minimum. Larger is better.) or age (over 5 years).

- ☐ Tracking error – check it's low. Manually compare index vs fund performance.

- ☐ Geographic exposure – ensure you're happy with the regions covered.

- ☐ Performance – quickly review the last 10 years, otherwise the last 5 years.

- ☐ Minimums – does the fund have a minimum? Ensure you're able to meet it.

- ☐ Full replication – check if each company on the index is purchased by the fund.

For a list of notable providers of index funds and ETFs, and tools to research them, see the resources section at the end of the book.

HOW TO CHOOSE YOUR INVESTMENT PLATFORM

Once you choose an investment platform, you're highly unlikely to ever move. If you take the time to do the research, you are ticking off one thing on your list that's necessary for you to build wealth. The investment platform that you choose to commit your money to will dictate how much it costs you to invest that money over time. In addition, it should be specific to you only because:

Pot size: If you have less than £10,000 to invest and someone else has £250,000, the type of platform that you and the other person choose will be vastly different.

Life goals: We all have different goals in our lives. You might be reading this and know that you need an investing platform that has ETFs, individual stocks or one that even has commodities. Another person might only want a platform with no-fuss, ready-made funds.

Strategy: The strategy you choose might be passive investing, it might be trading or it might be a simple buy-to-hold. This will influence the platform that you choose.

Here are four different things that we believe you should check out before you choose an investing platform to put your money into.

1. What will you invest in?

Let's say your investing strategy is that you are passive investing. You want to check that the types of platforms that you are considering have the specific types of index funds and ETFs that you are interested in.

2. Do they have the accounts you need?

You want to make sure they have the right tax-efficient accounts that will help your money be invested in a tax-efficient way over time. These are often referred to as tax-efficient wrappers. Examples in the UK include individual savings accounts (ISA), stocks and shares ISA, lifetime ISA, cash ISA and self-invested personal pension (SIPP). In the US, these include 401k, IRA (Traditional and Roth).

3. What service will you get?

Some platforms don't offer an app for investing, whereas some offer you a really useful investing app with research tools. We say consider the service offering very carefully, because buying cheap is not necessarily always the best thing to do. Balance the need for a good service with the need to pay for that service.

4. What will it cost you overall?

Fees charged by investing platforms will deplete your wealth over time. The lower the fees you pay, the bigger your portfolio gets over time. In fact, this is one of the main reasons you'll beat most active fund managers who charge high fees by investing your money passively using low-cost index funds. However, having a bias for low fees does not mean that you should just choose an investment platform because it's marketing itself as 'free'. Here is a summary of the different types of platform providers in the UK and who they're ideally suited to.

Category	Description	Ideal for	Investment platform providers
Full-service brokers	Offer a wide range of services, including research, advice and various investment products	Investors seeking comprehensive support and personalized advice	Hargreaves Lansdown, AJ Bell Youinvest, Interactive Investor
Robo-advisers	Automated investment management, usually based on algorithms and minimal human intervention	Investors who want a hands-off approach with automated portfolio management	Nutmeg, Wealthify, Moneyfarm, Moneybox, PensionBee
Share dealing	Facilitate the buying and selling of individual company shares and related securities	Traders and investors focused on buying and selling individual stocks	IG, Trading212, Freetrade, Barclays Smart Investor, Halifax Share Dealing
Fund platforms	Allow investors to buy, hold and manage a variety of investment funds	Investors looking to diversify through index funds and ETFs	Vanguard, Fidelity, Charles Stanley Direct
Social trading	Combine investing with social networking, allowing users to follow and copy the trades of others	Those who want to learn from and mimic the strategies of experienced traders	eToro, Plus500, Revolut Trading

We personally invest with Vanguard, Hargreaves Lansdown and Pen-sionBee at present, but we're always on the lookout for better platform offerings and will move platforms if we need to. None of these are personal recommendations to you, of course. Choose what works best for you using the guidelines we've provided.

HOW MUCH SHOULD YOU INVEST AND WHY?

At a basic level, if you're not already doing it, getting started with investing is a huge win. You can start with as little as £20 a month in the UK (or $1 in the US) or you can invest a lump sum driven by the minimums of the investing platform provider and how much you can afford. However, it will soon become clear that there is a gap between how much you're investing and how much you need to be investing in order to achieve your goals. If you're doing this properly, then you should be investing driven by certain assumptions around:

- How big is your financial goal in numbers and what is it for exactly?
- How long will you invest (the time horizon) to achieve that goal?
- What expected real return is realistic to assume annually after inflation and fees?

It's essentially a maths calculation using a simple compound interest calculator to gauge how much more you might need to invest to achieve your goals. You can download ours here: www.thehumblepenny.com/compound-interest-calculator/. This can all seem daunting and it's easy to get discouraged. We understand that, but it won't get us anywhere. Having answers to the questions above reduces the number of unknowns, keeps things practical and helps you to focus on what you can control. If you have a partner, this is also a good opportunity to discuss your financial goals.

WHAT ABOUT ETHICAL INVESTING?

There is a growing consciousness, especially among Gen Z and Millennials, about investing their money more ethically to align with their values, avoiding the likes of arms manufacturers or tobacco and gambling companies, or companies that damage the environment. We, for example, invested in a fossil fuel-free plan in one of our pensions with PensionBee as a way to get our feet wet, but it remains a small part of our overall portfolio. Ethical investing can be done in two ways.

- Screen out companies with certain characteristics
- Look at the activities of a company and select those companies which best fit your ethical criteria

Acronyms used in ethical investing product names include:

- SRI – socially responsible investing
- ESG – environmental, social and governance

You could try your broker's website as a starting point, but most don't have enough filters to zoom in quickly on the type of product.

For ETFs, go to www.JustETF.com and use the ETF screener[44] to filter by the 'social/environmental' equity strategy to see a list of socially responsible ETFs and filter further.

For index funds (OEICs in the UK), consider the Morningstar Fund screener[45] and select five-star rated funds. Then, 'broad category' as 'equity', 'Morningstar category' as 'Global Large-Cap Blend Equity', 'fund of funds' as 'No', OCF less than 1% and 'Max initial sales charge' as zero. This helps to narrow your search.

We're sharing these websites and products for illustration only and there are not a personal recommendation for you.

Ethical investing remains pretty niche and in some cases even politicized. You need to strike a balance between your desire to invest driven by your values and the type of performance you're willing to accept. Compared to the S&P 500, ethical funds are likely to underperform as some of them charge slightly higher fees and exclude companies that profit from some questionable activities. For example, over ten years, the UBS MSCI World Socially Responsible UCITS ETF A Dis generated a return of 138.6% compared to 229% by the S&P 500.

Interview: Sharmila and Matt

Sharmila Bain (half-Malaysian and British) and Matt Bain (British) are both 29, married and live in Cornwall. Sharmila is an entrepreneur who focuses on Christian art at SharmilaJoy.com and Matt is an accountant. Here is their up-and-down journey of aiming for financial freedom.

Sharmila: Financial joy means having a good relationship with money. It's not a burden or an idol, but rather something we steward because we believe God is our provider. We'd love to have a mortgage-free home and a passive income that covers our daily living expenses, not necessarily amassing great wealth. It's about having the resources to spend quality time with family and friends, raise our future family, and be generous with our time and finances.

Matt: Our journey has had its share of ups and downs. We started saving and investing together when we got married in September 2019 with a combined savings of about £30,000. We'd planned to invest in a property, but the pandemic forced us to pivot.

Sharmila: We decided to focus on our respective businesses instead.

Matt: We were also in the Financial Joy Academy, working to grow Sharmila's online art business and pursue property investments simultaneously. This two-pronged approach was our initial plan. However, when Covid-19 hit, things took a turn. I began researching stocks, shares and cryptocurrencies, and within a month I started investing in different stocks and crypto, which turned out to be quite profitable over the next 12 months. I didn't cash out everything but did take some profits. We had a significant amount of money invested and had made paper gains from our investments. That's when I decided to quit my job, a big step towards our financial freedom. This marked a high point in our journey.

Six months later, the markets took a significant hit. I also lost a substantial part of our cash savings due to a crypto company going bankrupt. This was a painful experience and a lesson learned. To make ends meet, I took on a couple of part-time jobs starting in September 2022 to cover our monthly expenses since our investments weren't sufficient.

On the flip side, Sharmila's art business was steadily growing year after year in the right direction. We still had a considerable amount of money invested in the markets, so it felt like two steps forward and one step back.

One positive aspect of our journey is that we moved to Cornwall, which improved our work-life balance. We were spending less than we were earning and Sharmila could run her art business from there. It was a promising progression, but there were undoubtedly some challenging moments.

Sharmila: Financial freedom doesn't happen overnight. It requires consistency, discipline and hard work. I've realized that I can do more than I thought I could. It's essential to make sacrifices, say no to unnecessary spending and stay dedicated to your goals.

Matt: I learned a valuable lesson when I lost a significant portion of our savings through a bad crypto investment. I had to re-evaluate where I placed my hope, security and trust. This journey taught me not to tie my happiness solely to financial success. My hope now rests in something beyond money, and I've learned the importance of not letting financial ups and downs define my self-worth.

Sharmila: I've learned about being a team. We had to make decisions together and avoid blaming each other when things didn't go as planned. It's about unity and having grace and forgiveness for each other, understanding that neither of us is perfect. Working as a team is crucial, and setbacks can sometimes motivate us to work even harder.

Matt: That loss made me realize I had become a bit complacent. I needed to kick back into work mode and stay consistent. The journey towards financial freedom taught me not to take success for granted and the importance of maintaining a strong work ethic.

WISH WE KNEW THIS ABOUT INVESTING MONEY WHEN WE WERE 20

Here are some life-changing insights that we've learned along the way that have not only encouraged us to invest more aggressively each month, but have also opened our eyes to how we could create generational wealth for our family.

Insight 1: compounding makes you richer
if you start investing early

Consider two investors, Ben and Lucy. They are the same age, but they decided to start investing at different times. Lucy started investing £2,000 ($2,600) per year at the age of 19 and did that for seven consecutive years. After those seven years and a total of £14,000 ($18,200) invested, she invested nothing until the age of 65. Ben started investing later, at the age of 26, investing £2,000 per year every single year until he became 65, with a total of £80,000 ($104,000) invested. Who will have the bigger portfolio at the age of 65, assuming both their investments generated an average 10% nominal return per year? We've kept the 10% return from the original 1950s example[46] by investment writer, Richard Russell. The results are astonishing.

Lucy invested only £14,000 ($18,200), but her net gains are £930,641 ($1,209,833) at 65. Her money multiplied a whopping 66 times. Ben invested £80,000 ($104,000), but his net gains are £893,704 ($1,161,815) at 65. His money multiplied only 11 times. Although Lucy only made seven contributions and stopped investing, she ends up with a larger net pot of money at the age of 65 than Ben does even with 40 contributions!

In case you wondered how this plays out assuming a 5% nominal return, Lucy will end up with net gains of £106,371 ($138,282) while Ben will end up with £173,680 ($225,784) at 65. Although Lucy ends up with a smaller pot this time around, her £14,000 ($18,200) invested multiplies eight times compared to Ben's £80,000 ($104,000), which multiplies only two times.

Note that although these examples illustrate people investing in their 20s, don't feel like you've missed the boat if you're in your 30s, 40s, 50s or beyond. The key thing is to start investing now not later.

Insight 2: how to become a millionaire by investing £10 a day

Have you ever tried to work out how long it will take you if you started to save money today to become a millionaire? If you saved £10 every single day, it would take an insane 274 years to reach £1 million. Even if you save £1,000 every single month, it will still take you around 83 years to become a millionaire. This tells us that saving money alone is not the way to go about becoming a millionaire, if that's your goal.

Investing £10 a day or £300 ($390) a month is an amount that most people can relate to, even on lower disposable incomes. Let's assume that you invested this amount in the S&P 500 or a low-cost global index fund generating an average annual return of 8%. Over a period of 40 years you'd return a total final investment of around £1,054,284 ($1,370,569). That includes total contributions in terms of monthly deposits of only £144,000 ($187,200) with the vast majority of that £1,054,284 return coming from compounding interest – so £910,000 ($1,183,000) coming from money working money over time.

Although this is a simplistic illustration (and needs to factor in inflation), it demonstrates how the power of money placed in the right environment can work and build upon itself to become a life-changing sum over time.

Conversely, it also demonstrates to us the opportunity cost of every £1 or $1 that's wasted and not invested. Assuming a 7% return, every £1 you don't invest would have doubled to £2 in ten years if you had invested it.

Insight 3: why your first £100,000 is the magical number for reaching £1 million

Getting to £100,000 is almost unimaginable for a lot of people and it was for us too in our 20s. However, if we understood why getting to that number mattered so much, it would have given us the motivation to avoid wasting money in our early 20s and invest even more intentionally. No matter your age and how little you have in the bank today, this insight will motivate and inspire you to gradually save and invest that first £100,000.

Several years ago, at an event, a young man asked the late Charlie Munger, business partner to Warren Buffett and billionaire investor, for some advice, because he was struggling to save, invest and see his net worth grow. Charlie Munger said this about saving that first $100,000:

'It's a b****, but you gotta do it. I don't care what you have to do – if it means walking everywhere and not eating anything that wasn't purchased with a coupon, find a way to get your hands on $100,000. After that, you can ease off the gas a little bit.'[47]

Here is why that first £100,000 matters.

Example: Daniel is 30 years old and has a 40-year investment horizon. He's looking to invest about £10,000 ($13,000) per year. Let's assume an average annual return of 7%. In case you're thinking 7% is an unrealistic return to achieve, we'll share shortly the exact funds we've invested in to achieve these returns. Using a compound interest calculator, it will take him around 7.7 years to reach his first £100,000. If he carried on investing £10,000 ($13,000) per year, every additional £100,000 will grow more quickly. The next £100,000 will take five years to happen. Then the next one will take 3.75 years to happen and so on. Below is a table and chart that shows how quickly each additional £100,000 is achieved.

Time taken to reach £1 million for every additional £100,000

Assuming 7% average return

(£/$)	Years	Years
100,000	7.70	
200,000	5.00	
300,000	3.75	16.40
400,000	3.00	
500,000	2.50	
600,000	2.08	
700,000	1.92	
800,000	1.58	
900,000	1.50	
1,000,000	1.33	13.90
	30.30	30.30

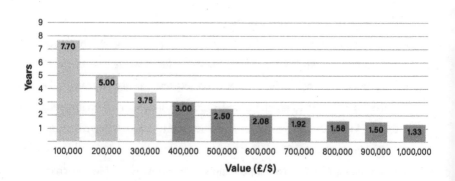

It took 7.7 years – the most difficult and longest period – to reach the first £100,000, compared to the last £100,000, which would take 1.33 years, giving a total of 30.3 years to reach £1 million. We thought that was remarkable until we took a much closer look at the numbers to see the power of compounding at work. Notice that the first £300,000 takes 16.4 years, more years than the last £700,000, which takes 13.9 years to happen. Why does this happen? There are three main reasons.

1. **Exponential growth:** The power of compounding requires time to work. If you invest £10,000 per year over 40 years at 7% average annual return, you'll end up with a pot worth £2,059,618. However, if you doubled your investment to £20,000 per year, but invested for half the time of 20 years at the same return of an average 7%, you only end up with £845,893. Research shows that 69% of the total return of the S&P 500 is attributed to dividends and the power of compounding.[48]

The power of re-investing dividends

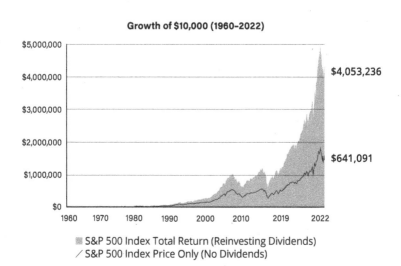

Growth of $10,000 (1960–2022)

S&P 500 Index Total Return (Reinvesting Dividends)
S&P 500 Index Price Only (No Dividends)

2. **Larger portfolio size:** This also partly explains why the rich get richer. Imagine you had £100,000 and you invested that and generated a 7% return of £7,000. A £7,000 addition to your original £100,000 is a significant amount, which itself then goes on to generate even more of a return. So, the larger £100,000 that you started with creates a snowball effect. As the years pass by, subsequent £100,000s are being generated faster, taking a smaller amount of time to achieve.[49]

3. **Healthy money habits:** There are so many changes in your habits and behaviours that lead to you becoming the person who, gradually and painstakingly over many years, gets to that point where you've saved and invested your very first £100,000. Those changes in your habits, behaviours and money mindset effectively build a solid foundation so that you're a person who not only saves and invests £100,000 one day, but you are likely become the person who sees their wealth grow consistently over time.

WHAT DO WE INVEST IN, EXACTLY?

We currently invest in these accounts in order: stocks and shares ISA (a tax-free account), lifetime ISA (a tax-free account), general investing account (a taxable account), self-invested personal pension (a tax-deferred account), junior ISA (a tax-free account for children), junior SIPP (a pension for children). We've done this as self-employed people in order to have access to our money before the traditional retirement age, while also prioritizing our pensions. Your order will be different depending on your circumstances.

Over many years, we've been investing across the following index funds and ETFs: Vanguard US Equity Index Fund Accumulation, Vanguard S&P

500 UCITS ETF (VUSA), Vanguard FTSE All-World UCITS ETF (VWRL), Vanguard FTSE Developed World ex-U.K. Equity Index Fund – Accumulation and, more lately, a fossil fuel-free fund. These gave us a heavy 90% bias for North America, 4.5% Europe, 0% UK, 3% Asia Pacific, 2% Japan and 0.5% Middle East and Africa. Our top ten holdings from these funds are Apple, Microsoft, Alphabet, Amazon, Nvidia, Meta, Tesla, Berkshire Hathaway, UnitedHealth Group and JP Morgan Chase & Co. In addition to these, we have individual stocks that we've owned for over a decade. Essentially, 100% stocks and 0% bonds with a big focus on the US. Will the US continue to have the dominance it has had until now given the rise of China? No one knows for sure, although history tells us that economic superpowers change over time. With that in mind, a safer approach is to invest globally. Remember, sharing what we invest in above or the mention of any funds in this book are not personal recommendations for you or financial advice. We'll continue to monitor our portfolios and invest even more globally.

RED FLAG AND GREEN FLAGS OF INVESTING

Let's wrap up with something fun by looking at some everyday red and green flags of investing.

Red vs green flags of investing

	Red flag	Green flag
Financial advice from your taxi driver, random family friends or distant cousin	✓	
The opportunity has low fees		✓
An investment with low risks and high rewards, for example £50,000 returns in three months or 21% return per month	✓	
The investment opportunity is regulated by the Financial Conduct Authority (FCA)		✓
An investment that has a deadline to act quickly in order not to miss the opportunity	✓	
You can access the money you have invested		✓
Platforms that have over-enticing offers, for example free shares	✓	
The potential losses from the investment opportunity match the amount you can afford to lose		✓
Unusually high fees attached to an investment	✓	
The opportunity is well diversified		✓
The investment opportunity is highly illiquid	✓	

We've shared a lot in this week with the goal of demystifying investing and helping you develop the confidence to not only invest now, for you and your family, but see it as an important vehicle for creating your life of financial joy.

Remember, your investments will go up and down daily, but over time, they will tend to go up overall. Don't panic during an inevitable stock market crash. Although it would seem counterintuitive, keep investing as you'll be buying units cheaper and losses during stock market crashes are paper losses, and only become real when you sell, so focus on buying more rather than selling. Happy investing!

WEEK 7: LESSONS AND ACTION STEPS

Three lessons for week 7

- You'll beat most investing professionals by investing your money yourself in low-cost, globally diversified index funds and ETFs. Ensure it is tracking a broad and well-known index and invest for the long term. Invest using tax-efficient accounts and automate your investing, so that you're investing each month without fail.
- Different assets play different roles in an investment portfolio, which means that your choice of assets and asset allocation matter for achieving your goals. If you're in the wealth accumulation phase and you have a long time horizon, don't be afraid to allocate mainly to equities. As you approach the wealth preservation phase of your life, you can introduce bonds to reduce your risks. Stay open-minded to other investment options, such as property (more on this later) and gold, as these are important in a world of high inflation and also offer diversification.
- Your first £100,000 or $100,000 will be the hardest to save and invest, but once you get there the power of compounding will be even more on your side as your wealth grows and snowballs faster.

Three action steps for week 7

Action step 1: Be clear on your purpose for investing your money.

```


```

Action step 2: Set your financial goals and time horizon, and state your vision for each one.

```


```

Action step 3: Follow these seven steps for super-simple investing.

- Choose a strategy. We suggest passive investing using low-cost index funds and ETFs that track a broad global index.
- Choose your investing platform using our guide above.
- Choose your investing accounts, for example stocks and shares ISA, pension, lifetime ISA, general investing account or your local equivalent.
- Decide on an amount to start with – either a lump sum vs dollar cost average (where you invest a set amount monthly and it helps to reduce your risk).
- Choose one to three index funds or ETFs to begin with, using our guide above.
- Automate your investing via a direct debit so you're prioritizing investing monthly.
- Monitor your investments every one to three months. Consider rebalancing once a year, but, overall, don't tinker too much with them.

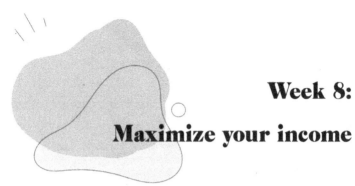

Week 8:
Maximize your income

A life of financial joy involves giving yourself
the permission to use your creativity to
make more money.

People usually aren't short on money, they're usually short on creativity, which is an important ingredient for making money. Our unique ability to create is dependent on our imagination, which we need to come up with ideas, but most people's imagination and thus their capacity for creativity has been depleted over time. In the most viewed TED Talk of all time,[50] Ken Robinson argued that our education system kills our creativity. However, this is only part of the story.

A creativity test designed by George Land and used by NASA to select the most innovative scientists and engineers was tried on 1,600 children aged four to five years old.[51] The research found that 98% of them were creative geniuses. This was a surprisingly high number, so they began testing the same children as they grew up. At the age of ten, only 30% of them were highly creative and by the age of 15 it had dropped to just 12%. The same research was conducted on over 1 million adults (with an average age of 31) and the trend downwards continued, with only a shocking 2% scoring as highly creative. Does this mean that the older we get the less creative we become?

The answer is no. If we zoom out and think about it, from the age of four to five, children spend almost all their time with other children. When they get to the age of ten, a lot of their attention shifts to gaming, music, homework and other activities, often in isolation. As they get older, further education and work takes over, again usually in isolation, and beats creativity out of them even more.

We believe that key to becoming more creative, even in adulthood, is connectivity. The more you spend time with others, and share thoughts and ideas, the more divergent thinking (generating a wide range of creative ideas and solutions by exploring multiple possible paths and perspectives) helps you come up with original ideas. However, you need to unlearn your lack of confidence, fear of failure, pressure to conform and negative self-judgement. When you operate under fear, you only use a small part of your brain. When you operate under logic, you use a bit more of your brain, but your brain lights up when you operate under creative thinking. We need to find that inner five-year-old.

Connectivity is necessary for your in-built creativity, and creativity is necessary for making money and building wealth. Tied to creativity and imagination are two other necessary ingredients for making money – optimism and communication. Without optimism, you won't believe that you can make more money, or be open-minded and willing to try. In our experience, gratitude is a catalyst for optimism. The more you appreciate what you have already, the more optimistic about life you'll be.

Other than your brain, your mouth is the most important organ in your body for wealth creation, which is why public speaking is one of the most important skills for wealth-building. Think about it: some of the most well-paid people in the world communicate their ideas by speaking well, and in our experience you need to become a good communicator to increase your chances of making more money. For example, whether you're seeking promotion or a new job, promoting your personal brand or marketing products or services for a business, communication is key. Here is a quick summary of the key ingredients for maximizing your income and practical things we've done to improve each area.

Creativity: You can increase this through more intentional connectivity with others to share ideas. We do this by being part of intentional groups such as paid memberships, masterminds or niche-focused WhatsApp groups. This connectivity also helps you to build important relationships.

Imagination: You can increase this by reading more good-quality books in different niches (including inspiring autobiographies) rather than watching TV.

Optimism: You can increase this by writing down three to five things that you're grateful for daily.

Communication: You can increase your public speaking ability by reading a good book out loud for 15 minutes a day, three to five times a week. Getting used to your own voice is half the battle.

These skills will form the foundation of the high-income skills that you need to maximize your income now and in the future. For this week, there are two broad ways in which we'll explore how you can maximize your income. First, we'll look at how to create a smart side hustle or business and, second, we'll look at career maximization and embracing portfolio work. Before we get into these areas, let's spend a moment looking at what we get paid for and how to break the employee mindset.

WHAT WE GET PAID FOR

Is it possible to make twice as much money as you're earning now by working less? Yes, by being twice as valuable. A big misconception is that people get paid by the hour. For example, if you get paid £20 per hour, the reason you're earning that income is because the marketplace has priced the value that you bring at a rate of £20 for one hour. Sticking with the example above, although one person could earn £20 in one hour, another person could do a speaking gig, for example, and get paid £20,000 for the same one hour. The difference is that the person being paid £20,000 for that hour is perceived to deliver a lot more value than the person being paid £20 for the same hour.

The good news is that you can shift your reality, but how do you become more valuable and earn more? There are two options. Option one is to do more work by putting in more hours. Basically, you grind more in your job. Rather than put more work into your job, option two is to put more work into yourself.

We know that what has made the biggest difference for us is option two. We've spent a lot of time and money improving who we are and what value we have to offer. That learning and growth has enabled us to not only earn more through our careers, but also to start businesses and side hustles, and invest in assets to grow wealth.

Interview: Tanuj

Tanuj Modasia-Shah (37) is a married father of one who lives in London. He's of Indian heritage and his parents were born in Kenya. He is state-educated and graduated from university in 2009 with a degree in electrical engineering. Today, he designs and builds technology systems for financial energy trading. Here is how he and his wife achieved financial independence in nine years through career maximization.

Financial joy for me is true freedom and security with little dependency on things external to myself. I want to be completely debt free, including mortgage free, irrespective of whether or not it's rational to invest that money or not. Daily joy for me is being active. We also love travelling and hiring a fancy car for a week. Finally, we have a list of philanthropy things that we give to.

As a couple, we manage everything jointly, reviewing our finances monthly via a detailed flowchart on Google Sheets. We deliberately avoid automating payments to maintain a conscious sense of achieving our financial goals. Monitoring our net worth and income keeps us on track.

I can trace what helped us achieve financial independence back to life after university in 2009. I focused on the highest paying job rather than on what I love to do. I learned social skills and put myself out there until I landed a graduate job with a £36,000 base salary. I lived at home, paid rent to my parents and focused on being frugal. I also focused on learning and getting better at my job to open up my options beyond promotions, and building confidence to get other jobs that paid more.

Around 2014, I had relatively bigger surpluses than I'd ever had before and was wondering what do I do with them? A friend of mine sent me financial independence blogs to figure out where to put my cash. I learned the formula: increase your earnings, reduce expenses and invest the surplus. We've mostly invested in index funds and once we grew in confidence, we worked hard on increasing earnings and our savings rate just went way up.

Our savings rate started at 10 to 15%, then jumped to 50% when we focused more on the financial independence process and peaked at 90% during Covid. Currently, it's about 65%. To increase my income, I focused on getting good at my craft and building a good reputation. Now, 14 years after graduating, my total compensation is ten times the annual income I started with, partly due to contracting, and that's before combining incomes with my wife. However, our costs are significantly lower as we have shared costs. In my industry, there is a window of earning of five to ten years and people typically burn out by age 50. So part of it is also squeezing it while it's there.

We have multiple income streams from our day jobs and a consultancy business. So far, we've achieved a basic level of financial independence, but we're now going for Fat FIRE – the luxury version of financial independence. As a couple, we have a list called Life After Kids (LAK) for when our children are at uni. For example, we're going to drive around the perimeter of Europe for three months.

For anyone trying to become financially independent, I'd say increasing your income is going to have a significantly greater impact than only focusing on frugality. Finally, have an idea of what you will do with your time and energy after you reach financial independence.

BREAK THE EMPLOYEE MINDSET

The employee mindset is something that we all get trained into as we grow up. Most people wait for payday to come once a month. Whose idea was it that you should earn an income once a month, rather than your income coming in a few times a month from different sources? As an employee, you wait for someone to direct you, guide you, tell you this is the piece of work you need to do and these are your areas of responsibility, and so on. We are not here to bash employees, because most people are employees and will remain so. For most of our working lives, we were employees and enjoyed our time as employees, even though there were many challenges that we faced. However, we realized a lot of people have a mindset that's holding them back from their future potential. Breaking the employee mindset with these four steps is key to growing your money and creating a path to financial freedom.

Step 1. Overcome limiting beliefs

In week 2, you identified your limiting beliefs. One of those limiting beliefs might be that starting a business is too risky. A way to reframe this is to realize that in your current job you are already using transferable skills, which will reduce the risk of starting a business. I (Ken) gradually overcame my limiting beliefs by seeking evidence of other successful business people in our niche and reaching out to them for answers and mentoring while offering value by way of suggestions that could improve one specific area of their business.

Step 2. Take calculated risks

When working for an employer, you are usually taking chances and making mistakes on their money and balance sheet. However, when you take a calculated risk on your own money, starting a side hustle or doing something else that diversifies your income, you've assessed the return you might get from it, the potential for failure and so on. This helps you to develop a different mindset, which is much superior to the typical employee mindset.

Step 3. Seek feedback and learn from failures

See the experience of trying things out, or even failing, as a way of seeking feedback. Wealthy people come to terms with failure, and are able to talk about it and learn from it. Failure should not be a taboo. Another way you can seek feedback is to volunteer for leadership roles at work or seek additional responsibilities. The more you put yourself out there, the more you become the person who gets used to being enterprising and creating opportunity.

Step 4: Focus on who you need to achieve your goals faster

The fastest way to get a result is to achieve it through other people, and it doesn't always cost money. Other people have better ideas, expertise and connections, and in a world where you're likely starved of time, relationships with other people is key to achieving your money and life goals. In all aspects of your life, you need a relationship map that will help you achieve each goal or flourish in that particular area. By thinking in conjunction with other people rather than just yourself, you'll expand your possibilities greatly and guarantee your results.

Following these four steps will help you to gradually fight the fear of failure, shift your mindset and, over time, break the employee mindset which is crucial for maximizing your income. Let's now take a look at the first way to maximize your income, which is to start a smart side hustle.

CREATE A SMART SIDE HUSTLE

With the rise in the cost of living, a growing number of people are exploring side hustles to make more money. Around 44% of Brits[52] and 39% of Americans[53] have at least one side hustle. However, not everyone actually makes money from a side hustle. Around 58% of Brits make less than £100 a week from a side hustle, 35% make between £100 and £600 per week, 5% make between £600 and £1000 a week, and 2% make over

£1000 per week.[54] A lot of people who start side hustles don't make money because:

- They are not committed to their side hustles and give up too early.
- They don't have specific side hustle income goals, so they don't have the motivation.
- They are doing side hustles that don't have the potential to make the kind of money they want to earn.

A smart side hustle is a way to make extra money on the side by using your skills and interests wisely. It uses modern technology and trends to make money, and it can even grow over time. Ultimately, a smart side hustle will help you to work less and earn more through passive and semi-passive activities.

Take the example of the Humble Penny, which we started as a blog with two hours a day while working in demanding full-time jobs and raising two young children. It connected with our desire to do something we were passionate about that would help lots of people one day, while having the possibility of creating an income in a sustainable way. Did we know it would work out? No! However, the desire to do something that we loved and the excitement to learn as we went along was enough to get us started.

The beauty of putting something like two hours a day into a smart side hustle is that you get to reap the benefits of compounding. Two hours a day works out at 730 hours or 30.4 full days in a year committed to one idea, which then snowballs. The compounding effect of those two hours per day are still being felt today, with the book you're reading being one of many outcomes from the time we've invested daily.

However, it's worth pointing out that it won't be easy, but it does get easier over time, a bit like learning how to drive a car or ride a bike. You'll get better at it, and acquire lucrative skills for today and tomorrow, while enjoying what you're doing.

There are three broad groups of smart side hustles:

Service-based side hustle: You offer a skill or expertise as a service. Examples include consulting, coaching, tutoring, graphic design and photography.

Product-based side hustle: You create and sell physical or digital products. Examples include handmade crafts, jewellery, artwork, clothing and printables.

Content-based side hustle: You create and share online content. Examples include, blogging, YouTube, podcasting, memberships and eBooks.

Here is a more detailed comparison.

Aspect	Service-based side hustle	Product-based side hustle	Content-based side hustle
Initial investment	Low to none – requires skills or knowledge	Moderate to high – for materials, production	Low to moderate – for equipment, tools
Income potential	Starts on day one, but is limited by hourly rate and availability	Depends on product demand, pricing and how much you invest	Limitless, but starts off very slow – depends on audience size and monetization strategies
Time commitment	Often requires active time and effort	Production and marketing	Consistent content creation and engagement

Scalability	Limited by time and personal capacity	Potential for scalability with demand	Potential for passive income
Market reach	Local or global, depending on service	Local to global, online platforms	Global through online platforms
Risk and returns	Service quality affects reputation	Inventory risk, returns and competition	Content quality affects engagement
Customer interaction	High – direct communication with clients	Moderate – customer support may be needed .	Online interaction and engagement
Example websites	Upwork, Fiverr, PeoplePerHour	Etsy, Shopify, Amazon FBA	WordPress, YouTube, Patreon

The choice of which one to start with will depend on your personality, income goals, available investment, time commitment, interests and skillset. For example, we started the Humble Penny because it's a content-based side hustle and we saw that as the way of the future in terms of reach potential. Although it involved 'putting ourselves out there', its potential outweighed our fears around that. In addition, it was an area that we had an interest in and knowledge about already. Find out which approach is most suited to you by taking our side hustle quiz at: www.thehumblepenny.com/BizQuiz

What was your quiz result? Did it match what you initially thought was your ideal type of side hustle?

Interview: Timothy

Timothy Armoo (28) is from Hackney, East London, but spent the first ten years of his life in Ghana. He is the co-founder of Fanbytes, a company he and his co-founders sold for tens of millions of pounds in 2022. This helped him achieve financial freedom. Here is his story and advice on starting, and growing, a side hustle.

I started with a company called Entrepreneur Express, an online media business, when I was 17. I ended up selling it for £110,000, which was a big deal for me back then. Four years later, at 21, I started Fanbytes, focusing on social media influencers and brand marketing. We grew it to a team of 80 people and sold it to Brainlabs in 2022. Right now, I'm semi-retired, doing some angel investing, advising and gearing up to build another successful company.

Financial joy means being able to enjoy life experiences without constantly worrying about prices. It's about travelling and not hesitating to fly business class. It's also about having the freedom to help people and make a positive impact. Financial joy, on a strategic level, is having optionality and the freedom to make choices.

Thinking about my relationship with money, initially, I had a scarcity mindset, worrying about every pound I spent. However, after my business success, I shifted to an abundance mindset. I've gone through different stages, from celebrating my achievements to realizing that the world continues to turn. Now, I focus on making more money and growing my wealth, rather than worrying about losing it. Transitioning from scarcity to abundance thinking was an iterative process. I became more comfortable talking about money and surrounded myself with people who had achieved significant financial success.

Growing up in a council block, I had quite big goals. I set a goal early on to have at least £10 million in my account before turning 30. The most influential thing I ever consumed early on was a video by Jim Rohn. He said, you get paid according to the value of the skills you provide to the marketplace. This opened my eyes. I believed that I could achieve this by mastering valuable skills. I focused on learning skills like sales, marketing, fundraising and copywriting. Business became the vehicle for me to deploy these skills to reach my financial goals.

My parents were not entrepreneurs. My mum didn't work and my dad worked for the council. I believe not everyone should start a business. Some people may not have the self-belief and determination required. But for those who are overwhelmed by where to start, my advice is to start small and lower the bar for success. The important thing is to get going and whatever you start with may not be what you end up with.

In terms of unusual things I've done to get here, I still don't have a house and I didn't learn to drive, and I still don't know how to. I focused on the money game first.

For anyone trying to create a side hustle or business that generates £5,000 to £10,000 per month in income, I'd say don't try to invent something new. Look at where people are already spending money and get a slice of it. For example, on platforms like Etsy, check out the best sellers in a category and then target a slightly different audience. Another approach is to help small businesses build an online or social presence if they lack one. People will pay for that because they don't know how to do it themselves. Content-based approaches can work, like affiliate marketing or building a presence on platforms like Instagram, YouTube or TikTok. You can create an audience and then attract brands and advertisers. However, it takes time to monetize.

CHOOSE A SMART NICHE

Now that you're clear on the type of side hustle that you want to create, you need to choose a niche to focus on. Our method for choosing a niche is the three-seed formula, which looks for ideas at the intersection of passion, talent and demand.

The three-seed formula for choosing a niche

A passion is an area of interest or something you easily do even if you were not getting paid for it. Areas of passion for us include travelling, cooking, reading, teaching and sharing ideas with others.

Write down ten different things that you're passionate about or have an interest in:

1.	6.
2.	7.
3.	8.
4.	9.
5.	10.

A talent is something that you're good at. Areas of talent for us include personal finance, investing, content creation, video editing and graphic design.

Write down 10 talents or things that you're good at below:

1.	6.
2.	7.
3.	8.
4.	9.
5.	10.

Next, you need to combine the ten different areas of passion and talent to create different potential niches that are worth exploring. For example, from our list of passions and talents, we took our passion for teaching and our talents for personal finance and investing, which led us to create the online platforms, the Humble Penny and Financial Joy Academy.

Write down combinations of your ten passions and ten talents. Use an additional notepad if you need to.

Next, you need to assess the above ideas for demand. In other words, is there sufficient interest out there for this to be worth your while and make you some money?

Use tools such as Google Trends, keyword research tools (for example, Ubersuggest), social media platforms, communities and forums, and surveys and questionnaires (for example, Google Forms). The presence of competitors is good news, as that often shows there is an active market and niche.

Next, validate your idea by creating a smaller, low-cost version of it to see if people show interest. Another low-cost way of gauging interest is to create a waiting list and market the idea on social media to see how many people are genuinely interested. This waiting list of people will become your first customers when you launch your side hustle.

SMART BUSINESS MODELS

Once you're clear on your niche, you need a way for what you're doing to make some money. In our experience, business ideas where you're directly swapping time for money, and without the potential to scale without putting in more hours, are not always worthwhile if you have limited time, unless you choose a smart business model. Here is a summary of smart business models worth exploring by business type:

Service-based business models

Group coaching: Rather than offering one-to-one coaching, it's far more lucrative to offer one-to-many in a small group. For example, you offer a six-week programme of transformation priced at £2,000 ($2,600) for two hours a week. If you had a group of ten people who you coached over six weeks, that's £20,000 ($26,000) made in six weeks, which is 12 hours in total.

Premium consulting: Offer consulting services using your existing skills to a more premium clientele. Deliver more value and charge more for doing this.

Product-based business models

Drop-shipping: Source products from suppliers and sell without holding inventory.

Subscription box: Regularly curate and deliver themed products.

Handmade/crafting: Create unique handmade products to sell via e-commerce.

Print on demand: Design and sell custom products without inventory.

Content-based business models

Memberships: You create a membership website behind a paywall where you use your existing skills to share your specialized knowledge and experience to a growing community, who pay monthly to access what you offer.

Brand sponsorships: Thanks to a growing creator economy, you can make significant amounts by collaborating with brands to promote their products. Brands are becoming more interested in micro-influencers with engaged communities. Creators make hundreds to thousands per post on social media.

Affiliate marketing: You make commission as a middle-person by promoting products or services created by others. These could be one-off or ongoing commissions.

Advertising: You can partner with an ad delivery platform such Google AdSense or Mediavine to deliver ads to your platform (for example a blog or a YouTube channel) and you generate revenue per thousand impressions (RPM – the M stands for *mille*, meaning thousand).

Digital products: Create your own courses, eBooks, planners and so on, and sell these on your own website or on platforms such as Gumroad or Shopify.

CREATE A VALUE LADDER AND A SALES FUNNEL

Have you ever wondered why, when you visit Ikea, you are directed to take a certain path through the store? That's because Ikea is effectively one giant sales system. A value ladder outlines the range of products or services you offer with increasing value. A sales funnel outlines the steps a potential customer takes to make a purchasing decision. Imagine walking through Ikea – everything from a cheap candle to a pricey kitchen. That's their value ladder. If you buy the cheap candle, you're a customer. Then you might get a table. If that's good, you might buy the kitchen. Ikea helps this happen with a simple sales system: one-way store layout, easy payment, delivery and loyalty rewards.

Every successful business or smart side hustle involves marketing (creating a value ladder) and sales (creating a sales funnel and sales system) – all done with integrity. Here is a step-by-step process for creating a value ladder and a sales funnel. Remember, these won't work overnight, but over time will enable you to create a smart side hustle that generates passive income.

Step 1. Understand your offerings

Identify the range of products or services you offer and categorize them based on value and pricing. Consider how each offering addresses different customer needs or problems.

Step 2. Define your target audience

Understand your ideal customer's demographics, preferences, pain points and buying behaviours. This will help you tailor your value ladder and sales funnel to their needs.

Step 3. Value ladder

Create a simple progression of offerings that starts with lower-priced or lower-commitment products or services and gradually moves to more valuable and higher-priced options.

For example, if your side hustle involves offering fitness coaching services, your value ladder might look like this:

- Free content: provide free workout tips and recipes on your social media – $0
- Low-cost eBook: offer an affordable eBook with a workout plan and nutrition guide – $7
- Online coaching programme: provide a four-week online coaching programme with personalized workouts and diet plans – $197
- One-on-one coaching: offer personalized one-on-one coaching with weekly check-ins and custom plans – $497

You can create your value ladder on a notepad or as a drawing or use a mindmapping tool.

Step 4. Sales funnel

Design a sales funnel that guides potential customers through the buying journey.

- Awareness: create content that introduces your side hustle and the problem it solves. Use social media, blog posts or videos to create awareness.
- Interest: provide more in-depth content showcasing the benefits of your offerings. This could be through detailed blog posts, webinars or case studies.
- Consideration: present your value ladder offerings and their benefits. Compare different options and explain how they address specific customer needs.
- Decision: provide social proof, such as testimonials or success stories, to build credibility. Offer limited-time discounts or incentives to encourage action.
- Action: make it easy for customers to make a purchase. Use clear calls to action (CTAs) and provide a smooth checkout process.

Useful tools include ConvertKit, ActiveCampaign, Mailchimp, ClickFunnels and Leadpages.

Step 5. Integration

Integrate your value ladder and sales funnel into your marketing efforts. Promote your value ladder offerings through your website, social media, email campaigns and other relevant channels. Create content that addresses the different stages of the sales funnel, providing value and guidance to potential customers.

Step 6. Measurement and optimization

Regularly track the performance of your value ladder and sales funnel. Monitor key metrics such as conversion rates, engagement and customer feedback. Refine and repeat.

Remember that simplicity is key, especially when starting out. Everything we've shared will take months to set up and that's okay. The key is to give yourself at least 12 months with one side hustle idea, and actually commit to it and make it work. We gave ourselves three years to either make the Humble Penny work or fail spectacularly. Knowing we were committed for this period gave us the patience to make it work.

Starting a side hustle can either generate active or passive income for you. The latter is far more desirable, but often overhyped on the internet. Let's explore it further.

MAKE YOUR FIRST PASSIVE INCOME

A lot of people would love to make passive income, but don't know how to start. Passive income is income generated from online or offline side hustles or assets. You put in some work initially, but, over time, you no longer have to swap time for money. However, there is almost always an element of maintenance with most ideas, making them semi-passive rather than 100% passive, and that's okay. The reality, though, is that making passive income is not easy! However, the biggest hurdle is making your first passive income. Here is how to begin:

Step 1: You need a strong desire

What would passive income do for your life? The more motivated you are by the life outcome, the more you'll put in the work.

Step 2: You need savings

Passive income begins with your savings, which you need to investigate a specific idea.

Step 3: Decide on the type of income you want

Which passive income source do you desire as your first one? And why? Does your personality draw you towards an offline idea (such as fixing up property to rent) or online ideas (such as blogging, dividend income and so on). Having clarity on this will help you to rule out a number of ideas and focus on a handful.

Step 4: Review your ten passions and ten talents

Look at the exercise you did earlier. This will help you identify an area that you could potentially explore for passive income, doing something that you enjoy and are good at.

Step 5: Start with one small thing that brings you joy as your goal

Imagine that the thing that brings you joy is buying a loaf of freshly baked sourdough bread once a week and it costs you £3 ($3.90) a week or £156 ($203) a year. This could be your motivation for passive income and you could think of one way of making enough passive income to replace this expense.

For example, you could explore how much you need to invest in dividend-paying stocks to produce £156 ($203) a year in income. Dividing this by a 4% dividend yield gives £3,900 ($5,070) invested to make enough in dividends to cover your sourdough bread expense. Once you've saved and invested enough to make this passive income, you could focus on the next small thing that brings you joy and try to replace that with passive income.

Step 6: Gamify it and make it fun

Performing experiments are fun and that's one thing that helped us explore ways to generate an income from our blog. If you have a partner, invite them into the game. You could aim to make 10% of your current net income from a side hustle source and give yourself a time horizon, say, six months, over which to achieve it.

Step 7: Rethink your time allocation

A great app for tracking your time is Toggl. Even if you track your time and activities for one week or one day, it will reveal what you're spending time on and help you see where you can redirect time towards making passive income.

Remember, although your first passive income will take time and will be the hardest, the second and subsequent passive income sources will be easier and quicker to achieve.

RANKING 21 PASSIVE INCOME IDEAS

Given that we now know passive income exists on a gradient from 'initial work only' to 'some ongoing work' to maintain assets, it means that the type of passive income ideas you choose to explore matters. They will have varying risks attached, returns expected, efforts required, money needed to start and liquidity levels (ease of conversion to cash). We'll score each passive income idea using the following guide:

- Risk – between 0 (high risk) and 10 (low risk)
- Return – between 0 (low returns) and 10 (high returns)
- Effort – between 0 (lots of effort) and 10 (small effort)
- Money – between 0 (lots of capital required) and 10 (small capital required)
- Liquidity – between 0 (low liquidity) and 10 (highly liquid)

The passive income ideas with the highest overall scores will be the best ones to explore. However, this will depend on what you prioritize. For example, you might prefer ideas with the highest return potential or least effort, and so on. Here is our ranking of 21 passive (and semi-passive) income ideas based on our personal experience of all of them, except creating an app, which is on our vision board to do one day:

21 Passive income ideas ranked

No.	Passive income ideas	Risk	Return	Effort	Money	Liquidity	Total
1	Rent Out A Spare Room	9	10	9	10	10	48
2	Rent Out Your Driveway	9	6	8	8	9	40
3	Start A Blog	9	8	5	9	8	39
4	Monetise Through Advertising	8	8	6	9	8	39
5	Invest In Index Funds or ETFs	8	8	9	5	9	39
6	Affiliate Marketing	9	7	5	9	8	38
7	Run A Podcast	9	8	5	8	8	38
8	Start A YouTube Channel	9	8	5	8	8	38
9	High-Interest Deposits (fixed)	9	7	9	5	7	37
10	Create An eBook	8	7	5	8	8	36
11	Bond Investing	10	5	9	5	7	36
12	Make and Sell Videos	8	3	7	9	8	35
13	Create Courses	6	7	6	8	8	35
14	Create A Membership Site	7	7	5	7	9	35
15	Real Estate Investment Trusts	6	6	7	5	7	31
16	Dividend Income Investing	5	7	5	5	8	30
17	Peer To Peer Lending	5	5	8	5	5	28
18	Start An eCommerce Store	5	5	5	6	6	27
19	Property investing	7	9	4	3	3	26
20	Create An App	4	4	4	5	7	24
21	Venture Capital Investments	3	6	5	5	2	21

In our experience, once you've got past making your first passive income, you'll find over time that around 20% of all the passive income ideas that you make money from will generate around 80% of all your passive income.

Interview: Sara

Sara Trezzi (45) is an Italian who has been living in London for 17 years. She's a food blogger at GatheringDreams.com. Here is how she went from nothing to a blog making multi-six figures a year in income.

I previously worked in the movie industry for 15 years, managing a team of 60 as head of production. But after seven years I realized I couldn't work in my job until retirement. I explored various ways to make money on the side, including selling tea online and investing in property. After working 50 to 60 hours a week, I decided that selling physical products wasn't for me. I even left my job to try to do it full-time, but properties aren't something you do every day, so I went back to work part-time.

I started to cook when I was six years old and this love for food led to starting my blog in 2017. Three months later, I made money through AdSense ads. At the time, I was putting in at least 40 hours a week, learning and absorbing. Right now, I make around ten times more than I was making when I started the blog, but I work only 15 to 20 hours a week. Compared to my old job, I earn twice as much as what I was earning in my daily job, which was 50 to 60 hours a week compared to 15 to 20 hours a week on my blog, with breaks of up to three months where I barely do anything.

Now, I wake up every day and can do what I want. Sometimes it's work, and sometimes it's relaxing, going for a walk or taking some time to travel. The biggest difference is that when you work in a corporate job, you have a certain fixed salary and you know how much time you put into it. In an online business, you frontload your efforts, investing a lot of time and learning at the start. However, once your business gains traction, you reap the rewards continuously. For example, there is an article that I wrote three months into my blogging journey and it still brings me money today, six years later. Even if you take breaks, the work you've already done continues to generate income.

My blog primarily earns through advertising and affiliate links. If you have 1,000 to 10,000 people a month reading your blog, you can start to make a little bit of money. For a one-person business without a team, I get between 500,000 and 600,000 people reading a month and, in the last year, about six million, with the vast majority reading from the US. It's just about knowing what you love and knowing where to look to see how people make a business out of it.

To embark on a journey like mine and make at least £1,000 or $1,000 a month, you should first identify your passion. It's essential to enjoy what you do. Find what makes you happy, whether it's cooking, running or any other interest. People often have something in their lives that brings them joy. You can turn your passion into a profitable online business.

When you've identified your passion, research how others have monetized similar interests. Observe their income sources, such as sponsored posts, advertising or selling products. If they're making money, there's a good chance you can, too. Focus on one income stream until it's successful and generating the income you desire. Then, consider branching out to diversify your revenue sources. Remember, you don't have to reinvent the wheel – just put your unique spin on what you love.

HOW TO GROW YOUR AUDIENCE

One of the most powerful assets that you can create for your side hustle is to grow an audience of people who know you, like you and trust you. That audience can either be grown on social media or via an email list or both. Although both are important, growing an email list is far more important, because you're in control of the data and you can communicate with your audience whenever you want. Over time, that audience becomes a community of people who rely on you for advice, guidance or they might purchase your products and services, thereby becoming customers. The best part is that you don't need a large audience to make sustainable income. Kevin Kelly popularized the 1000 True Fans idea[55] as a way to make a living doing what you love. If a thousand people who love what you're doing pay you £100 or $100 each per year, then you'll make £100,000 or $100,000. Knowing that all it took was a thousand true fans was liberating and made us realize that it is possible to create a successful side hustle and build an audience around it while generating income in a sustainable way.

Having started from zero and been on the journey of building an active audience of over 200,000 people (without paid advertising) in just over five years, we've learned the five ingredients that it takes to grow an audience of people who love what you do. Here they are:

Quality: Think of each piece of quality content that you create as a messenger with a megaphone broadcasting good things about you, your business and your brand. Start with your smartphone and good lighting.

Value: If people consume your content (video, blog, podcast, music) and get the transformation promised, then they'll leave having received value and share it with others.

Consistency: You could create good quality content and come across as authentic. However, if you're not consistent, you may as well not bother, because no growth happens without consistency.

CTAs: The only way you'll actually build an audience is to repeatedly give them CTAs, for example 'Click here to subscribe' or 'Join our newsletter'.

Authenticity: This is all about being yourself, telling your story (positives and not so positives) and letting your warm energy come through when you communicate with others. People are always seeking connection, so if you can come across relatable, you'll build an audience quite quickly.

Interview: Marvyn

Marvyn Harrison (39) is British-born with family roots in Jamaica and Antigua. He's a father of two, founder of Dope Black Dads and co-founder of Belovd Agency. Here is how he starts businesses by leveraging community and content.

I started at 13, washing cars for a fiver. I sold CDs in university to make ends meet. I've always worked, had my first job at 16 and moved out at 19. Eventually, I ventured into music management and digital marketing, running a successful live music and comedy event. Later, I worked at Betfair, Samsung and WPP. It was in this corporate world that my career took off and I ventured into my own businesses: Dope Black Dads and Belovd Agency, where I focus on cultural transformation for companies.

Some people start businesses to sell them or achieve specific financial goals. I'm motivated by solving problems. So the financial aspect comes last for me. However, I still have to be attentive to the profit and loss statement to ensure the business remains sustainable.

Building a community is vital for growing a business, but it's crucial not to build a community solely for profit. Monetizing the community should not compromise its integrity. You may need to say no to certain opportunities that don't align with the community's values. A better approach might be to create a closed user group (e.g. an email list), which is different from a community. A community should have power and influence, whereas a closed user group serves specific objectives.

My motivation to achieve our business goals comes from authenticity and passion. One of the best examples is my experience with Dope Black, which was a project I deeply loved. Even if there were flaws or challenges, we worked on the ground, reaching out to people and trying to make a difference. I'm motivated by creating solutions to problems that I've experienced personally. I aim to make these solutions sustainable. I leave these projects in the world to continue the conversation, even when I'm not directly involved. My authenticity fuels my motivation.

To earn an extra £1,000 to £2,000 per month from a side business, you should leverage your existing skills, like offering your services outside of your job, for example, by providing bookkeeping services privately. Additionally, become a content creator. Teach people about your area of expertise online and build an audience. Create merchandise related to your brand and consider going live or hosting in-person events to share your knowledge. You should also consider the intersection between your skills and passions. You may have a skill for numbers, but a passion for Arsenal. Your passion will drive you further than your skill for numbers. I would do an Arsenal podcast over an accounting podcast because you'll get more out of yourself in the Arsenal podcast with less chance of quitting.

To increase your side income from £2,000 to £5,000 per month, you can explore brand partnerships, monetize your content. Focus on platforms like TikTok and Instagram to grow your audience. Create merchandise and consider speaking engagements to increase your income. And don't limit yourself to your initial goal – aim to pivot and find a balance between work and income that makes you happy.

SIDE HUSTLES, EMPLOYERS AND COLLEAGUES

If you're in-between jobs, find a job with an employer who is open-minded to side hustles. If you're currently in a job and want to start a side hustle, make sure that you read your employment contract to ensure that you're not breaching any policies. In addition, observe the culture in your work-place to see if people are unofficially doing side hustles outside work to gauge if it's allowed or not. If you need to, speak with an employment lawyer.

If you're in a job and have already started a side hustle, it's worth mentioning this to your employer and making it clear to them that you don't do it during work time or using work assets. Be careful, though, because some employers might unofficially hold it against you and bring it up if you go through a disciplinary process for something else.

I (Ken) experienced challenges with an employer who wasn't happy that I was doing a side hustle alongside my day job, even though I was doing it in my spare time. I eventually left that company and was glad I didn't give up on my side hustle, because the Humble Penny would never have existed if I had! From personal negative experience, we also recommend not telling your colleagues about your side hustle, as they may not be as supportive as you would hope.

JOB SUCCESS SECRETS FOR A HIGH-PAYING, SIX-FIGURE INCOME

One of the often-overlooked levers for financial independence is your career. Many people stick in their jobs, getting the same pay every year or at best a pay rise in line with inflation. However, if you recognize your job as a really important pathway for accelerating your journey to financial freedom, you'll see that job and career very differently. A really important mindset for career maximization is to realize that before you can ask for anything, you must first know what you truly want, and give yourself the permission to go and get it. The same goes for making your ideal income.

Another way to think about it is neatly captured in this quote by Earl Nightingale, which says that 'Our rewards in life will always be in exact proportion to our contribution (or service).' In order to increase your income, it's important to ask yourself how you can raise your contribution in order to match your income goal. Although money isn't everything, it is a vehicle for helping you to create your version of freedom and more.

One thing you won't find on our LinkedIn profiles are the numerous low-paid jobs that we've done to get to where we are today. For example, I (Ken) have worked as a cleaner, waiter, receptionist, animal technician, shelf-stacker and sandwich-maker, while Mary has worked on the tills in retail, as a childcare assistant and as a production assistant for the education sector. Those jobs sowed the seeds of desire and convinced us that, in order to ultimately make a comfortable six-figure income, we needed to be bold and make career moves. We aren't, of course, sharing this to brag, but to give you some context.

Note that you don't need a six-figure income to design a life of financial joy. In fact, regardless of what you're earning, what truly matters is how much of your income you're able to keep. What we hope you'll get out of this section of the book is enough to help you get a pay rise that far exceeds inflation year after year, especially if you work in the private sector, because unfortunately some of the following tips won't be effective in the public sector.

Tip: Move jobs every two to three years

This especially applies if you're in your 20s, 30s or even 40s. The reason for moving so often is that the marketplace continues to evolve and re-values your skillset more quickly than your skillset is priced in your current employment. You might be thinking, what about loyalty? What we say to that is be loyal while you're in your job, but don't forget to look after number one and move jobs for your own good.

Tip: Get a VIP employer

There is a very direct link between the type of employer you have and the level of wealth generation you can achieve. Here we've sketched the different types of employers as we see them and how they link to your potential wealth creation.

Type of employers and their wealth-building potential

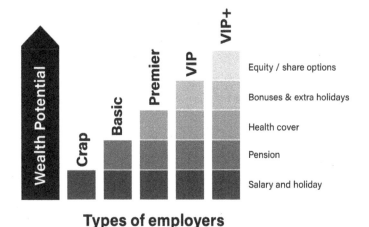

Looking at the chart above, the big question for you is, what type of employer have you got? The more you choose a favourable employer, the more you are likely to generate wealth with your career over time.

Where possible, avoid the crap and basic employers, and aim for VIP employers and above.

Tip: Ask for a paid qualification from your employer

We mentioned previously that I (Ken) did an Executive MBA through a previous employer, which cost approximately £75,000 for a two-year programme. Of that, 50% was funded by the employer after I pitched the idea to the board and 20% was funded by a bursary after I wrote an essay for the business school. You might be thinking, so you went and you did the course, and you learned some things. What does that have to do with money? Everything! My perceived value in the marketplace went up another £40,000+ per year in basic salary alone, plus pension contributions, as pensions are typically based on gross salary. The more money you make by doing a specialist qualification, the more money you are building towards your wealth overall.

Choosing to ask your employer to fund further studies is something that will potentially add value for life, provided they are paying for at least 50% of it. By the way, your colleagues are unlikely to bother asking for such sponsorship, so your chances of success will be high.

Tip: Become an intrapreneur

You're currently an employee at a company or a business. However, you could also become somebody who has a bit of an entrepreneurial flair within your organization.

For example, I used to work with a bunch of guys who made fairly good basic salaries – between £5,000 and about £8,000 net income per month. However, these guys also found a way of being able to negotiate for themselves 10 to 25% of any business that they were able to bring in. What that meant was that every single month when I was calculating their commissions they were earning stupidly large sums of money. On top of £5,000 to £8,000 per month of net income, they'd also be making £20,000+ per month in commissions alone.

The key lesson is that these people did what most people do not do, which is go to their employer or manager and say: 'I'm going to explore my networks and if I bring somebody into our business, look at all the value this could add to our company. For doing that, can I please have a 10% commission (one-off or recurring) for bringing that business in?'

This is how you start to change the game when it comes to your income. The key is to ask, and the worst response is a no. Then you need to find another way to ask, but keep asking.

Tip: Do your boss' job

Make it your business to learn one or two skillsets your boss has or take on an area of responsibility beyond those you have a remit for. This puts you in pole position for asking for pay rises that exceed the typical inflationary pay rises most people ask for. You should be the person asking for 10 to 15% pay rises because you took on some responsibility from your boss. You'll be seen as somebody who is forward-thinking and deserves that unusual pay rise.

In fact, to take this up a notch, ensure that at the start of every year you sit down with your boss and come up with a development plan. Then agree in writing that if you hit all your goals in a year, they'll agree to a conditional pay rise of 15%, for example. The key is to put you and your boss into a win-win negotiating position where you both stand to gain something defined that clearly links effort to reward.

In conclusion, maximizing your income is never given to you, you have to fight for it and get what's yours. It will require employing creativity, shifting your mindset and working smarter, but more than you can imagine is possible if you give yourself the permission to make more money.

In week 9, we'll work on helping you to prepare for a comfortable retirement, with the option to retire early when you want to and not when you have to.

Interview: Thando

Thando Jacobs (33) was born in Zimbabwe and moved to the UK when he was 12. He's married to Lindie and they have one child. He currently works as a business analyst and is a dream-maker at Financial Joy Academy. Here is how he grew his income by around 900% in 12 years.

Financial joy is about empowerment. It means being able to provide for my family, fulfil our needs, and have the freedom to chase our dreams and ambitions. It's about not only securing our own needs, but also helping others and supporting causes we believe in.

My career journey began when I joined Barclays as a cashier at 22. I spent seven years in retail banking, working my way up from cashier to relationship manager. After that, I switched to tech as a business analyst, where I've been for the past five years. Recently, I transitioned to be an independent business analyst contractor.

My journey began with a salary of £16,000 as a cashier and slowly climbed as I progressed through different roles. The key was switching to tech and becoming a business analyst. I went from £35,000 to £50,000 by developing skills and certifications. Then, as a contractor, I jumped to £100,000 and recently to between £130,000 to £145,000 with my new contract.

The early stages were tough, especially in retail banking, with high competition and limited job opportunities in my area. Switching to tech made it easier due to a broader market, but it wasn't without its challenges. The key was improving my skills and making myself more attractive to hiring managers, which took about two years. It required a mindset shift, especially when I became a contractor. The switch from retail banking was driven by the desire for more financial rewards and faster progression. Retail banking didn't provide the financial growth I was looking for. The switch to tech was about empowerment. I wanted to choose my projects, income and work schedule. As an employee, I couldn't make those choices. The push came from wanting more control over my career.

My wife's support was crucial. She backed my career journey. Networking and building relationships on LinkedIn also played a significant role. Talking to professionals in the field and asking for guidance opened my mind to new possibilities. Interactions with colleagues and friends exposed me to different career paths, which motivated me to make changes.

Increasing our income has moved us away from living paycheque to paycheque. It provides room in our budget for savings, investments and supporting others without sacrificing our financial stability. It also opens up the possibility of making different life choices, like my wife considering not returning to employment after maternity leave to focus on family and our side hustles.

Balancing my career and side hustles involves focusing on outcomes rather than inputs. I'm strategic about where I invest my energy and effort, ensuring I make progress even if I get distracted. Having a clear vision and staying committed to my passion project keeps me on track. Over the last five to ten years, I've developed my skills through various methods. I've put myself in challenging positions, accepted new opportunities, networked, joined webinars and attended boot camps for intensive learning. Getting certifications, like the BCS Business Analysis Foundation Certificate, has also been instrumental in my career growth.

My advice to those looking to grow their income to achieve financial freedom through their career would be: first, be strategic in your career choice. Look for industries that offer higher salaries and lower barriers to entry, like tech or financial services. Second, go above and beyond the average employee. Network, get certifications and build your authority in your field. Finally, focus on outcomes and put in the work to demand higher salaries, which will aid your financial freedom journey.

WEEK 8: LESSONS AND ACTION STEPS

Three lessons for week 8

- People usually aren't short on money, they're usually short on creativity, which is key to making more money and building wealth. To become more creative, you need more connectivity in your life, because creativity is never done in isolation, it's done with others.
- Breaking the employee mindset even if you remain an employee is key to helping you to earn more and accelerate your journey to financial freedom. It will allow you to explore smart side hustles, and tried and tested ways to earn above-inflation pay rises in your job and throughout career.
- Passive income isn't always 100% passive and that's okay. What matters is making your first passive income and that will take some time to achieve. However, it snowballs after that if you persevere and work hard at it.

Three action steps for week 8

Action step 1: Choose an approach for maximizing your income. Will you be focusing on starting a smart side hustle or career maximization?

Write your answer below and explain why.

```



```

Action step 2: If you want to make passive income, what is the one small thing that brings you joy that you'd like to generate passive income to replace first? And which one of the 21 passive income ideas will you explore first and why?

```



```

Action step 3: If you'd like to create a smart side hustle, follow the steps that we outlined earlier in this week, starting with the ten passions vs ten talents exercise, to figure out one idea that you'll explore to make more money. Ensure that you check whether there is demand for that idea and validate it. Remember to give yourself six to 12 months to properly commit to an idea.

PART 3

Looking ahead to financial freedom

Goal: Aim for financial freedom while seeking joy.

Week 9:
Plan for financial joy
in your retirement years

*A life of financial joy aims for financial independence
and the option for early retirement, so that you can
ultimately do what you love when you want.*

On a flight back from Rhodes after a family holiday, I (Ken) got up to use the bathroom and while queueing, as you do at 35,000 feet, a guy sitting to my right recognized me from our YouTube channel and said, 'I'm in my 40s, married and would love to retire in ten years, but I have so little saved. If you were in my shoes, what would you do?'

This is a relatable dilemma that speaks to people of different age groups. However, few people proactively seek out solutions to their retirement conundrums because they are either too busy navigating life's challenges or they simply don't know where to start and it's far easier to kick the can down the road. My fellow passenger's question reminded me of two important mindsets that dream-makers should adopt as they work towards retirement: stay hungry and stay humble.

Staying hungry speaks to the desire to seek creative ways to solve your problems and take risks, but also the need for financial bravery as you work towards your financial independence or retirement goals.

Bravery with money is following a plan that works no matter the weather. For example, following the ten-week plan in this book because it's coming from people who have actually achieved what they're sharing.

In addition, it is about making unconventional choices that get you to where you want to get to. For example, lifestyle choices around where you live, what car you drive, how much you spend vs how much you invest monthly. Exercising the power of choice by itself is an act of financial bravery.

We believe financial bravery is also about living a purpose-driven life while spending intentionally, having fun and ultimately living a life of financial joy, even if you're far from achieving your goals.

Stay humble means setting realistic goals and making reasonable assumptions. Don't expect your income to always carry on rising on a straight line and expect the unexpected, for example a stock market crash or a global pandemic. Consider that your health might not always remain as good as it is now, stay flexible and keep learning as things change.

With these mindsets, our goal this week is to help you to dare and take the leap to aim for financial independence and the *option* for early retirement. Even if you choose to retire conventionally, in your 60s or later, what we share this week will give you the confidence, inspiration and focus to work towards your goals.

CHALLENGES TO BEING BRAVER WITH MONEY

While aiming for financial independence and the option for early retirement is possible, it doesn't come without unique challenges that affect us all in different ways. Figuring out ways to navigate these challenges daily, while keeping our eyes on our goals, helps us to grow and become the people we need to become to reach our goals. Here are some of the challenges you may need to deal with to be braver with money.

- Inflation can lead to tough choices, such as forcing you to relocate to a cheaper area.
- The Black Tax burdens Black households striving for success while supporting struggling family members, hindering financial progress due to historical and systemic racism.
- Wealth gaps persist: Black Africans and Caribbeans possess only 10% and 27%[56] of the wealth of White British households, affecting retirement prospects.
- Gender pension gap and singles tax heighten financial disparities, impacting women and singles' retirement outcomes.
- Financial abuse causes savings loss, damaged credit and affects retirement plans.
- Raising children affects retirement due to associated costs, but it shouldn't deter parenthood.
- Unexpected life events like recessions, divorce or bereavement influence retirement plans.
- Immigrants face financial struggles in new countries due to lack of resources and legal status.

With all these challenges, seeking financial independence or the option for early retirement can seem impossible and it might even make you feel like giving up. For us, giving up was not an option. We had to see financial independence as the only destination and even if we aimed for it and fell short, the worst-case scenario was that we'd end up with a lot more financial security than we started with.

We have been on that journey over a decade and we have experienced most of these challenges and more, yet we have persisted in our pursuit of financial independence, so we know this journey is possible, but can be frustrating. We felt motivated to write this book because we believe very strongly that our message of financial joy will help you enjoy your life in small ways each day, as you gradually work towards your goals, knowing that the journey is a race with yourself and not with others.

HOW MUCH IS ENOUGH FOR YOUR RETIREMENT?

Deciding how much money you'll need for a retirement that might seem far away and uncertain is difficult. Research show that 77% of people do not know how much they need in retirement and 51% of people are focusing on their current needs and wants at the expense of providing for the future.[57] This is totally understandable as getting by daily is hard enough. However, an encouraging statistic is that 70% of people believe that having targets will help them to save more.

For this section of the book, we want to help you figure out how much you need for retirement or your financial independence goals, and understand what gaps you have (if any), in order to decide how much you may need to invest each month having made some reasonable assumptions about future returns.

We'll look at two options. Option one is if you want to retire in the traditional sense at around the age of 66 or 67, when you start getting the state pension. You will also have had access to your private pension for about ten years already.

Option two is if you want financial independence and the *option* to retire early while continuing to work doing what you love. This is our take on the FIRE (Financial Independence Retire Early) movement. You can retire at 55 (or 57 from 2028) with pension access or retire before 55 without pension access.

To determine how much is enough for retirement or your financial independence goals, let's work through some steps:

Step 1: How much annual income do I need?

Retirement savings should provide you with a steady income to cover expenses – without running out. Given we're thinking about future income, we need to think in real (post-inflation) terms. One sensible way of doing this is to use a percentage of your expenditure today (for example, 80% of today's net income), then apply real returns to your calculations. For example, we worked out that given we've already paid off our mortgage, we only need an annual after-tax income of £24,410 for both of us to fully cover our living expenses, including various costs like holidays, energy, food, insurance and more.

Another visual way of looking at retirement is to consider the Pensions and Lifetime Savings Association's retirement living standards (RLS). It covers three levels of expenditure (minimum, moderate and comfortable), designed to help you realistically work out how much you will need in retirement. To make sure the numbers were realistic, extensive work and research was conducted with focus groups made up of real people all over the UK.

According to the RLS, here is how much you need in annual income after tax to cover your expenses at retirement depending on your lifestyle option.[58]

The retirement living standards

Lifestyle	Single	Couple
Minimum: Covers all your needs with some money left over for fun.	£12,800 (outside London) £14,300 (inside London)	£19,900 (outside London) £22,400 (inside London)
Moderate: Offer you more financial security and stability.	£23,300 (outside London) £28,300 (inside London)	£34,000 (outside London) £41,400 (inside London)
Comfortable: Offers you more financial freedom and some luxuries.	£37,300 (outside London) £40,900 (inside London)	£54,500 (outside London) £56,500 (inside London)

All numbers above assume that you're mortgage free or rent free at retirement. Account for mortgage status or potential renting in your calculations. Also, remember costs will rise due to inflation over time.

How much annual income after tax do you think you'll need in retirement to cover your annual expenses?

Step 2: How big is your retirement or financial independence pot?

You want a pot that's large enough to either provide you with an annuity from an insurance company that gives you an income for life or a draw-down to provide income annually and cover your costs.

The second option involves drawing down a certain percentage of your pot to live on each year. However, choosing a safe withdrawal rate (SWR) that makes sense depending on what part of the world you're in is incredibly important. Most of the literature in this area of financial planning focuses on the idea of a '4% rule' (most reference 1998's Trinity Study[59]), which simply says that withdrawing 4% of your retirement portfolio balance in the first year and adjusting the amount for inflation annually has historically provided a 95% probability of success – in other words, not running out of money – over a 30-year retirement period.

It's important to note that the 4% rule only applies to US investors and should not be blindly applied to the UK or other countries. That's because the original research (by William Bengen in 1994) and analysis did not factor in fees. It also only looked at a 30-year retirement, while in reality this will vary for each retiree. Furthermore, historical returns for UK investors (and those in other parts of the world) differ to those for US investors. For example, the American market in much deeper than in the UK and the US equity market typically delivers an average of 1% real return above the UK.

In short, having spent many hours reading all the research papers in this area of choosing a SWR, we've concluded that a sensible withdrawal rate for the UK is between 2.5% and 3.5%. We'll focus on 3.5% and assume that you're investing in global funds, which allocate mostly to the US market. If you're in the US, use 4%. If you're invested only in the UK (for example, 50% equity and 50% bonds), you'll want to lean closer to

3%. If you're outside the UK or US, an initial SWR of around 3% to 4% adjusted for local inflation could serve as a starting point.

With this number, you can then work out how large your retirement or financial independence pot needs to be. Using our personal required after-tax income of £24,410, we worked out that our freedom number is £697,429 or £24,410 divided by 3.5% (0.035). This is also roughly the same as multiplying your number by 28.5 (100% divided by 3.5%).

What is your required retirement pot or financial independence number, aka freedom pot? Work it out below:

Using the RLS in the UK, here are the required retirement pots for singles and couples according to a 3.5% SWR.

Estimated retirement pots for singles and couples in the UK by lifestyle

	SINGLE					
	Minimum	Minimum	Moderate	Moderate	Comfortable	Comfortable
SWR per annum	(Outside London)	(Inside London)	(Outside London)	(Inside London)	(Outside London)	(Inside London)
	12,800	14,300	23,300	28,300	37,300	40,900
3.50%	£365,714	£408,571	£665,714	£808,571	£1,065,714	£1,168,571

	COUPLES					
	Minimum	Minimum	Moderate	Moderate	Comfortable	Comfortable
SWR per annum	(Outside London)	(Inside London)	(Outside London)	(Inside London)	(Outside London)	(Inside London)
	19,900	22,400	34,000	41,400	54,500	56,500
3.50%	£568,571	£640,000	£971,429	£1,182,857	£1,557,143	£1,614,286

Although these numbers are a rule of thumb and should help guide you in determining what your number should look like, as everyone's personal circumstances are different, reading them can feel both scary and overwhelming.

If you're planning to retire at the traditional age of 66, at which point you get the state pension, you won't need as much as the numbers above imply. Here is a breakdown of the pension pot that's required for a single person as well as a couple, according to the RLS.

Table 1: Fund sized required to reach different retirement living standards (RLS)

Retirement living standard	Annual expenditure	State pension*	Pot income	Total income pre tax	Total income post tax per person	Approx fund size required if purchasing an annuity**
Comfortable	£37,300	£10,600	£32,882	£43,482	£37,300	£530,000
Moderate	£23,300	£10,600	£15,383	£25,983	£23,300	£248,000
Minimum	£12,800	£10,600	£2,258	£12,858	£12,800	£36,500

* Full state pension for 2023–24

** Rounded indicative figures based on an annuity of £6,200 per £100,000 (see below)

Let's explain these numbers assuming you want a comfortable lifestyle (for example) at retirement. This table is saying that:

- A comfortable lifestyle needs a £37,300 after-tax income.
- For this, you require income from two sources: state pension and personal pension.
- If retiring at 66 with a £10,600 yearly state pension, you need an additional pre-tax income of £32,882 annually.

- This additional income of £32,882 must come from a private/workplace pension pot.
- To estimate the needed pension pot, use an annuity formula: £6,200 per £100,000 in the pension pot.
- This calculation suggests a required pot of £530,000: £32,882 divided by £6,200 and multiplied by £100,000 (as shown in the table).

To find the figures for moderate or minimum lifestyles (£248,000 and £36,500 respectively), follow the same process as previously described. These figures presume retirement at 66 (state pension age). If seeking financial independence with the option to retire early, you'll need a larger pot as the state pension won't be available. Instead of buying an annuity, you'd draw down on your portfolio, considering the 3.5% SWR.

Table 2: Fund size required for a couple to reach different retirement living standards

Retirement living standard	Annual expenditure (couple)	State pension* (both)	Pot income (both)	Total income pre tax	Total income post tax per person	Approx fund size required if purchasing an annuity**
Comfortable	£54,500	£21,200	£40,640	£61,840	£27,250	£328,000
Moderate	£34,000	£21,200	£15,016	£36,216	£17,000	£121,000
Minimum	£19,900	£21,200	£0	£21,200	£10,600	£0

* Full state pension for 2023–24

** Rounded indicative figures based on an annuity of £6,200 per £100,000 (see below)

Note that the numbers on the right-hand side of the table are per person, so:

- Comfortable lifestyle requires post tax income of £54,500 (£27,250 × 2) a year and a pot of £656,000 (£328,000 × 2).

- Moderate lifestyle requires post tax income of £34,000 (£17,000 × 2) a year and a pot of £242,000 (£121,000 × 2).
- Minimum lifestyle requires post tax income of £19,900 a year (£9,950 per person) and a pot of £0 (the state pension of £10,600 per person per year covers it).

Couples often have financial advantages compared to singles. For a moderate lifestyle, a single person needs a £248,000 pension pot, while a couple requires a lower total of £242,000. Even for the minimum lifestyle, a couple needs £0 additional funds compared to the £36,500 required for a single person, after the state pension. While not everyone desires a relationship, this difference is notable.

Additionally, annuity formulas change over time, affecting the numbers provided. To achieve financial independence and early retirement without pension access, consider using the 3.5% SWR (or a suitable alternative) and carefully plan when to start drawing down funds, which impacts pension accessibility and tax considerations.

Step 3: How much do you have saved and invested already?

In week 4, your net worth gave you a clear picture of what your existing pot looks like. Consider combining resources with a partner to calculate a joint household net worth. This calculation reveals the gap between your current position and the target in step 2.

Assess various places where your money is invested or saved:

- Tax-deferred accounts like pensions (defined benefit or defined contribution workplace pension, SIPP – self-invested personal pension, SSAS – small self-administered scheme, 401k and Traditional IRA

(US), superannuation fund (Australia), registered retirement savings plan (Canada) and so on).

- Tax-free accounts such as ISAs (lifetime ISA, stocks and shares ISA), (US: Roth IRA).
- Other investments like general investing account, property equity, commodities, digital assets and so on.

For those aiming for financial independence with early retirement, exclude your primary home's equity and defined benefit pension transfer value. However, property equity apart from the primary residence counts as part of your saved and invested amount. How much do you have saved and invested in total?

Step 4: How long do you need to invest for?

Do you aim for a traditional retirement at 66 or seek financial independence for an earlier retirement at 55, 57 or even sooner? The timeline for investing might not be as straightforward as it seems.

Our experience and that of our community members shows a gap between expectations and reality as people age. You might think that you will carry on working until you're 66 (or 67 as the state pension age increases), but the reality is that many employers are somehow managing to quietly get rid of their older, highly experienced and often expensive staff members in favour of the younger and less expensive.

Other factors like health issues may force an earlier retirement. So, it's crucial to carefully assess how much you need to save and the realistic time available to build your savings.

How long do you have in years before you need to retire or achieve FI?

Step 5: What is a realistic portfolio return?

Stay reasonable and consider inflation and fees (approx 0.5% annually for passive index funds and ETFs). Longer time horizons and more equity allocation generally lead to higher expected real returns, typically between 4% to 7% for investments spanning 10 to 20 years or more. While better returns are possible, it's best not to exaggerate these rates. Review week 7 for sound investment advice.

Step 6: When will you reach financial independence or have the option to retire early?

The key to achieving financial independence and optional early retirement is your savings rate – what portion of your after-tax income you save and invest monthly. A higher rate accelerates your path to financial independence, reducing the years until retirement. For instance, we maintained a

65% savings rate during our journey, gradually increasing it from zero to 10% by simplifying our lifestyles and focusing on boosting earnings without lifestyle inflation.

In order to figure out when you'll achieve financial independence and the option for early retirement, you'll need to figure out how much you'll need to contribute each month for that to become a reality. To make this easy for you, we've built a retirement calculator that you can download here: www.thehumblepenny.com/Freedomcalculator. We've made it flexible enough for you to change the inputs and currency to match your location.

Given everyone's spending and savings rates are different, driven by different lifestyles, let's look at some real-life case studies and see how different savings rates influence when different people can achieve financial independence and the option for early retirement.

Sophia, 35, and **Andrew, 32,** are newlyweds renting in London Zone 3. They envision a future of travelling and working remotely. With a joint after-tax income of £50,000, they currently save and invest 15% (£7,500) due to their love for travel and an active social life, spending £42,500 annually. Their goal is financial independence with a freedom number of £1,214,286. With £45,000 saved and investments at a 5% real return, at a 15% savings rate, they project retirement at 72 and 75. If they upped their savings rate to 40%, they could achieve financial independence 20 years earlier at 53 and 56, with a pot of £857,143 on a more frugal lifestyle.

Daniella, 29, is a marketing manager who is single and renting in Essex. She plans to relocate to St Lucia upon achieving financial independence. With an annual after-tax income of £30,542, she maintains a 30% savings rate, saving £9,163 and spending £21,379. Her goal is financial independence with a freedom number of £610,840. At a 30% savings rate and a 5% return on investments, she anticipates retiring at 54, but by increasing her savings rate to 40%, she could achieve financial independence in 20 years, aged 49, with a pot of £523,577.

Chidi, 45, and **Ola, 40,** have been married for 15 years and own a mortgaged home in Kent. Chidi, an entrepreneur, and Ola, a lawyer, work long hours and have three children in state schools. Their joint after-tax income is £82,342 and they practise a frugal lifestyle, saving 55% (£45,288) annually while spending £37,054. With a net worth (excluding home equity) of £120,000 and a freedom number of £1,058,683, they anticipate achieving financial independence in 13 years at 58 and 53. By increasing their savings rate to 65%, they aim to achieve financial independence in ten years at 55 and 50, targeting a pot of £823,420 due to a less expensive lifestyle.

Priya, 50, and **Rahul, 52,** are married. Priya is a physiotherapist while Rahul recently returned to work in IT after being a stay-at-home dad. Residing in Birmingham, their household income totals £77,000, providing an after-tax income of £60,404. They have a 50% savings rate, saving £30,202 and spending the same annually, with a net worth of £95,000 (excluding home equity). Their goal is financial independence with a freedom number of £862,914. At a 50% savings rate, they aim to retire at 65 and 67, coinciding with state pensions. By increasing their savings rate to 60%, they plan to reach financial independence at 61 and 63, in 11 years, targeting a retirement pot of £690,331.

Download our calculator here: www.thehumblepenny.com/Freedom-calculator. At what age will you achieve financial independence and the option of early retirement? Tweak the savings rate in the calculator to see how much earlier you could do it if you made some lifestyle changes.

WHAT ABOUT MINI-RETIREMENTS?

For the people of our generation, Millennials and Gen Zs, and a growing number of others, the idea of working until you're 66 or 67 and then supposedly retiring and starting to enjoy your life is dead. It's not appealing and we much prefer getting a taste of retirement sooner rather than later. When we look at our parents, who are aged in their 60s, 70s, and 80s, a common trend we notice is that retired life is too lonely. They want to have fun, but do some work and keep their minds active. As a result of that, they've unretired and focused part of their time on their small businesses as it gives them a sense of identity and a way to feel like they're still contributing to society.

Although early retirement is appealing, a middle ground is a mini-retirement, which offers the best of both, because you get a taste of retirement now while doing work you love. We see a future of more mini-retirements or cycles of retirement for people who are designing a life of financial joy. To put this idea to the test, we began taking August off every year as a mini-retirement to see what it felt like to have a complete break from work, knowing that we'd return to work that we actually enjoyed after our break. It has since become a part of our family culture and we've increased our one month to three months off each year. Starting small is key, though, with annual leave from work.

RETIREMENT SAVINGS OPTIONS

Navigating investment options can be overwhelming, especially when considering various accounts like pensions vs ISAs and others like the lifetime ISA, and general investing accounts. The debate on which to prioritize can be confusing, particularly in planning for financial goals like early or traditional retirement or buying a first property. Each account comes with its unique benefits and constraints, making it crucial to understand their nature and then determine their priority based on your specific financial goals.

Account 1: Pension

Examples include workplace pensions, private pensions such as the self-invested personal pension (SIPP) in the UK or equivalents in other countries as mentioned earlier.

Used for: Saving for retirement.

Key benefits include:

- Tax relief depends on your tax band:
  - Basic rate: Every £100 investment costs £80.
  - Higher rate: Every £100 investment costs £60.
  - Additional rate: Every £100 investment costs £55.
- Free from 40% inheritance tax (if death occurs before age 75).
- If you're not earning, you can pay up to £2,880/year into a SIPP and get tax relief of £720 (total £3,600).
- Eligible for employer contributions and matching.

Annual allowance: Up to £60,000 per year if earnings permit. Lower for very high earners.

Money access: Available at age 55 (age 57 from 2028).

Risk: Potential future rule changes, complexity and limitations on money access. Also, only 25% is tax free and 75% is taxable in retirement.

Account 2: Stocks and shares ISA

Used for: Investing in stocks and shares, funds and ETFs for various goals, for example, house purchase, financial independence, retirement.

   Key benefits include:

* No capital gains tax on profits from selling.
* No income tax on dividends.
* No tax upon withdrawal.

Annual allowance: Presently £20,000 per year across all ISAs.

Money access: Accessible anytime without incurring taxes.

Risk: Loss of annual allowance if not entirely utilized annually.

Account 3: Lifetime ISA (LISA)

Used for: Saving and investing for property purchase (first-time buyers) or retirement. You can only open one before your 40th birthday.

   Key benefits include:

* Tax-free account with a 25% government bonus on savings up to £4,000/year.
* The government bonus is paid annually until age 50, offering up to £33,000 in free money from age 18.
* Types include cash LISA and stocks and shares LISA.

Annual allowance: £4,000 per year with a potential £1,000 bonus.

Money access: Access is allowed for a property purchase or wait until age 60 for retirement without incurring taxes.

Risk: Inaccessibility of funds until age 60 for retirement.

Account 4: Dealing or general investing account (GIA)

Used for: Taxable account used to invest in stocks and shares, funds and ETFs. No tax benefits. Also called a fund and share account.

Key benefits include:

- Access your money at any time.
- Use annual capital gains tax (CGT) allowance for profits.
- Use annual dividend allowance and personal savings allowance.
- Can be used by individuals, companies, investment clubs and trusts.

Annual allowance: No annual limit to your investing or withdrawals.

Money access: Any time.

Risks: You'll pay tax above your tax-free allowances, which are on the decline. Currently £6,000 (to be halved to £3,000) CGT tax-free allowance per individual per year or £12,000 (to be halved to £6,000) for married couples or civil partners. Currently £1,000 (to be halved to £500) per year tax-free dividend allowance and £1,000 and £500 personal savings allowance for basic rate and high rate taxpayers respectively.

Account 5: Junior SIPP

Consider the Junior SIPP as a long-term saving option for your child's retirement. Its annual allowance allows up to £2,880 yearly, supplemented by a government top-up of £720 basic tax relief (20%), totalling £3,600. It complements Junior ISAs for children, although funds cannot be accessed until retirement, making the Junior ISA, with an annual tax-free allowance of £9,000, the primary choice for us before the Junior SIPP.

ORDER OF INVESTING FOR EARLY RETIREMENT VS LATER RETIREMENT

Remember, this is our guide, so feel free to change this up if you prefer:

Scenario 1: Employee aiming for traditional retirement

Let's first look at the basic rate taxpayer in this scenario, assuming you're not trying to buy a property and instead saving for retirement, but access to your money is important to you, too.

Scenario 1A: Basic rate taxpayer without employer-matched pension contributions

Invest in this order:

1. Stocks and shares ISA: maximize for tax benefits and immediate access to your money.
2. Dealing account or GIA: maintain access to funds and enjoy tax-free allowances.
3. LISA (lifetime ISA): if you have more money, invest in a LISA.
4. Pension: invest remaining funds here as tax relief is not as beneficial and you're not getting employer matching.

Please note: When investing in a LISA, your £4,000 annual allowance is part of the total £20,000 ISA allowance. However, prioritizing the LISA offers a £1,000 bonus if you contribute £4,000, totalling £21,000 annually, but you give up accessibility until age 60. If you get substantial pension contributions and tax benefits through salary sacrifice, it might rank higher.

However, if accessibility is crucial, prioritize the stocks and shares ISA for immediate access.

Scenario 1B: Basic rate taxpayer with employer-matched pension contributions

Invest in this order:

1. Pension: max out your pension and take the all-free money from your employer.
2. Stocks and shares ISA: max out S&S ISA for tax-free benefits and accessible money.
3. Dealing account or GIA: invest in your dealing account to keep access to money and also use tax-free allowances.
4. LISA: if you have more money, invest in a LISA. You get all of it tax free, but at the age of 60. It also has the same 25% tax relief as for a pension for basic rate taxpayers.

Scenario 1C: Higher rate taxpayer with or without employer-matched pension contributions

Invest in this order:

1. Pension: max out your pension despite the lack of employer contributions for higher government tax relief.
2. Stocks and shares ISA: max out S&S ISA for tax-free benefits and accessible money.
3. Dealing account or GIA: invest in your dealing account to keep access to money and also use tax-free allowances.

4. LISA: the tax relief is better with a pension at 40% vs 25% LISA bonus and you also access your money sooner. However, if you have more money to contribute beyond your maximum allowance for tax relief in a pension, you can use a LISA. Other high earners who are worried about potential lifetime allowances on pensions also make contributing into a LISA a priority. However, the lifetime allowance charge is expected to be abolished in April 2024.

Scenario 2: Employee who wants to become an entrepreneur/optional early retirement route

The most important things to you here will be access to your money early, as well as minimizing tax. We're also assuming here that you're not buying a property.

Invest in this order:

1. Stocks and shares ISA: this account is gold for financial independence and the option of early retirement.
2. Dealing account or GIA: prioritize to maintain accessibility and tax-free allowances.
3. LISA: consider for tax-free benefits, but locked until age 60.
4. Pension: prioritize earlier, especially as a higher or additional rate taxpayer if you've built up enough accessible money in your stocks and shares ISA and dealing account.

Scenario 3: Main goal is buying your first home

Invest in this order:

1. LISA: maximize the government's 25% bonus up to £5,000 annually.
2. Stocks and shares ISA: invest up to the £20,000 tax-free allowance.

3. Dealing account or GIA: utilize the account to invest beyond ISA limits and benefit from tax allowances.
4. Pension: any money here will be locked away until retirement.

Scenario 4: Self-employed and investing for retirement

The assumption here is that you're mainly saving for retirement. As someone who is self-employed, you won't benefit from a workplace pension or employer matching. Here is our suggested order of investing.

For higher rate taxpayers:

1. Stocks and shares ISA: max out for security with accessible funds.
2. Pension: utilize high tax relief.
3. Dealing account or GIA: use for additional tax-free CGT allowances.
4. LISA: consider based on personal preference.

For basic rate taxpayers:

1. Stocks and shares ISA: prioritize for liquidity.
2. Dealing account or GIA: invest to maximize annual tax allowances.
3. Pension: assess if it's better than a LISA considering personal circumstances.
4. LISA: consider as a final option.

Scenario 5: Director of a limited company

Assuming here that you're not trying to buy a property and instead saving for retirement, but access to your money is important to you too.
Invest in this order:

1. Pension: max out pension (if you can) via limited company pension – Up to £60,000 a year is 100% tax deductible, and saves you money on corporation tax.
2. Stocks and shares ISA: contribute from dividends and salary payments.
3. LISA: gain a £1,000 bonus on a £4,000 investment.
4. Dealing account or GIA.

Please note: Your investment order may evolve with changing circumstances and goals, so adjust as needed.

HOW WE ACHIEVED FINANCIAL INDEPENDENCE

To achieve financial independence we started by learning about financial freedom, first from Robert Kiyosaki's book, *Rich Dad Poor Dad*, and in 2007 and 2008 we were also following a number of American blogs. These began to shift our mindsets about what was possible, especially for people with our cultural and economic backgrounds. We started investing in individual stocks in 2010, where we made money and we still hold some of the stocks that made us money (e.g. Amazon, Apple) and lost money (e.g. EasyJet, Tesla) due to timing the market. We learned a hard lesson, figured out how index funds and ETFs worked, started investing in the S&P 500 and would, over time, add other more globally focused funds to our portfolio.

Parallel to all this, we used some of our savings to get on the property ladder and decided that paying our mortgage off was a key part of our financial freedom journey. With very low interest rates, although technically our money could have got us a better financial return elsewhere, we chose to focus on paying off our mortgage early and would eventually achieve this in seven years.

This was a very difficult undertaking, because it required deferring gratification and doing something most people were not doing, including those who laughed at us for making such a move during times of record low interest rates. Making this move with low rates meant that we were paying off mostly capital rather than interest, helping to further speed up our journey to mortgage freedom. Parallel to overpaying, we continued to simplify our lifestyles, living mainly on part of my income and consistently investing the rest each month, plus Mary's income, in mortgage overpayments and in the stock market.

While doing all this, we knew financial independence was possible, but it seemed too far away. So we explored side hustles to make more money and invest more. This paid off. In addition, we were improving our skills at work, doing various qualifications, which led to numerous salary increases that raised our joint income from around £47,000 in 2009 to six figures in 2012. It would remain at this level for years as we continued to work hard and keep an eye on our goals. This was a big leap from my first wage of £80 a week doing a cleaning job in 1999.

We stayed focused and invested around 65% of our net income monthly. This high savings rate was only possible because we bought a relatively cheap house outside London and we maintained a simpler lifestyle while working hard to make more money. In addition, I took loans with my parents and siblings to start a nursery business because childcare was too expensive for all our children. This one scary move alone turned out to be one of the most game-changing things for our finances as it not only provided a career for Mary as a nursery manager for seven years, but it saved us thousands on childcare costs. Those savings went towards helping us get to financial independence faster. We still own those nurseries today, but we don't get involved on a daily basis. This successful joint venture gave us a foundation to repeat the approach with property and other opportunities.

In summary, getting to financial independence has required:

- Shifting our mindsets from scarcity to abundance thinking.
- Improving our skillsets over many years to generate better career outcomes and business opportunities that have created more income to invest aggressively.
- Moving away from self-reliance to a focus on unity that led to joint ventures.
- Focusing on a ten-year plan that began with a foundation laid by our personal development journey in 2007 and 2008.
- Using what we had to take risks to create more wealth, especially when others were not willing to.

The point on unity and joint ventures need not be limited to family. Friends or community members work, too. For example, at Financial Joy Academy, dream-makers have built trust over time and invested in property and started business ventures together. Relationship capital is crucial on the financial independence journey.

Achieving financial independence did not happen overnight as it took a decade to cross our freedom number. We also did it using a mixture of strategies, which showed us that becoming financially free isn't just about investing in the stock market. Different approaches will work for different people, depending on your attitude to risk and how you choose to navigate the economic circumstances that you find yourselves in.

Reaching financial independence eventually led to us quitting our traditional career paths and focusing on work we love, which includes our work with the Humble Penny and Financial Joy Academy, and other business and volunteering activities, as a way of giving back to our communities, while also enjoying our lives. We don't class ourselves as 'retired' in the traditional sense, because we still work four days a week, but we've just chosen what type of work we do and don't have any plans to stop work altogether in the future as we see what we do as a calling.

Interview: Olumide

Olumide Ogunsanwo (38) lives in Miami, but grew up in Lagos, Nigeria. He emigrated to America as a teenager and started his career in 2006 as a chemical engineer. He then worked at McKinsey and Google as a strategy consultant for about a decade and retired early in 2022 to focus on personal projects. He is a venture capitalist investor, podcaster and the author of Firedom: Financial Independence Stories of African Immigrants. *Here is how he achieved financial independence in 14 years through career maximization at age 35.*

Happiness is all around you if you create the right circumstances. I feel very happy and fulfilled, and have financial joy because I'm living the life of my dreams. I had a vision of the life I wanted to live and developed the mindset and took the actions needed to get me there.

But it didn't happen automatically. I had my first job when I graduated at 21 with $56,000 a year income, and at some point I was let go from that job. I realized that life was like a chessboard, and I needed to develop a strategy that would grant me more freedom instead of being a mere pawn. So I started to do research and became fixated on becoming financially independent.

I eventually ended up getting business degrees from the University of Oxford and MIT, then my focus was on how to get the best possible job to maximize income. By 2012 at McKinsey, my income rose to $130,000 to $150,000, later higher at Google. Next, I learned about investing. I explored investment options and settled on a stock market investment strategy that aligned with my personal situation.

However, I would not recommend that people invest the same way I did. A better approach would be to investigate different investment options and select the ones that fit your personality, interests, background and location. Then experiment with multiple investments simultaneously until you find the investment path you can follow for decades.

In addition to investments, savings played a large role in my financial independence journey. I had an after-tax savings rate of 80% to 90%, and a gross savings rate of 50% to 60%. I also made a lot of decisions that other people weren't willing to make. For example, reducing my housing costs. For my entire career, it was $300 to $500 per month for 7 years, and then $1,000 to $1,500 for the last 10 years. I chose to rent because the numbers were heavily skewed towards renting for me. I lived in a three-bedroom house and chose to have two housemates. If I had bought a house, I don't know if I would be financially independent now.

I didn't have a car for 60% of my career. I walked or took the Google bus to work but some of my friends had fancy cars. 'I'm a vegetarian and make my own food, which is cheaper than eating out. As an engineer, I think of it as an optimization game. I focused on value-based spending only on things which brought me joy, not what would make me fit in with the expectations of others.

Financial independence requires intentionality and planning – living an autopilot life is not likely to get you there. Life unfolds probabilistically, and I tilted the probabilities in my favour by developing a lifelong interest in personal finance, finding ways to maximize my income, having a high savings rate and developing an investment philosophy that fit my life goals.

STRATEGIES FOR INVESTING IN PROPERTY FOR FINANCIAL FREEDOM

When you read most books about FIRE, the core focus is usually on investing in index funds and ETFs, which we covered in week 7. This is a great approach as it's passive and easy for most people to get involved in at all income levels, and we highly recommend it. An alternative approach is to explore property in addition to investing in stocks. As we mentioned in week 6, debt is used by the wealthy to invest in assets such as property using other people's money, usually the bank's and potentially that of other investors.

Part of the reason why most people don't consider property is because it is perceived as complex and requires capital. The other big reason is because people typically don't know what strategies to focus on. If you think about it, the security offered by property (or, more appropriately, land ownership) is one thing that we can all easily understand and, with demand far outstripping supply in the UK and in other major cities around the world, property will always be in demand. In addition, in a world of above average inflation, property and rents rise as inflation rises.

On top of that, it is a brilliant way to achieve some diversification away from stocks. You can invest in physical property for either income or capital appreciation. Alternatively, you can invest in REITs (real estate investment trusts – see page 196) via the stock market and benefit from dividend payouts. Either way, exposure to property is another way to preserve or build wealth long term and you shouldn't let the fact that there is capital involved put you off. Naturally though, this won't be for everyone as there are interest rate rises and taxation changes among other things to consider. Plus to invest in property you need to be brave and good at project management.

So, what we're sharing in this section of the book is the practical knowledge of what to do and how to do it if you aspire to invest in property one day, even if you don't have the money yet. It often takes just investing in one property for you to get more comfortable with it and to do it well, but you need to focus on a specific strategy and be clear on your goals. Before we share six strategies for investing in physical property for financial freedom, here are some important things to consider in order to decide whether investing in property is for you or not:

Horizon: Property investing will favour you if you have a horizon of more than 20 years ahead of you, so that you can recover from any economic declines or adverse changes while also seeing your money grow.

Returns: Ensure that the historical property ROI surpasses the mortgage interest rate, even though past performance is not a predictor of the future. The ROI can be calculated by dividing total annual profits (rental income after all expenses) by your initial investment. For instance, investing £75,000 ($97,500) in a £300,000 ($390,000) property yielding annual profits of £7,500 ($9,750) results in a 10% ROI (£7,500 divided by £75,000), excluding capital appreciation. If the buy-to-let mortgage interest rate is 5%, this might be a sound investment, especially if rates decrease and rental income rises. Assess the viability of your investment by factoring in all costs, including maintenance and void periods. If the long-term returns don't justify the effort, it might not be the right opportunity for you.

Money commitment and leverage: To invest in property in the UK, you generally require an income of at least £25,000 ($32,500). Banks consider rental income potential for lending. Prepare for a 25% deposit and a 75% mortgage to leverage your returns, as using all your own money would yield lower returns. Avoid putting all your savings into the 25% property deposit. Maintain a six-month emergency fund and be ready for contingencies. Joint ventures can help raise funds and diversify risk. Document agreements in a contract.

Interest rate: Run what-if scenarios (worst case, base case and best case) for interest rate rises. For example, if the base rate is 5%, assume 7% for your worst-case scenario and make sure you're adequately prepared to take the risk if rates are rising. Get a fixed-rate mortgage to remove uncertainty and predict your expenses.

Net worth: Ensure your asset-to-liability ratio (ALR) is at least 2 before investing more in property. For instance, if your total assets amount to £500,000 and total liabilities are £350,000, your ALR would be 1.67 (£500,000 divided by £350,000). This ratio signals caution, particularly if your net worth includes your home. Aim for your home equity to represent, at most, 50% of your net worth, ideally decreasing over time to enhance liquidity for retirement. If home equity significantly exceeds 50% of your net worth, consider diversifying into other assets, such as stocks. A higher asset-to-liability ratio is vital during economic declines when asset values drop in relation to debt, yet a smaller ratio can suffice during times of boom.

Bank stress tests: To meet the bank's stress tests when considering a property purchase, let's imagine you're buying a property at £300,000 ($390,000) and seeking to borrow 75% of that value, which is £225,000 ($292,500). The bank assesses the viability of lending based on the property's potential rental income. They calculate the annual mortgage payment at an assumed interest rate of around 6%, which amounts to £13,500. For basic rate taxpayers, the expected annual interest-only mortgage payments are multiplied by 1.25, making it £16,875. For higher rate taxpayers, the multiplier is 1.45, resulting in £19,575. These annual figures are then divided by 12, indicating the necessary monthly rental income. For the bank to lend the full 75% (£225,000) on a property costing £300,000, it should generate a minimum monthly rental income of £1,406 (basic rate taxpayer) or £1,631 (higher rate taxpayer). Perform the same calculation for any property you're considering.

Get advice: Seek tailored tax advice from an accountant or financial adviser, and consider the guidance of various other experts such as a mortgage broker, solicitor, builder, estate agent and more.

Time: Investing in property comes with a lot of hassle as you're effectively running a property business. You can, of course, outsource to a property management company at a cost, but that eats into your margins. Property investing is nothing compared to investing in stocks. It creates a lot of headaches, but if done well over the long term, it could help you achieve financial freedom faster.

Now that we've got past the most important things to consider, your goals should come next and they need to be absolutely crystal clear. For example, 'In ten years' time, I want to make £500 a month in net income per property from five properties to cover my £2,500 a month cost of living.' If you plan to invest in property, write your exact goal below:

Now that you're clear on your goal, you need to choose a strategy that's most suitable, depending on whether your goal is income- or capital-focused. Four of the strategies we'll share are income-focused, while the remaining two are capital appreciation-focused. These are not the only strategies that exist, but ones that we know are reliable paths to financial freedom:

Strategy 1: Live frugally, save lots and buy a property every two years for retirement

Goal: This strategy is focused on gradually building a growing income stream, which you reinvest monthly to buy more properties as momentum builds. If you have a ten-year horizon, for example, and buy every two years, you could potentially buy up to five properties. The properties you choose to buy will vary in price depending on location. For example, if you have a smaller deposit of, say, £25,000, you can focus on buying properties in the Midlands or North. The key is to make sure that you remove your emotions from the purchase and make sure that it all stacks up numbers-wise with a focus on monthly cashflow and ROI as your key metrics.

Who is it ideal for? It's ideal if you have a long-term horizon but want the simplicity of saving and investing in property without too much hassle, although the effort you need to put in will increase over time as you're effectively running a growing property business. You'll likely also want to consider whether you buy these in your own name or via a limited company, with the latter usually more suited to higher rate taxpayers with more than four properties.

Capital required: Medium to high as you need to stump up 25% each time, in addition to legal fees and additional rate stamp duty if you own a second property without selling your main residence.

Example: Imagine that with the £25,000 deposit mentioned above, you invest in a property costing £100,000. After all expenses (mortgage interest, repairs, void periods), you generate a profit of £250 a month or £3,000 a year (before tax). This is an ROI of 12% (£3,000 divided by £25,000). For simplicity, if you repeated this every two years over ten years, you'd have total annual income of £15,000 a year (before tax). This is purely an illustration and there will be other costs to factor in, such as management fees, but you get the point. It will not be easy, but it's possible with a plan. You also have to bear the risks in mind, because using bank leverage can work against you, especially as interest rates rise, so make sure that you're not overborrowing and you have adequate buffers in place.

Strategy 2: House of multiple occupancy (HMO)

Goal: Generate a lot of income from a handful of properties by renting out rooms individually.

Who is it ideal for? It's ideal if you only have a few years until retirement and the traditional path of investing in stocks and waiting 20 years or more won't work. You could also explore this if you want to quit your job or career long term and rely on property income as your main source, but you want to do it sooner rather than later. Essentially, if you want a quick return in a short period, this might be the option for you.

Capital required: Very high, as you usually need to invest in properties with the potential for refurb work that would create four or more rooms. Given you're renting individual rooms, you'd need to create a large communal space and kitchen, which means money usually needs to be spent on extending a property. This will usually require planning permission, in addition to costs of acquiring a HMO licence. This is a big deal and not for the faint-hearted! However, the key is to do it in an area with low-ish cost of purchase (relative to other areas), but with a high rental demand and yield, for example university towns or locations with professionals and proximity to train links. Places like Birmingham, Liverpool, Manchester, Bristol, Nottingham and Newcastle are popular examples. In addition to the capital required, you'd need to put a lot of effort in, especially if you're managing it yourself.

Example: Here is a real life example from the Humble Penny community. Gary and Jane bought a three-bed house in a not so desirable part of Zone 4 in London for £350,000, putting down a 25% deposit of £87,500, stamp duty of £15,500 and legal fees of £2,000. The property has two reception rooms and needed £10,000 of refurb work done to it. This brought the total invested to £115,000. All five rooms are rented to young professionals working in London and generate rent of £850 per month, giving a total income of £4,250. Gary and Jane managed to secure a five-year fixed rate mortgage at 3.5% interest-only rate (before rates rose significantly) and pay a monthly mortgage of £766. They also have to pay bills (gas, electric, insurance, council tax) for the property of £615 and allow 10% (£400) for repairs. The total monthly income of £4,250 less these costs gives them £2,469 per month (£29,628 per year) in profits before tax. This works out to be an ROI of 25.76%. This is significantly higher than renting the property to one single family, but requires a lot of work managing it themselves weekly. Note that the ROI figure above does not include returns from capital appreciation.

Strategy 3: Rent-to-rent or guaranteed rent

Goal: You rent a property (by contract) from the owner rather than buy it and you pay the owner a guaranteed rent. You then take on the property and rent it out for income, to others, at a premium, usually as an HMO (strategy 2), and make a profit room by room. In effect, you get the income return not the capital appreciation as you don't own the property. This is all completely legal. However, you need to operate ethically.

Who is it ideal for? This is ideal if you don't have a large deposit to buy a property and convert it into an HMO, but you want to make property income from room lets. You can start with little money and become profitable fast with recurring monthly cashflow. In addition, you can get access to the names and addresses of landlords who will be willing to rent their property to you for you to then rent it out to others. Once you start the rent-to-rent business, over time you can re-invest the profits that you make into buying your own properties. However, do note that you have to be hungry, prepared to do the work and put the time in (one to five hours a week) for things like speaking with agents, landlords, doing viewings and so on.

Capital required: Low, as you don't get to own the properties, but you'll need to spend some money on refurbishments. There is also your time commitment to be factored in, although you could systemize things and outsource various aspects, such an ongoing management and cleaning.

Example: Here is a real-life example of a rent-to-rent deal done by a community member at Financial Joy Academy. Stephanie rented a property in Newport from a landlord who had previously used the property as a student let, but it wasn't working out. The landlord simply wanted someone who could look after the property and pay rent consistently. Given the location of the property, the rent was quite low. The total monthly outgoings on the property are £1,316 and the total income from the housemates is £1,921, resulting in a total monthly cashflow of £605 or £7260 a year. By itself, this might not seem significant. However, as the returns compound over time, it really builds up. After five years, her profits before tax became £43,308. She also applied the learning to build up a small portfolio of five properties (houses and flats) via rent-to-rent and, after five years, her monthly profits before tax were £3,638 a month or £218,280 over five years. Remember, she has done this without owning any of these properties, but has now built up enough to invest in her own properties and own them. In her example, five properties over five years was the magic number.

However, the key takeaway here is that you don't need many properties for this to be worth your while. You can do this as a side hustle and even managing one or two properties will make a huge difference to your retirement outcomes. Working out your numbers, which remains a running theme with all things to do with property, is critical. Aim for profits of at least £100 per room per month after costs. Note that you can either do this in your own personal name or in a limited company for tax purposes, depending on your personal circumstances. This also applies to all the other strategies.

How do you find the landlords to rent property from? All councils maintain a list of HMO landlords (name and addresses), which you can write to your council for. In addition, you can find these lists online simply by searching for 'name of local authority' followed by 'council HMO licence register'. You then need to write them a letter with a focus on what is in it for them rather than you. You could mention helping them to reduce voids, guaranteed rent, free refurb of their property, any examples of what you've done before and so on. Keep the letter simple and end it with a call to action for them to call you.

Any specific property types to focus on? You need an area that's a people hub with transport links, shops, cafés, hospitals, schools and so on. In addition, you need a property that can be an HMO and meets the minimum room size requirements required by the council.

Is this a good time to do this? Provided demand for property still far exceeds supply, people will always need a place to rent. There will never be a perfect time. Even with interest rates rising or if there is a recession, there will always be an opportunity. The key thing is deciding if you're prepared to take the risk and learn from others as you go along. The answers you need are always out there so find a community of others investing in property and keep learning. Consider strongly if this is for you and take the leap by applying what we've shared. Start by either setting up the business first (limited company or sole trader) or finding a property to see if this is really for you or not. Remember, in the worst-case scenario you can give a property back after your contract ends if it's not for you. Finally, remember that you're providing a good quality home for people, so this should remain top priority over profit.

Strategy 4: Buy, refurbish, refinance, rent (BRRR)

Goal: Create an income stream by finding properties that need work done to them, then do the work to increase the market value using short-term lending, then refinance using a mortgage and rent out the property, thereby less of your own money is used to buy the next property.

Who is it ideal for? You want to create a regular income stream, but you also want to release and recycle your money, so that you can invest it into other properties.

Capital required: Medium with low ongoing investment.

Example: You find a property (two-bed maisonette) that's in poor condition and in need of a major refurb. You negotiate to buy it for £60,000 with the plan to spend £12,000 to refurbish it and bring it to the market value of similar properties valued at £100,000. This presents an opportunity for you with enough margin for you to make a decent profit.

Given the short-term nature and size of this purchase, a traditional mortgage would not be suitable. Instead, you'd use short-term bridging finance (typically costing 1.5% per month) for 70% of the purchase price for seven months and later on you'd need to refinance using a mortgage, which is suitable for properties held for the long term. The numbers are: £30,000 deposit, £12,000 refurb, £2,000 purchase fees, £3,000 stamp duty, £7,350 financing cost. That makes a total of £54,350 that you have to fund, with £42,000 (70% of £60,000) coming from the bridging finance.

Make sure all the work is done to the property within six months so you can get rid of the expensive bridging loan and refinance to a normal mortgage. In the meantime, you can get a tenant for the property as you prepare to refinance. When you do refinance, aim for the new mortgage to be 75% of the new value of the property of £100,000 i.e. £75,000. This amount will pay off the £42,000 that you borrowed for the bridging loan and give you £33,000 left.

Notice that you invested £54,350 in total. However, you now have £33,000 in your bank account, leaving only £21,350 of your money tied up in the property. This means that if you want to make another similar investment similar in 24 months' time, you already have £33,000 to start with and you'd need to save up another £21,350 (£890 a month), which you can partly save from the existing property that you'll be renting out, in addition to personal savings from your job.

The big takeaway from this strategy is that you found an opportunity that you bought at a significant discount, put the work in to raise the market value, chose the right financing option to start with, then refinanced later at a higher level and created equity that you can now use to invest in another property.

Note though, as ever with property, things can go wrong as you're taking a risk! Getting a mortgage could take longer to happen, refurbishments could cost more than you expected or you could be doing this while property prices are falling, so you might not get the value you want for the property when you try to refinance. You have to be prepared for these possibilities and more. However, if you did the first transaction fully by cash without the bridging loan, you'll save on the financing costs and things are more likely to work out in your favour.

Strategy 5: Flipping for profits

Goal: You're buying, fixing up and selling property in the short term for profit or lump sum capital.

Who is it ideal for? You're not interested in investing and renting property for monthly rental income. You simply want to trade property – buy, fix up, sell and cash out and then repeat this maybe one to three times a year. This is ideal if you want a substantial profit now to help you quit your job or build up your savings or retirement pot faster. This strategy is also ideal if you don't have a large deposit to buy a property, but you can access short-term bridging finance or money from a family member or friend at low cost. People who do this are risk-loving and enjoy the process of transforming a property quickly.

Capital required: Medium to high, as you must renovate property to a high enough spec for someone else to pay you a premium for it. Depending on the location, you can get away with a smaller budget.

Example: You identify a rundown property to buy for £100,000 ($130,000) with your money as a deposit (£30,000) and a bridging loan (where you can usually borrow around 70% of the property value). You borrow £70,000 at a cost of 1.5% per month for six months to allow time for refurb and sale. The total bridging finance cost is £6,300 (£1,050 per month for six months). The property needs £10,000 of work and you do a lot of the work to save money. Legal and other upfront costs will cost £2,000 and stamp duty is £3,000. The total cost is £51,300.

After all the refurb work, you expect to sell the property for £150,000 having done your research and spoken to a few local estate agents. Once you've sold the property, your profit before tax is £150,000 minus £70,000 (borrowed) minus £51,300 (total costs) minus £2,000 (selling costs) to give £26,700. Typically, people make such transactions through a limited company, so you'd then pay corporation tax and the remaining profits after tax could be drawn as salary, dividends or pensions, or reinvested for another flip.

Strategy 6: Invest for capital growth and forget it

Goal: Invest in property in an area with appreciating property prices with the primary goal of capital appreciation. You'll need to make sure that the property generates income to cover costs. However, your main focus is on generating a big return from capital appreciation in 10 to 20 years, so that you can either sell and cash out at a huge profit or end up with a property that's mortgage free and producing an income. This strategy makes a key assumption, which is that property prices will rise on average over time. For this strategy to work for you, you have to deliberate about where you invest with a focus on prime locations – ideally major cities with transport links.

Who is it ideal for? People who strategically prefer capital appreciation over rental income long term.

Capital required: High but with low ongoing financial commitment and effort. Some people raise this capital by taking equity from their own home. We prefer raising such capital from savings, joint ventures with others or refinancing another property if you have one.

Example: We'll use large numbers here so that you can see how time and leverage can work for you. However, you can also get similar results using smaller amounts. Let's assume you have £200,000 to invest and you have a 20-year horizon. Rather than invest it into one property, you invest £50,000 each (including a 25% deposit and all costs) into four two-bed houses in the Midlands costing £160,000 each.

For each property, you need to put down a 25% deposit of £40,000, pay stamp duty of £4,800 and legal fees of £2,000, and spend £3,200 on a light refurb and other costs. The total is £50,000. For each property, you took out a 5% interest-only mortgage on the £120,000 borrowed per property and are paying a mortgage of £500 per month for each property. For simplicity, let's assume that when you rent all these properties, each one generates rental income of £995. After paying your mortgage (£500), management fee (assume 10% or £100), repairs (assume 10% or £100), and void for two weeks, you end up with £283.65 a month or £1,134.61 a month in profits before tax for all four properties.

While this isn't a huge ROI from the income, this wasn't the main focus. Fast forward 20 years from now and let's assume conservatively that each property has doubled in value. Four properties at £160,000 each (total £640,000) would be worth £1,280,000. However, the debt on the property will remain the same at a total of £480,000 (£120,000 multiplied by four). Notice that over those 20 years, your rental income would have been increasing and so will the property value, while the debt remains the same, demonstrating the power of leverage. You'll have built up equity of a whopping £800,000. At this point, you can sell the properties, pay capital gains tax and then live off the rest for retirement after deducting your original £200,000 invested. Or you can sell two properties and use the profits after tax to pay off the two mortgages on the two remaining properties, making them mortgage free and enabling you to live off the larger monthly rental income and profits left over from selling the two properties. Given rents rise with inflation, you'll keep getting paid an income in real terms each month for your retirement.

If you're going to explore property investing, which of the six strategies will you start with and why? Ensure this aligns with the goals that you set for yourself earlier.

Which properties should you buy?

Avoid any property with fewer than two rooms and focus on the cheaper part of a good location. Plus, avoid flats or apartments with expensive and uncontrollable service charges. If you can find a maisonette with no service charge or ground rent, then these are worth buying as you can attract market rate rents, but buy them cheaper relatively speaking. However, note that flats don't usually go up in value as quickly as houses with three bedrooms or more. The more rooms there are in a property, the better, especially as rents will continue to rise in the future and renting by room will become more of the norm. Also, although buying older properties usually means better build quality, you may need to spend more in the future to improve energy efficiency.

When should you buy a property?

Basic economics tells us that there is a property cycle at play in a world where demand for property far outstrips supply. According to one idea, popularized by Fred Harrison, there is an 18-year property cycle made up of seven years of recovery, seven years of an explosive phase and four years of the recession phase.[60] By understanding these phases, you're able to get a sense for where we are in the cycle and decide whether to invest now or not. While we're not fans of future predictions of house price crashes, which usually end up being wrong, one key observation from each phase of the property cycle is that each one ends with property prices at a higher level than the previous phase. This has helped us to come up with some general rules about when to buy.

- The ideal buying time is at the end of a recession or the start of a recovery, but long-term buying during a stable market is fine if you don't buy during a hype.
- For a home, choose a good location, avoid overborrowing and commit to staying for many years.
- For investment, prioritize running the numbers and ensure the returns align with the risk. Never buy high and sell low.
- Accumulate savings and be ready to buy during low confidence periods when prices fall and banks limit lending.
- Ignore media noise and focus on informed decisions, as savvy investors make strategic moves quietly.
- Consider a long-term approach, holding the property for at least 20 years to navigate different phases of the property cycle.

How should you start investing in property?

We love this quote by Napoleon Hill, which can be applied to all aspects of wealth-building: 'Whatever your mind can conceive and believe, your mind can achieve.'

First, you need to believe that investing in property is possible for you, even if you don't have the money yet and people around you are doing everything possible to put you off. Second, write your property investing goals and why this will change your life, and look at it daily. Third, find a property opportunity while you're saving money. This will take months, but you'll learn a lot as part of this process. Do this yourself or use a property sourcer. Finally, begin making a list of potential sources of capital, for example, 75% will come from the bank and 25% will come from you and other sources. You need to be creative and remember that the quickest way to achieve your goal is by using the expertise and resources of other people. Joining a community of other people investing in property will help you keep learning as you go on this journey.

Overall, as exciting as it is, property investing isn't for everyone. It should be part of a balanced portfolio for your financial independence and retirement goals. The key thing beyond learning what to do is to be one of the few rare people who actually takes action. Finally, think long term and consider an exit plan. Will you hold your properties forever to create generational wealth? Or will you sell all of it or some of it? Whatever you decide to do, remember your why for doing this in the first place and always seek advice.

Interview: Nemi

Nemi Woghiren (48) is as an IT consultant who moved to the UK from Nigeria at 21. She lives in Kingston with her husband and four children. She's also a dream-maker at Financial Joy Academy. Here is her journey of trying to achieve financial freedom through property investing.

Financial freedom is being completely debt free and having banks chase me to offer me money, rather than the other way around.

I want the freedom to borrow when I need to explore business opportunities without feeling subservient to the banking system. I find happiness in progress and making life more enjoyable. Frustration is my driving force. I also think about the dynamics in Black families where one person often becomes the sole provider and eventually gets drained. I'm working towards financial freedom not just for my children, but for generations to come, so they don't rely on a single superhero. I'm actively involving my family, reaching out to family and in-laws, and encouraging collaboration. I want to open more taps and ensure everyone in the family gains the experience to create wealth and handle financial setbacks together.

One unusual step we took on our financial freedom journey was buying property during the lockdown, when banks were tightening lending and many people were reluctant to invest. We saw an opportunity when others were hesitant and purchased a property that hadn't been sold in an auction. We viewed the property before making an offer and it was a former bakery converted into four one-bedroom flats, going for less than £100,000 in the East Midlands.

Securing a mortgage was challenging. However, I found a mortgage broker who was starting out on YouTube, and he helped us obtain a bridging loan to purchase the property, later converting it into a mortgage. I've always believed that going against the grain is where you often find opportunities. We carried on this trend of multi-units and bought a commercial building that we converted into four flats and a shop. One hard lesson was that people will try to take advantage of you. As the saying goes, 'Be as wise as a serpent and as gentle as a dove.'

These recent property investments have significantly contributed to our journey toward financial freedom. We're now earning an additional couple of thousand pounds per month from one of our properties, bringing us closer to our goal. The hard work and challenges have made me realize that one of my most lucrative investments is my own home.

We have a five-bedroom house in London and my older children have gone to university, so we signed up for a guardian scheme to host international students during weekends, earning around £700 per weekend with three available rooms. I'm taking it a step further – when we go on holiday in August, I'm listing my property to rent out during that time. The projected earnings for August from the three rooms are £4,800. If I were to rent out my entire house for a full month, I could make up to £9,000. It's hard work, but it's a significant opportunity I've been sitting on. I now want to do it for expats in my area and split the earnings.

HOW TO REDUCE YOUR TAX LEGALLY TO MAXIMIZE RETIREMENT SAVINGS

When you choose to retire will dictate what accounts you choose to prioritize first, which, in turn, determines whether your retirement income will be taxable. Let's look at some scenarios:

You plan to retire before the age of 55 (or 57 from 2028)

In this situation, you won't have access to your pension or lifetime ISA. Your income will come from various sources with different tax treatments, such as tax-free stocks and shares ISA, tax-free savings within your personal allowance, taxable dealing or general investing account, taxable property, taxable income from a business or side hustle, taxable part-time work (above personal allowance), taxable income from getting a lodger (above £7,500 a year tax-free allowance) and taxable income from other assets.

You plan to retire between 55 (or 57 from 2028) and 66

Upon accessing your workplace and private pensions, with 25% tax-free and 75% taxable, avoid the common mistake of withdrawing the entire 25% and storing it in current or savings accounts. Instead, withdraw only what you need to utilize your annual personal tax allowances efficiently, ensuring you minimize unnecessary taxes. Leaving your money invested provides the best opportunity for above-inflation growth. However, if you require the 25% tax-free lump sum for purposes like paying off your mortgage in retirement, withdrawing it would be sensible.

You retire on or after age 66

Upon retirement, the state pension becomes accessible, but it's taxable if your total income exceeds the annual personal allowance. Regarding inheritance tax, if you pass away before 75, your pension pot is typically considered outside your estate, exempt from inheritance tax. However, converting it into an annuity prevents inheritance by loved ones. Note that the state pension age is expected to rise in the future.

With these scenarios in mind, aside from moving abroad, which we touched on earlier, here are legal ways to reduce your tax as you plan for financial independence and the option to retire early:

Invest more into ISAs: They offer tax-free savings and investment gains, shielding you from increased capital gains tax outside ISAs. Considering potential future changes or caps on tax-free allowances, maximize your ISA contributions before any rule alterations, as changes are unlikely to be applied retrospectively.

Contribute more into pensions: Pension contributions receive tax relief at your highest marginal rate and the initial 25% withdrawal is typically tax-free. When accessing different pension pots, plan strategically to minimize tax implications. Be cautious, as withdrawing the full 25% tax-free lump sum followed by taxable withdrawals triggers the money purchase annual allowance (MPAA) at £10,000, replacing the current £60,000 annual limit with tax relief. To maintain the £60,000 allowance in retirement, avoid triggering the MPAA by:

- Taking only up to 25% of your DC pension as a tax-free lump sum.
- Taking the tax-free lump sum and purchasing a lifetime annuity.
- Receiving income from a DB scheme if available.

Invest in venture capital trusts (VCTs): This offers up to 30% income tax relief on the invested amount, capped at certain limits. A £10,000 investment, for instance, could reduce your income tax bill by £3,000, providing a tax-efficient boost to your retirement savings. Additionally, tax-free dividends and capital gains can enhance your retirement income without incurring extra tax liabilities.

Invest in enterprise investment schemes (EISs): These offer immediate income tax relief (up to 30%) for retirement planning, reducing your tax liability upon investment. They present potential capital appreciation if invested in successful early-stage companies. Moreover, reinvesting gains in an EIS-eligible company allows you to defer paying CGT, aiding portfolio rebalancing near retirement. Shares held for two years in such companies may qualify for inheritance tax (IHT) relief.

Note that both VCTs and EISs are higher-risk investments, and their tax benefits are subject to certain conditions and limits, and may not be suitable for everyone. Consult with a financial adviser.

Marriage allowance: Applicable to spouses or civil partners, this allows the lower earner (currently with a personal allowance of £12,570) to transfer 10% of it to the higher earner. This is feasible if the partner earns under £50,000 or pays basic rate tax, potentially saving £252 annually. The calculation involves taking 10% of £12,570, resulting in a £251.40 reduction in the recipient's tax bill. The allowance can be backdated up to four years for eligible couples who were married during that period, offering additional savings.

Salary sacrifice: From a pension perspective, salary sacrifice is where you give up some of your monthly pre-tax income and your employer puts it towards your pension for you. Doing salary sacrifice has some interesting advantages:

- Reduced National Insurance contributions: You and your employer pay less National Insurance.
- Lower taxable income: Pay less tax due to being taxed on a lower income.
- Increased take-home pay: Experience a boost in take-home pay by paying less National Insurance and income tax.
- Automated tax relief for higher rate taxpayers: Higher and additional rate taxpayers benefit from automatic tax relief without the need for self-claiming through self-assessment.
- Child benefit protection for higher rate taxpayers: Higher rate tax-payers using salary sacrifice can keep their full child benefit by reducing taxable income to avoid the high income child benefit tax.
- Mitigation of 60% effective tax rate for £100,000–£125,000 earners:

Salary sacrifice helps earners in the £100,000–£125,000 range reduce their taxable income, preventing the unofficial 60% effective tax rate caused by the tapering of personal allowances, so you lose £1 for every £2 above £100,000 and lose it all when you earn £125,140. Encourage your employer to offer salary sacrifice if it's not available.

Sharing assets: Take advantage of the spouse exemption to transfer income-producing assets between spouses (married or in a civil partnership) without incurring a tax liability. This allows both partners to optimize their tax allowances, such as income tax and capital gains tax, minimizing overall tax payments. By redistributing assets between yourselves, you maximize the use of these allowances, and any surplus assets can be held by the individual with the lower tax rate. With the reduction in tax-free allowances, this is not as attractive as it used to be but it still remains an option.

WITHDRAWING MONEY AT RETIREMENT: SEQUENCE OF RETURN RISK

So far in week 9, we've focused on wealth accumulation and how to navigate your way to a life of financial independence and optional early or traditional retirement. We've looked at some of the challenges along the way such as investing in assets and navigating taxes. However, one of the biggest dangers to consider is what happens when you start to withdraw your money in retirement. The biggest of these risks is what's known as the sequence of return risk, which is the risk that the order of your investment returns could be unfavourable.

Although this risk exists during your wealth accumulation phase, it is amplified at retirement. Research in this area[61] for UK retirees (and applicable to other countries) shows that the returns you get in the first decade of your retirement are the biggest driver of a sustainable income over a 30-year retirement and beyond. If you get a good average return in the first decade of retirement, you're unlikely to run out of money in retirement. However, if you don't, you are likely to run out of money even at a modest withdrawal rate of, say, 4%.

Given this risk and the fact that no one can predict the future, what withdrawal strategies give us the best chances of mitigating this risk in retirement? To consider a potential solution, it's important to understand the reality of what happens at retirement vs what our perceived expectations are.

We looked at an extensive research paper by the International Longevity Centre UK called 'Understanding Retirement Journeys: Expectations vs Reality',[62] where they analysed two large datasets, the Living Costs and Food Survey and the English Longitudinal Study of Ageing. They found that, contrary to popular perceptions, as people get older, they spend progressively less on consumption, regardless of their income. A household headed by someone aged 80 and over spends, on average, 43% less than a household headed by a 50-year-old. Much of the decline in consumption is explained by falls in spending on non-essential items such as recreation, eating out and holidays.

This is consistent with research by Morningstar in the US,[63] which looked at the true cost of retirement and found that retiree expenditures do not, on average, increase each year by inflation. The same paper also cited other US-based research, which found that consumption-expenditures decrease by about 2.5% when individuals retire and expenditures continue to decline at about a rate of 1% per year after that.

These have important implications for how we approach drawing down money for our retirement. In an ideal world, a SWR should mirror the typical spending pattern in retirement with a higher withdrawal rate early in retirement, which then progressively falls in real terms later in retirement. Having researched six different strategies for withdrawing money in retirement while mitigating the sequence of return risk, the one dynamic method that has been tried and tested, and is designed to make your retirement savings last the longest while being aligned with the research on retirement spending declining as people get older, is known as the Guardrails Withdrawal Strategy,[64] which was devised by financial planner Jonathan Guyton and computer scientist William Klinger.

The approach, which can be applied in the UK, US and in other countries, aims to make withdrawals in retirement sustainable over a much longer period of 40 years. The Guardrails Withdrawal Strategy proposes four decision rules that can be applied individually or combined together, including what to do during the good times and downturns in the stock market. Here are those rules.

Decision rule 1: During times of prosperity – an upward market

You should raise spending in the current year of retirement by 10% if the SWR in this current year (adjusted for inflation) falls by more than 20% below the prior year SWR.

Here is an example of this in action for someone in the UK. (For the US and other countries, use a starting SWR between 3% and 4% as appropriate and in your local currency.)

Imagine that you have £1 million portfolio in year 1 of retirement and a starting SWR of 3.5% or £35,000. At the start of year 2, imagine that your portfolio grows to £1,400,000, which means that you would take a £35,000 income plus, say, 2% inflation uplift, so £35,700. When you work out £35,700 as a percentage of £1,400,000, this works out to be an implied SWR of only 2.55%. As 2.55% is a 27.1% decrease compared to the original 3.5% that you started with, it is a fall of more than 20%, which qualifies you for a 10% uplift in current year spending, so you can increase the £35,700 by another 10% to £39,270 as your withdrawal.

Decision rule 2: During times of a down market – capital preservation

You should cut your spending in the current year of retirement by 10% if SWR in the current year (adjusted for inflation) rises above 20% of the prior year's SWR.

Here is an example of this in action. Let's say that you're withdrawing 3.5% (£35,000) from a £1,000,000 retirement portfolio in year 1 as in the previous example. However, you immediately hit a stock market crash and your portfolio falls by 30% to £700,000 at the start of year 2. Your withdrawal in year 2 on a pretest basis would have been £35,700 assuming a 2% inflation uplift (£35,000 multiplied by 1.02). However, when you divide £35,700 by £700,000, this would imply an SWR of 5.1%, which is a 45.7% increase from the original 3.5% SWR. Given 45.7% exceeds 20% as suggested by the guardrail decision rule, you should cut your spending in the current year by 10%, so reduce the £35,700 amount by 10% to give a withdrawal amount in year 2 of £32,130.

Decision rule 3: Portfolio management

The rule says that you should withdraw the gains from the asset class that performed the best in the previous year and use that to provide an income for yourself in the current year. In addition, beyond withdrawing what you need, you should move any excess gains into cash, so that it will help you to fund future withdrawals. For example, if your equity allocation has strong performance and exceeds your target equity allocation, you should sell any excess equity and keep it in cash.

Decision rule 4: Inflation withdrawal or adjustment rule

You should increase withdrawals by inflation each year. However, if the previous year's total return turned out to be negative, don't increase withdrawals by inflation.

In summary, decision rules 1 and 2 act as guardrails and strike a pleasing balance, which helps retirees to consume more during the good times without putting their futures at risk and reduce their spending gradually during the bad times without an immediate shock if they experience a bad sequence of returns.

In addition, this dynamic approach better aligns with what the research has shown us about how retirees spend in retirement. Decision rules 3 and 4 provide that extra layer of protection and help to manage cashflow volatility. Note, though, that this is not a set-and-forget system for managing withdrawals in retirement. It will need ongoing review and calibration for your own personal circumstances. We recommend that you consider speaking with an independent financial adviser (IFA), financial planner or coach as you explore the best strategies for withdrawing money in retirement.

ORDER OF ACCOUNT WITHDRAWAL
IN RETIREMENT

So far, we've established that one of the biggest challenges faced by retirees is how to convert their accumulated savings into a retirement income that will last at least 30 years. Choosing a sustainable withdrawal rate (UK: 3.5%, US: 4%, for example) is a good starting point, with the option to reduce spending and work longer as alternative options. Another way of improving your retirement outcomes is to tax-efficiently choose which accounts to spend from first in retirement in order to improve the after-tax return of your portfolio.

Given we're not retired and haven't started drawing our retirement funds yet, we've had to lean on the research of reputable sources to figure out the most effective order of withdrawal in retirement here in the UK. Here is what Vanguard concluded in a recent paper:[65]

'Managing taxes on retirement portfolios can have a significant impact on an investor's ability to meet their retirement goals. One way investors with multiple pots can reduce the taxes paid on their retirement assets is selecting the correct withdrawal order among their accounts. Our analysis shows that, generally speaking, the most effective withdrawal order strategy is to deplete the GIA first. This withdrawal order, combined with an annual crystallization strategy, where possible, can significantly improve retirement outcomes across a number of success metrics. Once the GIA is depleted, we found very little difference in outcomes between spending the ISA or DCP first, however, other factors such as IHT treatment and protection from creditors will likely mean most investors are better off drawing down their ISAs first.'

We, too, agree with this approach of focusing on the taxable general investing account (GIA) first, followed by the tax-free ISA and then the partly taxable DC pension, although the exact order you choose will depend on your personal circumstances.

HOW TO ENJOY YOUR MONEY GUILT FREE

Do you still remember how to have fun? Pause for a moment and reflect on that question. In a world where financial worries often weigh heavily on our minds, it's easy to forget the simple joy of enjoying the fruits of our labour without guilt or apprehension.

Here is our five-step guide to help you to enjoy your money guilt free:

Step 1: Identify your personal values for values-driven spending

Whether we admit it or not, the way we spend our money often reflects our deepest values and priorities. Understanding and aligning your spending habits with your personal values is the first step toward enjoying your money guilt-free. Here is how to identify your values and make spending choices that resonate with your core beliefs.

Small task: Self-reflection

To embark on a journey of guilt-free spending, take a moment for self-reflection. Answer these questions:

What makes me truly happy and fulfilled in life?

> [blank box]

What do I value most – family, experiences, security or personal growth? Or something else?

> [blank box]

If money were no object, how would I choose to spend my time and resources?

> [blank box]

What causes or charities do I feel passionate about supporting?

> [blank box]

Small task: Prioritize your values

Once you've reflected on your values, it's time to prioritize them. Your values may encompass a range of things, from financial security to adventure or community involvement. List your values in order of importance. For example:

- Freedom
- Family and Relationships
- Financial Security
- Personal Growth
- Travel and Adventure
- Giving Back to the Community

List your values in order here:

This prioritization will serve as your compass when making financial decisions.

Small task: Align spending with your values

Now, it's time to put your values into action. Review your spending habits and identify areas where they align with your values and where they may diverge. For example, if family is a top priority, you might find that spending quality time with loved ones brings more happiness than buying material possessions. To align with financial security, you can create a budget, save and invest wisely to ensure a stable future.

Identifying your personal values and aligning your spending choices with them is the cornerstone of guilt-free money management. When your spending is in harmony with your values, you'll find that every pound or dollar spent brings a sense of purpose and fulfilment.

Are there any expenses that you currently incur, which could be redirected to better align with your values?

Step 2: Set realistic spending goals

Now that you've identified your personal values and understood what truly matters to you, it's time to translate those values into actionable spending goals.

Small task: Break down your values into specific goals

Your values provide a broad framework for your spending, but you'll need to break them down into specific, actionable goals. Let's take a closer look at how this works:

Value	Specific goal
Family and relationships	Plan a weekend getaway with family every quarter

Financial security	Save 20% of your monthly income in an emergency fund
Personal growth	Enrol in one online course every six months to acquire new skills

By converting your values into specific goals, you'll have a clear roadmap for your spending. Complete the table below with your values and specific goals:

Value	Specific goal

Small task: Prioritize and allocate resources

Once you've established specific goals, prioritize them based on your values. Not all goals are equally important, and it's crucial to allocate your resources (time and money) accordingly. Consider factors like urgency and long-term impact.

- Priority 1: family getaway – allocate a portion of your savings and set aside specific weekends.
- Priority 2: financial security – make saving a non-negotiable part of your joyful spending plan aka budget.
- Priority 3: personal growth – allocate funds for courses and dedicate time to learning.

Which spending goals are you prioritizing?

(blank box)

Step 3: Make enjoyment part of your joyful spending plan

In week 5, we suggested allocating a minimum of 5% of your after-tax income as guilt-free spending and then increasing this over time depending on your personal circumstances. For example, being 100% debt free, we currently allocate around 20% of our after-tax income to guilt free spending on travel and other activities that bring us joy. Another way to calculate this allowance like this:

Total monthly income – (essential expenses + saving/investing + debt repayment) = joyful spending allowance

What is your joyful spending allowance per month?

(blank box)

This allowance can then be allocated each month to the goals that you prioritized earlier.

Step 4: Embrace the 'travel now, not later' mindset

Often, we find ourselves postponing travel plans, believing that the right time will come someday, for example when you've reached retirement or achieved financial freedom. However, waiting for the perfect moment might mean missing out on incredible experiences. Here is why it's important to embrace the 'travel now, not later' mindset and make travel an integral part of your life.

Many of us fall into the trap of waiting for the 'perfect' time to travel – when we have more money, more annual leave days, or fewer responsibilities. The truth is, there's rarely an ideal moment, and life is unpredictable.

Studies have shown that experiences, like travel, tend to bring more lasting happiness than material possessions[66]. Rather than accumulating more stuff, consider investing your resources in experiences that will create cherished memories. Travel allows you to learn about different cultures, meet new people and gain a deeper understanding of the world.

Travelling now doesn't mean throwing financial caution to the wind. With smart planning and budgeting you can embark on affordable adventures that align with your values. Consider these strategies:

Set a travel budget: Allocate a portion of your income to a dedicated travel fund. Even small contributions over time can add up to meaningful trips.

Take advantage of deals: Keep an eye out for travel deals, discounts and rewards programs that can significantly reduce your expenses. Sometimes, we're also able to travel business class for the price of economy by collecting Avios points and companion vouchers yearly using a credit card for planned purchases and booking travel 12 months ahead to save thousands. Other travel hacks include booking multi-city trips rather than single return trips. For example, a multi-city trip on Skyscanner from London to Cairo to Dubai to Rio and back to London (with one week in each country) costs £1,685 ($2,190) per person with at most one transit, whereas, a return trip from London to Rio costs £1,447 ($1,881) per person on a direct flight.

Optimize your itinerary: Plan trips that maximize your experiences while minimizing costs. Consider off-peak travel, staycations or exploring nearby destinations.

The 'travel now, not later' mindset is a reminder that life is meant to be lived in the present. By prioritizing experiences, planning wisely and valuing the moments spent exploring the world you can enrich your life and create a treasure trove of memories that will last a lifetime.

Step 5: Sharing with others

One of the most profound ways to find joy in your financial journey is by using your resources to make a positive impact on the lives of others. We're reminded of the saying that, 'It is more blessed to give than to receive.'[67] Whether it's through charitable giving or supporting causes that align with your values, sharing with others not only benefits those in need but also enriches your own life. We can testify first hand to how fulfilling it is for us to give mostly to strangers we'll never meet through our work at the Humble Penny. It not only gives us a sense of purpose, but it has also unexpectedly opened unimaginable doors.

There are many ways to give, even on a modest budget, whether that is volunteering your time and skills to organizations in need, or donating used items of clothing or toys directly to a charity or cause that you care about. You don't have to be a millionaire to make a difference.

Phew! We've covered a lot in this week and it's clear that retirement planning is complex. However, we believe that the latest insights we've shared will help you to improve your likelihood of achieving financial independence and the option of early retirement, and maximize your savings such that you never run out of money. Having a plan for your financial independence and retirement goals is one thing, persevering over many years to achieve your goals is quite another, which is why it's important to find small ways to enjoy your money and your life daily guilt free. Remember: stay hungry and stay humble.

WEEK 9: LESSONS AND ACTION STEPS

Seven lessons for week 9

- Although achieving financial independence and the option of early retirement is possible for everyone, there are unique challenges that make it harder for a lot of people to be braver with money. Having been on the journey ourselves and experienced most of these challenges, it really is possible to create your custom life of financial joy and make it your reality one day at a time. In fact, we'd argue that the life lessons from these challenges make you more self-aware and expand your capacity.

- The biggest driver of your chances of achieving financial independence and the option of early retirement is your savings rate. This means that even if you earn the average national income, financial independence is still possible for you at your lifestyle level and you're more likely to achieve financial independence compared to a higher earner with a more expensive lifestyle and consequently a lower savings rate.

- Although financial independence is often presented as a goal of self-sufficiency and doing it all yourself, reaching financial independence requires embracing other unusual principles, such as unity, community, self-awareness and personal development.

- There are a number of critical things to consider as you plan for retirement, for example your asset allocation and investing tax efficiently, driven by when you plan to achieve financial independence. When you come to retire, the risks don't stop there. You're faced with the sequence of return risks, for which we offered you a solution that involved creating guardrails to manage withdrawals during the good times and bad. In addition, the order in which you withdraw money from your retirement accounts will help you to improve the after-tax return of your portfolio.

- Money is meant to be enjoyed as you earn it. As you get your finances in order, commit to allocating 5% of your after-tax income to enjoying your life guilt free. Enjoyment doesn't have to be expensive or become a burden. The key thing is to spend intentionally on the small experiences that bring you joy, while saving and planning in advance for bigger expenditures.

- Travel now, not later. Start by travelling small and ask yourself, where would I go in the world if it were the last destination I could visit? Such questions will help you to focus on the quality of the travel experience, ensuring that you're immersing yourself in local culture and that your adventures are filled with memorable activities.

- Although it's natural for us to mainly think of ourselves when spending our hard-earned money, there's beauty in giving and sharing with others. It's more blessed to give than to receive. Giving your money, time and talent to causes you're passionate about will give you a sense of purpose, connection and enhanced well-being.

Three action steps for week 9

Action step 1: How much money do you need for your retirement and why? This is the same as your financial independence or freedom pot. Refer back to steps 1 and 2 in the section on how much is enough for your retirement (see page 273–279).

> [blank box]

Action step 2: At what age will you reach financial independence and the option for early retirement?

Use our free calculator: www.thehumblepenny.com/Freedomcalculator. Refer back to steps 3 to 6 in the section on how much is enough for your retirement (see page 279–283).

> [blank box]

Action step 3: What changes do you need to make about the order in which you're currently investing for your retirement?

> [blank box]

Week 10:

Creating your financial legacy by protecting your wealth and planning your estate for the next generation

A life of financial joy appreciates life daily and intentionally prepares for the worst.

Sometimes in life, it takes catastrophic events for us to be forced to stop, appreciate our lives and take radical action to prepare for the worst. The dates 31 December 2018 and 14 March 2023 will forever be etched in our memories as the days that our lives changed. What we're about to share with you is very personal. However, we're going to share it in some detail because we want you to truly understand why this topic is important.

On 31 December 2018, Mary and I were in Lagos, Nigeria with our family on holiday. It was a beautiful sunny day and our home was filled with laughter and good vibes. There was that positive New Year feeling on the horizon. Unknown to me, I was about to begin the worst New Year of my entire life. My mum, dad, sisters, brother, uncles and aunties were all there – a proper African gathering of family members eating and sharing food – but suddenly, around 7pm, something unthinkable happened right before our eyes. My mum and life hero suffered a catastrophic brain haemorrhage; something we'd later learn was an aneurysm or subarachnoid haemorrhage. Imagine staring at someone you love dearly suddenly faint and stop breathing before you. That moment, the fight for her life began.

When you're on holiday, you never expect these things to happen. In under 24 hours, Mum went from being super energetic and filled with entrepreneurial drive to losing 100% of her mobility, memory and eyesight all at once. She was now in a wheelchair and not only could she no longer see us, she could not remember us. I was crushed and so were my siblings, my dad and other family members with us. In that part of the world, there is no NHS. If you don't have any money, there is no treatment. Period! For the next three weeks, we slept on the hospital chairs as various neurosurgeons got to work. The best neurosurgeons in the country cost a lot of money. Before we knew it, we'd spent around £50,000 we hadn't prepared to spend. We had to find that money. I saw a side to me that I'd never seen before. I was determined that I would not lose my mum this way.

I fought for her and so did my dad and siblings. You know how in a family there is always one person that is good at the admin work? That person is me in our family. As my mum couldn't speak or do anything, I got to work to look through her life admin. This is where this week's learning on protecting your wealth comes in.

Here are three things that my mum did well. She had travel insurance, critical illness insurance and life insurance. Thankfully, as the boring one in the family who talks about this stuff, I knew she had these policies, so I got to work and brought fighting spirit to the weeks of arm-wrestling that would follow with these insurance companies. They looked for every opportunity not to pay out, but, long story short, with a lot of persistence, we won the battle.

Mum had no idea that we were fighting for her. In late January 2019, she survived her brain surgery and after much battling with the airlines (given the complexities of flying such a delicate patient at 35,000 feet), she was allowed to fly back to the UK. The bills kept on piling up, but the battle that I won with the insurance companies not only paid her medical expenses, but also paid out a significant sum to help with her recovery. Five years later, she is still recovering and has battled a lot, including a complete lifestyle change, to get here. She has regained her eyesight, mobility and memory. She survived and we're able to tell the story. We might have had a different story to tell if she hadn't prepared adequately for life's emergencies.

I literally broke down in tears again writing this as I recalled what happened on 14 March 2023. The day started like normal. Mary and I took our children to school, and got back home to start our work. Then we got a phone call to say that my dearly loved brother-in-law (39, with the exact same date of birth as me), who had been in hospital with breathing issues for a few weeks, was getting worse. I quickly rushed to the hospital and saw him in an unbelievable state.

It also happened to be the day that doctors were striking in the UK for pay rises. The one doctor who was managing multiple wards and looked really stressed pulled me and my other sister to the side and very casually said to us, 'I have no hope that he'll make it in 24 hours. In fact, we'll need to take him off life support, because there is too much demand for our overstretched resources.'

This was the most crushing pain I'd ever experienced in my life. We all couldn't stop crying as we felt so helpless. Everyone was praying with every hour that passed. We had faith that he'd make it, because he was still able to communicate well and was even making jokes and encouraging us all that he'd be home in two days, but he didn't know what the doctor had said.

While I went out for a walk to clear my head, I felt led by an inner voice to remind my sister about wills. She asked me to call their solicitor and ask him to send me a copy of their unsigned will for her and her husband to consider and sign in front of witnesses. They'd discussed wills before, but never got round to actually finalizing one. The solicitor acted fast and within 30 minutes, according to their wishes, I'd given my sister and her husband their wills to review and sign, which they did in front of witnesses.

Within 24 hours, in all the hospital panic as they tried to move him from a ward to the intensive care unit, they unplugged his oxygen from the mains, but the smaller tank they'd given him couldn't sustain him. After multiple tries at resuscitation, our dearly loved brother, father, husband, son and friend passed away.

We were due to celebrate our 40th birthdays together. My sister was inconsolable. Her 'superman', as she'd call him, was gone forever, leaving her and their two young sons, parents and friends behind. I still remember me and his wife begging him not to leave us as we shook him, hoping he'd wake up. His beautiful face was at peace as he had no more pain.

None of us saw this one coming. Who expects to die at the age of 39? On top of the horror of watching his wife, parents and all our family members cry, the image of him wrapped up in white cloth with the date of death taped to his chest right next to his date of birth, which we shared, still leaves me shaken. It made me realize that could have been me. It literally could have been any of us. He'd left behind loved ones, multiple assets, his beautiful car, which he adored, friends, literally everything he spent all his life's energy trying to acquire.

This is where life insurance, which he had through work and lost when he left his job, but sadly couldn't get privately anymore because of recurring illness, could have played a role in helping my sister and nephews carry some of their financial burden. Thankfully, they'd applied our teachings for years and had become mortgage free in eight years, a big achievement that left a softer financial burden for my sister and her children to carry.

What should we take away from these stories?

- Accept that the worst can happen: Life is unpredictable, but your financial future or those of your loved ones doesn't have to be if you have a safety net. Think the worst and prepare for it, then hope or pray for the best.
- You can never have too much insurance: It's shocking that we work so hard to acquire assets and build wealth, but we don't work as hard to protect those assets from being taken away.
- The earlier you start the better: Being young and healthy affords you cheaper cover for various forms of insurance. Each day that passes, your future life and those of your loved ones gets more expensive if you don't have adequate insurance cover.
- Appreciate your life: Everyday you wake up to a boring and normal day is a gift that should be appreciated. Not everyone was fortunate enough to be able to do the same.
- You can't take it with you: The hard reality of life is that it eventually comes to an end at some point and other people will start to enjoy your hard work. So you have the choice of enjoying your money now coupled with intentionally thinking about what legacy you want to leave.

Now that we've understood the importance and urgency of preparing for emergencies and protecting our wealth, let's now take a look at the different ways that we can do so, depending on your circumstances.

CHOOSING THE RIGHT INSURANCE AND ESTATE PLAN STRATEGIES

Planning for the future, as we've established, is a crucial aspect of financial responsibility. This includes selecting the right insurance policies and creating a comprehensive estate plan to protect your assets and provide for your loved ones. However, this can all seem overwhelming to the point that most of us simply avoid it all. In this section, we'll provide you with a step-by-step plan to help you make informed decisions about your insurance and estate planning needs.

Step 1: Assess your financial situation

Before diving into the world of insurance and estate planning, it's essential to have a clear understanding of your current financial situation. Take the following steps:

- Evaluate your assets, liabilities, income and expenses (weeks 4 and 5 – see pages 90 and 113)
- Determine your short-term and long-term financial goals (week 4 – see page 90)
- Consider the unique needs of your family and dependents.

For the third point, consider how much money they'd need if something happened to you, the debts they might inherit and who would get what from what you leave behind, all while considering their emotional needs too. Your insurance and estate planning should be tailored to address their specific circumstances.

Step 2: Identify your goals

The next step is to identify your specific goals for insurance and estate planning. Common goals include:

- Providing for your family's financial security.
- Minimizing tax liabilities.
- Leaving a legacy or supporting charitable causes.

What are your main goals when it comes to insurance and estate planning?

Step 3: Choose your insurance policies and estate planning needs

Here is a simple decision tree for choosing the right insurance:

Q1. Do you have dependents or financial responsibilities?
If, yes, proceed to Q2. If, no, skip to Q4.

Q2. Do you need life insurance?
Whether you answer yes or no, consider what you need from the options below and then move to Q3.

You typically need life insurance if you have a mortgage and/or dependents. Broadly speaking, you can either get term or whole life insurance.

Term life insurance provides coverage for a specified period, such as 10, 20 or 30 years. If the policyholder passes away during the term, the insurance pays out a lump sum to the beneficiaries. It's one of the most straightforward and cost-effective life insurance options, making it ideal for covering financial responsibilities within a specific timeframe, like a mortgage or children's education.

Whole life insurance, also known as permanent life insurance, provides coverage for your entire life. It offers a guaranteed payout as a death benefit to beneficiaries. Whole life insurance is typically more expensive than term life insurance, but offers long-term financial security. We personally have term life insurance as it's more cost-effective for us, the amount we pay each month is fixed and will become insignificant over time due to inflation. However, it covers us until our mid 80s with significant sums payable to our family if a claim is ever made. We also took out two single policies rather than one joint policy to give us the option of claiming twice over different years rather than once.

Life insurance is more than a safety net; it's a promise of financial security for your loved ones. These are the points to consider:

- Consider your income, debts and dependents to determine the coverage amount needed. Typically, you need around 10–15 times your annual income.
- Choose between term life insurance and whole life insurance and compare quotes from reputable insurance providers.
- Consider additional features such as critical illness or disability insurance, which are often sold as a bundle with life insurance. More on this below.
- Ask your life insurance provider to put your life insurance in a trust for you free of charge. Doing this keeps any future payouts outside of your estate for inheritance tax purposes.

Q3. Do you need additional insurance types?

Whether you answer yes or no, consider what you need from the options below and then move to Q4.

We also suggest considering carefully what coverage you already have through your job to see if it's adequate or not. However, we recommend not relying solely on employer-provided insurance, because you could lose your job and those benefits. Here are other types of insurance to consider:

Health insurance complements the declining state of the NHS, offering quicker access to GP appointments and private hospitals, providing a backup plan for urgent specialist care. We opted for it to secure future health needs despite our current good health. While private health insurance may seem costly, quotes could surprise you. As a family of four, we pay around £200 ($260) monthly for cover, with the potential for cheaper options if premium hospital lists aren't prioritized. The essential idea is to think about having at least some cover rather than none. These are the points to consider:

- Evaluate your health needs and consider private health insurance alongside what you already get through the state.
- Research and compare health insurance plans and premiums to find the best fit.
- Tailor the policy to your medical needs and pre-existing conditions.

Critical illness insurance pays out a lump sum upon the diagnosis of a critical illness, such as cancer, heart attack or stroke. It is designed to help cover medical expenses, lost income or other financial burdens during a health crisis. While not strictly life insurance, it complements other policies by providing support when needed most.

Income protection ensures financial stability during illness or disability, offering a portion of your income (around 50% to 65%) until you return to work or as per the chosen policy term. If you are unable to work due to health reasons, support from your employer might last for a while, transitioning to statutory sick pay (SSP) within six months. In cases where savings are inadequate or for self-employed individuals lacking SSP benefits, income protection becomes crucial. However, if ample savings or familial support exist, income protection may not be necessary.

Overall, we say assess your specific needs for these different forms of insurance in addition to others such as home, car, travel, disability insurance, over 50s life insurance and so on.

It can seem overwhelming, especially if your budget is already stretched to the max. However, we say you should stay encouraged and focus on where you have the most need. For example, we started with life insurance and focused on looking after our health, so we didn't need income protection insurance for years. It's only in the last 12 months that we actually took the leap to buy health insurance as our approach had always been focused on prevention being better than cure. It was also made more urgent for us as we're self-employed and no longer have employee perks.

Which one type of insurance has the highest level of priority in your life right now? What action do you need to take next?

Q4. Do you have estate planning needs?

Whether you answer yes or no, consider what you need from the options below.

WILL AND GUARDIANSHIP

Writing a will often feels uncomfortable in some cultures, leading to delays or misconceptions about its necessity and who should create one. There's a common assumption that wills are for older individuals, creating a procrastination effect, but the truth is, life's uncertainties require early consideration. Writing a will enables you to decide how your assets are distributed, who cares for your dependents, and how your affairs are managed after you're gone. Options to create a will without a substantial cost include:

Simple wills: These cost around £10 to £50 through DIY kits or online services, but ensure it accurately reflects your wishes and is legally valid.

Solicitor-drawn wills: These can cost from £150 to £500 or more and are recommended for complex financial situations or substantial assets, providing added legal security.

Mirror wills: Created by couples, these wills leave assets to each other and then to children or beneficiaries, offering cost-savings compared to individual wills. For instance, we've created mirror wills.

The decision on whether you should get a professional to write your will is an important one. According to the UK government website,[68] you can get advice from a professional if your will is not straightforward, for example:

- You share a property with someone who is not your husband, wife or civil partner
- You want to leave money or property to a dependant who cannot care for themselves
- You have several family members who may make a claim on your will, such as a second spouse or children from another marriage
- Your permanent home is outside the UK
- You have property overseas
- You have a business

In our experience, don't think about the money it will cost you to write a will. Focus on doing it properly and having the peace of mind. These are the actions to take:

- Consult a solicitor to create a legally valid will, especially considering any cultural concerns by seeking advice from professionals familiar with local laws and cultural context.
- Appoint an executor and guardians for minor children.
- Regularly update your will to match changes in your life and assets.

TRUSTS

Trusts are essential tools for managing your legacy and reducing inheritance taxes. They involve the transfer of assets by one person or entity (the 'settlor' or 'grantor') to another person or entity (the 'trustee') to benefit individuals or other entities (the 'beneficiaries'). Trusts play a vital role in estate planning, helping with the orderly distribution of assets, potentially reducing inheritance taxes, and bypassing probate. Different trust types suit various purposes and financial situations. Seeking guidance from legal and financial experts specializing in estate planning is crucial to establish and manage a trust that aligns with your objectives.

INHERITANCE TAX PLANNING

Inheritance tax planning is a necessity to protect your assets and pass on wealth effectively. In the UK, there are specific rules and regulations regarding the gifting of assets, particularly in the context of inheritance. Here is a summary of the key points:

- Seven-year rule: Gifts (for example, property and other investments) are tax-exempt if the giver survives seven years after the gift; otherwise, inheritance tax on a sliding scale (taper relief) may apply.
- Exempt gifts: Certain gifts, like those between spouses, to UK charities and political parties, are free from inheritance tax.
- Annual gift allowance: Each tax year, individuals can gift £3,000 without incurring inheritance tax and unused allowances can be carried forwards for larger gifts.
- Small gifts exemption: Gifts of up to £250 per recipient are free from inheritance tax.
- Nil rate band: Estates below £325,000 per individual (£650,000 for married couples) avoid inheritance tax.
- Residence nil rate band (RNRB): Aimed at reducing inheritance tax when a main residence is left to direct descendants, it's £175,000, combining with the nil rate band for a potential £500,000 threshold per individual (£1 million for couples).
- Spousal or civil partner exemption: No inheritance tax on transfers between married or civil partner couples.
- Normal expenditure out of income: Regular gifts made out of income, not capital, are free from inheritance tax, like those for family support.
- Gifts with reservation of benefit: If the giver continues to benefit from a gifted asset, inheritance tax might apply.

It's advisable to consult with a qualified professional or the UK's HMRC for up-to-date information and guidance on inheritance tax planning due to potential rule changes.

LASTING POWER OF ATTORNEY

Lasting power of attorney (LPA) is the plan when life doesn't go as planned. It's a legal document that appoints individuals to make decisions on your behalf if you're unable to due to physical or mental incapacity. It covers two broad areas of decision-making.

The health and welfare LPA allows appointed individuals to make decisions about your healthcare, treatments, daily care and end-of-life decisions, while the property and financial affairs LPA enables appointed individuals to manage your finances, like bill payments, investments and property transactions, in case of mental incapacity. These are the actions to take:

- Appoint someone to make decisions on your behalf if you become incapacitated.
- Create lasting powers of attorney for health and welfare, and property and financial affairs. You can do so via this government guide.[69]

TIPS FOR EFFECTIVE PLANNING FOR YOUR ESTATE AND LEGACY

Now that we have covered all of the main aspects of protecting the wealth you've built and making provisions for your loved ones if the unthinkable happens, we wanted to round off with a few general tips to keep in mind:

Seek professional advice

If in doubt or dealing with complex situations, consult solicitors, financial advisers, and insurance brokers who specialize in insurance and estate planning for personalized guidance. Start by seeking recommendations from friends or family members first.

Educate yourself

Understanding the nuances of different insurance policies and estate planning options empowers you to make informed choices.

Organize important documents

Your documents' safety is your family's peace of mind. Keep your insurance policies, will, trust documents and other estate planning papers in a secure location. Inform trusted family members or executors about their whereabouts.

Communication

Regularly communicate your intentions, and the details of your insurance and estate plan, to your family, ensuring they understand your wishes.

Monitor and adjust

Your estate plan is a living document, not set in stone. Regular reviews are essential to keep it aligned with your life's changes. Generally speaking, as your family dynamics and financial situation evolve, and as laws change, so should your estate.

Stay informed

Staying informed keeps your insurance and estate plan agile and up to date with ever-changing laws. Practical ways of doing this include keeping an eye on the annual budget announcements from the government, as they often include changes in taxation and financial regulations that may affect estate planning and insurance. In addition, check-in with experienced solicitors, financial advisers and accountants who specialize in insurance and estate planning. They can provide personalized advice and keep you informed about relevant legal changes.

RAISING FINANCIALLY SAVVY CHILDREN

When we think of legacy and generational wealth, we like to think of it beyond money alone and also see it as something that includes passing on to our children the knowledge and experiences we've acquired, along with the processes and tools that have helped us get to where we are today. In our experience, the most natural way of doing this in order to raise financially savvy children is to start as early as possible and weave this knowledge and experience transfer into the fabric of everyday life. Here are practical ways we recommend doing this.

Co-investing with children

When our children receive money from grandparents, godparents or other family friends, we've taught them to always invest a third of that money and we co-invest with them by matching what they invest. This way, they learn the importance of putting some of their money to work and it also gives us an opportunity to incentivize them to save and invest, while also getting them involved in the physical act of investing their money in the stock market. We started this from birth by buying them individual stocks in major companies with birthday monies. However, as they grew up, we got them involved and they now see investing in index funds and ETFs as a way for money to work for them.

We also make a point about ensuring that aside from saving and investing a third of their money, they also spend at least a third on whatever they want and give from some of the remaining third. This way, they are also learning how to budget and they use interesting phrases like 'this one is above my budget' when we visit a toy shop.

Use everyday things around you

When we do the school run, we try to spot everyday things around as a way to teach a principle. For example, we once spotted a fish and chip shop and we asked our children how that shop makes money? This created an interesting dialogue with our children and taught them the principle that money doesn't just come from the bank, but it comes from the creation of value through the selling of a product or service that solves a problem.

Help them become entrepreneurial

We don't just give our children pocket money, we try to connect it to something that shows them that they can create their own money. A recent example was when we set our second son, who is learning the violin, a challenge to play 'Time' by Hans Zimmer by the end of the summer for £100. Although he's not usually enthusiastic about playing the violin, this challenge created a different outcome. He was so incentivized he found various tutorials on YouTube to help him learn this piece all by himself. This challenge taught him to solve a problem while making money at the same time. Other examples include setting up an eBay account for our boys to sell old toys and furniture, and they get, say, 20% of the proceeds for getting involved taking photos and creating the eBay ad.

Have themed conversations at home

A recent example is a conversation we had was talking about the concept of income and how income is created, for example, earned income (working from nine to five) and unearned income (income from assets). This raised an interesting conversation around, 'What is an asset, Daddy?' and 'Why do some assets make money and some don't?' This set of conversations indirectly helps them to understand what assets create wealth and which ones waste wealth.

Get organized and plan ahead for things

Creating money pots for things is a visual way of teaching children to get organized while also planning ahead for things. These could be in physical money jars or by creating pots online with a bank account. Examples of pots could include, 'bicycle', 'game console', 'business', 'giving', and so on. This also teaches them to delay gratification and budget.

Talk about money as though they are adults

Sometimes as adults, we feel the need to hide the reality of our financial situation from our children. In our experience, talking about your progress and challenges with money helps them to understand and empathize with the fact that things aren't easy for adults. Plus, it helps children to develop good money habits and a positive money mindset.

WEEK 10: LESSONS AND ACTION STEPS

Five lessons for week 10

- Comprehensive insurance and estate planning are essential components of your financial future. By following these steps and seeking professional guidance, you can create a robust plan that secures your family's well-being and protects your assets.
- It can all seem very overwhelming, but the key is to focus on one thing at a time. Remember, wealth-building is like doing admin.
- Although it is a hard reality to accept, tomorrow isn't guaranteed. Even when you do make it to tomorrow, unexpected things can happen, so embrace today as the best time to act.

- A key part of creating generational wealth is raising financially savvy children who grow enough wings to fly on their own, build their own wealth as well as multiply what you entrust to them.

- Finally, remember that we're all passing through this experience called life and cannot take anything with us. To do life well, we need to strike a balance between living our best lives today, while taking practical steps to leave a worthy legacy and transfer our assets to the next generation without giving it all away to taxes.

Five action steps for week 10

- Review your insurance coverage and consider any gaps. Do it today. Follow the steps outlined above.

- Ask friends and family to recommend an estate planning lawyer or solicitor, or find one online in your local area. This will help you to not procrastinate when it comes to getting these tasks done. This will help you to initiate conversations on all the areas we've covered this week, such as trusts and wills.

- If you've not written one already, write your will. If you have a partner, make this a point on your money day conversations and discuss your wishes. Speak to a solicitor if you have a complex situation. Then, begin this process with your parents and pass the knowledge on to your siblings.

- Get a power of attorney[70] for yourself and initiate that conversation with your parents if they don't have one already.

- If you have children, decide on which of the practical things we shared you would focus on first as part of raising financially savvy children.

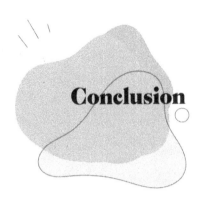

Conclusion

Thank you from the bottom of our hearts for going on this ten-week journey with us, dream-maker.

Financial joy is not just a destination – it's a movement and a countercultural way of doing life well that's accessible to everyone. You can have both wealth and well-being now, not later, so start today to create your life of financial joy. As you build that purpose-filled life by taking faith walks, remember that your journey is individual but will be powered by unity. Stay generous, stay thankful always and take others along with you.

To God be the glory for the opportunity to write this book. May it be light to your feet, a blessing to you, your family and your generations to come. Pass it on to others.

Love, Ken and Mary ♡

Useful resources

The Humble Penny:

Blog: www.thehumblepenny.com
YouTube: www.youtube.com/thehumblepenny
Instagram: www.instagram.com/thehumblepenny
TikTok: www.tiktok.com/@thehumblepenny
Twitter/X: www.twitter.com/thehumblepenny
Facebook: www.facebook.com/thehumblepenny
LinkedIn (Mary): www.linkedin.com/in/mary-okoroafor
LinkedIn (Ken): www.linkedin.com/in/ken-okoroafor/
Email Us: Book@thehumblepenny.com

Financial Joy Academy:

Membership community of Dream-Makers achieving Financial Freedom:
www.FinancialJoyAcademy.com
Instagram: www.instagram.com/financialjoyacademy

WEEK 6

Debt Charities

Step Change: www.stepchange.org/

Christians Against Poverty (CAP): www.capuk.org/

Citizens Advice: www.citizensadvice.org.uk/

WEEK 7

Notable Providers of index funds and ETFs

Vanguard: www.vanguardinvestor.co.uk

BlackRock's iShares: www.ishares.com/uk/

Find and research index funds and ETFs: www.morningstar.co.uk/uk

Notes

1   Stephen R Covey, *The 7 Habits of Highly Effective People*

2   www.pnas.org/doi/10.1073/pnas.1011492107

3   www.pnas.org/doi/10.1073/pnas.2016976118

4   www.pnas.org/doi/10.1073/pnas.2208661120

5   news.harvard.edu/gazette/story/2017/04/over-nearly-80-years-harvard-study-has-been-showing-how-to-live-a-healthy-and-happy-life/

6   Hebrews 11:1, New King James Version

7   www.openknowledge.worldbank.org/entities/publication/46bb9132-2a47-5d3f-968f-81021fbb1ef6

8   www.youtu.be/tPBFVlxnbDw

9   www.en-gb.facebook.com/business/news/insights/how-instagram-boosts-brands-and-drives-sales

10   www.statista.com/topics/3236/social-media-usage-in-the-uk/#topicOverview

11   jamesclear.com/quotes/habits-are-the-compound-interest-of-self-improvement

12   www.12weekyear.com/

13   www.ons.gov.uk/peoplepopulationandcommunity/personalandhouseholdfinances/expenditure/bulletins/familyspendingintheuk/april2021tomarch2022#

14   Matthew 25:14–30.

15   In the US, this might be a 401(k) or equivalent.

16   In the US, this might be a Roth IRA or equivalent.

17   Annual Equivalent Rate (AER) is the actual interest rate a savings account will yield after taking the effect of compounding into account.

18   www.kwik-fit.com/press/motorists-costs-running-at-one-hundred-and-sixty-two-pounds-per-month-excluding-cost-of-the-car

19   www.thecalculatorsite.com/compound

20   www.ons.gov.uk/economy/inflationandpriceindices/bulletins/housepriceindex/april2023

21   www.stampdutycalculator.org.uk/

22   www.mortgageable.co.uk/mortgages/history-of-mortgage-interest-rates/

23   This assumes 1%, but typically between 1% and 4%: https://www.airtasker.com/uk/costs/general-maintenance/house-maintenance-cost/

24   www.moneysupermarket.com/home-insurance/

25   www.checkatrade.com/blog/cost-guides/cost-renovating-house/

26   www.reassured.co.uk/life-insurance/average-life-insurance-cost-uk/

27   www.gov.uk/government/statistics/council-tax-levels-set-by-local-authorities-in-england-2023-to-2024/council-tax-levels-set-by-local-authorities-in-england-2023-to-2024#

28   www.familyandchildcaretrust.org/sites/default/files/Resource%20Library/Childcare%20Survey%202023_Coram%20Family%20and%20Childcare.pdf

29   www.openaccessgovernment.org/the-cost-of-raising-a-child-has-increased-for-families/136613/

30   www.gov.uk/childcare-calculator?utm_source=childcarechoices&utm_medium=microsite

31   www.helpforhouseholds.campaign.gov.uk/

32   www.insight.kellogg.northwestern.edu/article/key-to-happy-marriage-joint-bank-account

33   www.ons.gov.uk/peoplepopulationandcommunity/personalandhouseholdfinances/incomeandwealth/bulletins/householddebtingreatbritain/april2016tomarch2018

34   https://www.ons.gov.uk/peoplepopulationandcommunity/
personalandhouseholdfinances/incomeandwealth/bulletins/
householddebtingreatbritain/april2016tomarch2018

35   www.thedecisionlab.com/reference-guide/psychology/pain-of-paying

36   www.thebehavioralscientist.com/glossary/denomination-effect

37   www.citizensadvice.org.uk/debt-and-money/help-with-debt/dealing-
with-your-debts/work-out-which-debts-to-deal-with-first/

38   www.hbr.org/2016/12/research-the-best-strategy-for-paying-off-credit-
card-debt

39   www.businessinsider.com/warren-buffett-wins-million-dollar-bet-
against-hedge-funds-2018-1?r=US&IR=T

40   www.londonstockexchange.com/raise-finance/etps/etfs

41   www.vanguardinvestor.co.uk/investments/vanguard-ftse-global-all-cap-
index-fund-gbp-acc/portfolio-data

42   www.vanguardinvestor.co.uk/investments/vanguard-ftse-global-all-cap-
index-fund-gbp-acc/overview

43   www.ishares.com/uk/individual/en/products/251850/ishares-msci-acwi-
ucits-etf

44   www.justetf.com/uk/find-etf.html?assetClass=class-equity&groupField=in
dex&equityStrategy=Social%2B/%2BEnvironmental

45   www.tools.morningstar.co.uk/uk/fundscreener/default.
aspx?Site=uk&LanguageId=en-GB

46   www.cmgwealth.com/wp-content/uploads/2015/11/Rich-Man-Poor-
Man-Richard-Russell-Nov-2015.pdf

47   www.uk.style.yahoo.com/b-gotta-charlie-munger-says-140000516.html

48   www.hartfordfunds.com/dam/en/docs/pub/whitepapers/WP106.pdf

49   www.investopedia.com/ask/answers/042415/what-average-annual-
return-sp-500.asp

50   www.ted.com/talks/sir_ken_robinson_do_schools_kill_
creativity?language=en

51   www.youtu.be/ZfKMq-rYtnc?si=_R6IN4euMbB5SQoa

52   www.finder.com/uk/side-hustle-statistics

53   www.bankrate.com/personal-finance/side-hustle-survey/

54   www.finder.com/uk/side-hustle-statistics

55   https://kk.org/thetechnium/1000-true-fans/

56   www.ons.gov.uk/peoplepopulationandcommunity/
personalandhouseholdfinances/incomeandwealth/articles/
householdwealthbyethnicitygreatbritain/april2016tomarch2018

57   www.retirementlivingstandards.org.uk/details#examples

58   Ibid.

59   This is another name for the article 'Retirement Spending: Choosing a
Sustainable Withdrawal Rate,' by Philip L Cooley, Carl M Hubbard and
Daniel T Walz (who are all professors at Trinity University in Texas).

60   www.thisismoney.co.uk/money/mortgageshome/article-12417859/
House-price-guru-predicted-2026-crash-inflation-high-rates-thrown-off.
html

61   www.amazon.co.uk/Beyond-4-Rule-retirement-portfolios/
dp/1985721643

62   www.ilcuk.org.uk/understanding-retirement-journeys-expectations-vs-
reality/

63   www.morningstar.com/content/dam/marketing/shared/research/
foundational/677785-EstimatingTrueCostRetirement.pdf

64   www.cnbc.com/select/guardrails-approach-retirement-withdrawal-
strategy-how-it-works

65   www.vanguard.co.uk/content/dam/intl/europe/documents/en/
whitepapers/withdrawal-order-making-the-most-of-retirement-assets-
uk-en-pro.pdf

66   https://news.cornell.edu/stories/2014/09/doing-makes-you-happier-
owning-even-buying

67   Acts 20:35

68   www.gov.uk/make-will

69   www.gov.uk/power-of-attorney

70   Ibid.

Acknowledgements

We thank God for the opportunity to write this book. We know it wouldn't have been possible without your blessing and favour. May the works of our hands continue to bring you glory.

Ken:

To my loving parents, Ogbuzuru Dr Ken Okoroafor and Ogbuefi Mrs Stella Okoroafor, thank you for taking risks and sacrificing so much for me, teaching me all that I know. You've always been there and helped me believe that I can achieve anything. You continue to inspire me with your courage, hard work ethic and focus on enjoying life every weekend even in your 60s and 70s. Thank you for your love and blessings.

To my siblings – Jennifer, Pamela and Kingsley – we've been through so much together and managed to find light at the end of the tunnel. This book wouldn't be possible without all the experiences we shared together and all your support. Thank you for believing in me, and being there for me and our family always. I love you all and may we always be united as a family.

Mary:

Deepest gratitude to my loving parents, Mr Matthew Obadina and Mrs Martina Obadina, my pillars of unwavering support, inspiration, selfless love and prayers that have shaped my journey. Thank you for always reminding me to put God first, for believing in me, and for all the sacrifices you've made. I'm forever grateful.

To my siblings – Funmilola, Ade, Andrew and Shola – this book wouldn't be complete without acknowledging the people who have shaped me in more ways than I can express. I've watched, learned, and benefited from your triumphs and the wisdom that comes with navigating the bumps along the way. Your mistakes became my lessons, and your victories fuelled my aspirations. Thank you for your love and support. Love you.

To our extended family and friends, we love you more than you know. Thank you for continually supporting us, checking in on us and giving us feedback and ideas for our book. We also appreciate the practical love you've shown us such as providing childcare on the many random occasions we needed it urgently. Our lives wouldn't be the same without our friendships.

To our editor, Emily Arbis – you are a rare gem. You've been an incredible pleasure to work with and it warms our hearts to think of how well we worked together. You've worked very hard alongside us, encouraged us from start to finish and gone above and beyond. We've also laughed together and we're proud of what we've created. We couldn't have had a better editor. Huge thank you.

To our literary agent, Oscar Janson-Smith – we're honoured to have worked with you on this book. You're genuine, full of interesting ideas and you've always looked out for us. We also appreciate your commitment to confidentiality in all matters. Thank you for fighting hard for us and already thinking of our future plans. We love every moment of our conversations.

To our book cover designer, Anna Morrison – every time we look at our finished book cover we smile because you achieved the balance we wanted of a money book that's authoritative, a joy to hold and look at and one that stands out. It's like looking at a beautiful front door. Thank you for bringing your creativity to this work.

To our illustrator, Robert Brandt – the illustrations in the part openers and across the book are a delight to look at. You beautifully captured the essence we wanted to come across when people look at those illustrations. They're simple and empowering. We love them so much that we're framing them as artwork in our home in addition to the cover design by Anna. Thank you for your patience in helping to capture the illustrations just how we wanted them.

To our copyeditor, Lisa Hughes – before this process, we didn't understand the purpose of a copyeditor until we received your comments for us to review. You thought of everything we hadn't considered from the perspective of the reader to make sure that they were always taken along without assumptions, ambiguity or complex language. We thank and appreciate you.

To our publicity manager, Emily Patience – we still remember visiting the London office and after celebrating the book together, you pulled out your laptop with your PR ideas. We were so impressed by your ideas and hard work in helping to gain us and our book the right visibility. Thank you for keeping up the momentum with our book's publicity and always keeping us updated on the progress.

To our marketing manager, Charlotte Gill – thank you for working together with Emily Patience to get our book in front of so many people. Everything from creating all our marketing assets to promoting our book on socials and other media platforms. We appreciate your creativity, ideas and hard work.

Finally, to you, the dream-maker reading this book. Thank you for picking up this book and following our 10-week plan. Our work and community would not exist without people like you who support us, read our blogs, watch our videos, podcasts etc., and overall, give purpose to our lives through this work. We thank you deeply from the bottom of our hearts.

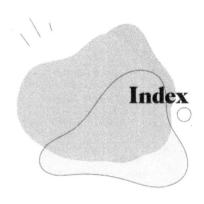

Index

About the Authors

Ken & Mary Okoroafor are a married couple who achieved financial independence by age 34, 100% debt-free, having paid off a £380k mortgage. They are the founders of The Humble Penny and The Financial Joy Academy to help others achieve financial independence. Ken is a first-generation immigrant, Chartered Accountant, MBA and former CFO. Mary was born in London to hard-working immigrant parents of Nigerian heritage. They live in South East England with their two children.

Website: www.thehumblepenny.com
Email: Book@thehumblepenny.com
Socials @TheHumblePenny

Follow us on:

YouTube   Instagram   TikTok   Facebook

Join the Financial Joy Academy, a membership community of Dream Makers achieving Financial Freedom:

https://FinancialJoyAcademy.com